Praise for *The Complete Book of Triathlons*

"If you want only one triathlon book—a combination of great technical info and interesting, relative training stories—buy this book!"

—Scott Tinley,
two-time Ironman World Champion, author, and lecturer

"Sally has left absolutely no stone unturned in this book. It is easily the most comprehensive look at what it takes to be involved in the triathlon lifestyle. She has made the challenge as easy as stepping out the door. This book is an essential part of any aspiring athlete! Another awesome piece of work by the most committed athlete in our sport's history."

—Paula Newby-Fraser,
Ironman Triathlon World Champion

"The succinct style, the practical advice, and the vast experience Sally Edwards has accumulated throughout her long and illustrious career are overtly evident. If I were preparing for a triathlon, I can't think of anyone else I would want as my trainer."

—James Raia,
syndicated journalist and long-distance runner

"As usual, Sally Edwards is the curve in the sport of triathlon. She knows the sport, she knows the athletes, and, more importantly, she knows how to communicate to new triathletes. She's the Pied Piper of the sport."

—Murphy Reinschreiber,
president, PCH Sports and Ironman finisher

"No one in the sport of triathlon has been any more central to its foundation and growth than Sally Edwards. It is only right that her latest contribution should be an almost perfect blend of how to train your body and mind with the more important aspects of using the sport as a tool for personal growth and satisfaction."

—Jim Curl,
president, Event Media

To Paul, Mom, and Nancy—your love and support make it possible

To Jim Whigham, for keeping me sane

To my parents, for instilling the dream

the complete BOOK of triathlons

Sally Edwards

with Rebecca Brocard Yao
and Kaari Busick

PRIMA PUBLISHING

Published by Prima Publishing, Roseville, California. Member of the Crown Publishing Group, a division of Random House, Inc., New York.

Illustrations by Pamela Tanzey and Audrey Miller
Photo Credits: Nigel Farrow (chapters 9, 11, 14, 16, 18, 20); Photosport.com (chapters 1, 3, 5, 7, 8, 10, 12, 13, 15, 17, 21, and the appendix); brightroom Inc. (chapters 2, 6, 19); Sports Instruments (figure 5.1, page 42)
Design by Melanie Haage

Library of Congress Cataloging-in-Publication Data
Edwards, Sally.
Complete book of triathlons / Sally Edwards.
p. cm.
Includes index.
ISBN 0-7615-3527-6
1. Triathlon—Handbooks, manuals, etc. I. Title.
GV1060.73 .E39 2001
796.42'57—dc21 2001052351

02 03 04 HH 10 9 8 7 6 5 4 3 2
Printed in the United States of America

First Edition

Visit us online at www.primapublishing.com

Contents

Acknowledgments

Thanks to the reviewers who were there from the start, when the manuscript was oh so very young: Jim Curl, Pilla Leitner, Rachel Herold, Paul Yao, Susanne Achtenhagen, and Jill Seaman.

Thanks to the technical reviewers who caught the big ones. We'll take responsibility for the rest: Estelle Gray and Kim Cunningham, for the bike sections; Matt Sellman, for the swim sections; Debbie Smith, for reading it all while training for her first Ironman; Annemieke Hiemstra, for reviewing the Staying in the Game chapter; Steve Power, for help with swim technique.

Thanks to the folks who supplied gear to test: Emily Banks of CCS/PR, for the Aqua Sphere goggles; Thierry Rouillard of Piel North America, for wetsuits; Bonnie Buol of the late great SportBrain, for gizmos; Melon Dash of Transpersonal Swimming Institute, for the *Conquer Fear* video; and Maggie Sullivan of Danskin Inc., for the fine athletic apparel.

A huge thanks to the sidebar writers and content contributors for the choicest bits in the book. It wouldn't be "complete" without you: Ken Glah, Sue Latshaw, Frank Cokan, M.D., Jim Curl, Terri Schneider, Scott Molina, Barb Linquist, Estelle Gray, Anne Q. Coloma, Dave McGillivray, Jackie Gallagher, Ben Bright, Sarah Springman, Lew Kidder, and Tom Benson.

In addition, I'd like to thank that invaluable wordsmith, Donna Thomas, and my training partners, Estelle Gray, Lori Bursati, Ellen Karpay, Ardis Bow, Richard Ongerth, and Bill Brewster.

And finally, thanks to the entire team at Prima Publishing/ Random House: Denise Sternad, Tara Mead, Jennifer Dougherty Hart, and Stacey Curran.

Foreword

"Triathlons are fun." At first glance, the statement seems an athletic oxymoron, a play on words, a bad joke. It makes no sense—like having your birthday party at the dentist's office or standing in line at the post office for a leg workout. Everybody knows that triathlons are hard, they hurt, they can cause you any amount of physical pain, but they sure as heck aren't fun.

But what is "fun"? Does it always have to involve physical pleasure and the unbridled joy of a trip to Disneyland? Or can fun take on a much deeper meaning? Can it not only stand beside such other noble words as "courage," "tenacity," and "commitment" but also include them in some unique application of the term when used in a description of the sport of triathlon?

I guess what I'm asking is, Can triathlons really be fun? We all know they can be challenging and difficult, and those of us who have achieved some tenure in the sport have found that indeed they can teach us those desirable traits of courage, tenacity, and commitment. But fun? I suppose that's a decision that you alone must make on a journey of your own choosing.

There was a time, many years ago, when I thought there could be nothing as fun as the sport of triathlon. To set a goal, come up with a well-thought-out plan, buy all the groovy gear needed to complete the task (and look good in the process), and head out in the crisp newness of a spring day with a few friends, riding your bike down the road like you were 12 years old and possessing that same lightheartedness: This was fun. To watch your body morph from some sad resemblance of what it once was into a newer, leaner, and healthier vehicle that could carry you into the next phase of your life with style and strength, and then to finally have that big day arrive, carrying with it a strange combination of trepidation, excitement, fear, and anticipation: This was fun.

Ah, and the race itself. I wouldn't go so far as to label every moment enjoyable. How could it be? If every day were a weekend, there wouldn't be any weekends. But what better opportunity in this day and age to go out to find what you're made of, to have all your strengths and weaknesses laid out for all the world to see, and to know that no matter what your time or place, you were a better person for having passed through those gates of self-discovery. Fun may not be the best term for this, for there are other more telling descriptions. The awards party is where you can fully appreciate the true meaning of fun.

I may have forgotten much of this in my quest to be the fastest triathlete I could be. I suppose I could be forgiven while competing under the guise of professionalism and a "winning is the goal" attitude. But I remember it now, how fun triathlons were in the early days, and more important, how fun they are again.

Sally Edwards' book helps facilitate that process, not only for the beginner looking to avoid the trials and tribulations of learning something of significance for the first time but also for those who have lost sight of what the sport is and can be about. Her simple, direct, and honest approach comes out in her writing style only because that's her style in life.

And she has a hell of a lot of fun along the way.

—Scott Tinley

1982 and 1985 Men's Ironman Winner, 50 Ironman finishes
Author of *Triathlon, A Personal History*
www.scotttinley.com

chapter 1

the extraordinary world of triathlon

Or Why We Do This Crazy Thing

Many years from now, you'll look back on your life in triathlon and marvel at how it all got started. That's the sneaky genius of the world of triathlon. One day you're safely reading a book, and the next year you're looking over your splits from your fifteenth triathlon.

The purpose of this book is to show you how to become healthier and to have a lot of fun in the world of triathlon. No matter how tall, thin, fat, short, or goofy you think you are, a place is reserved for you at a triathlon starting line. With proper preparation and a few tidbits and tricks, you'll be able to enjoy all that this challenging and quirky sport has to offer. Perhaps you've tried other exercises or sports and quit. Put that in the past. Whatever you may have done before, nothing is quite as remarkably life changing as triathlon is. I know; I've been there.

If you're already a triathlete, even a very good one, this book will acquaint you with other parts of the world of triathlon, places

How the Triathlon Bug First Bit Me

Coming from a running background, I was limited in the number of hours my body could train. When I realized how long I could train per week and the overall fitness level I could achieve while still staying healthy and injury free, I knew triathlon was the sport for me.

—Ken Glah, of West Chester, Pennsylvania, is an 18-time Ironman Hawaii finisher, with 14 finishes in the top 12.

you may not have gone to yet. You, too, can get fitter, have more joy, and be better able to take advantage of all triathlon offers.

Whether you are an experienced triathlete looking for new information or someone new to this sport, these pages will teach you:

- how to feel better and look marvelous
- the ins and outs of the participatory triathlon lifestyle
- where you are today with your fitness and where you can go, even if you've never done any exercise at all
- how you can use a heart rate monitor to increase your energy
- training plans and tips and tricks for swimming, biking, and running—the backbone of triathlon
- conquering the open water swim
- how to eat more and weigh less
- how to incorporate triathlon into your lifestyle comfortably

You will, in short, discover much about yourself that has lain hidden or dormant, awaiting the day when you begin to reap the beneficial effects of training for triathlon. Sure, it sounds like a tall order, and you may think I'm completely full of it. When I first looked into the world of triathlon, I was looking for a new challenge to properly slake my competitive spirit. As an accomplished runner, I'd won prizes in races for many different distances, including the Western States 100 Miler. My first triathlon was a run, bike, swim race that I did not finish. Still, I was hooked. In the process of opening myself to this new challenge of triathlon, I found a love of swimming and biking that I didn't know existed.

Typically, a person begins an exercise program in search of fitness: to lose weight and to feel better. With this book, you've taken that first step into the extraordinary world of triathlon. You can approach exercise beginnings in a new way: training for triathlon. The benefits of triathlon—more outdoor time, planning for a desired outcome, toning and conditioning your body,

How the Triathlon Bug First Bit Me

In 1982, I was a track runner for Indiana University and was at my parents' house for a holiday break from classes. I was stretching in front of the TV after my Sunday run, switching channels. I eventually tuned in to *ABC Wide World of Sports* and sat transfixed the rest of the morning while the drama of the Ironman Hawaii unfolded. Julie Moss and Kathleen McCartney were like unknown but immediately recognized sisters to me! The level of will, determination, and un-self-consciousness that they showed during this new, amazing event was something I had never had words or images to match with what I knew lived inside me. That day, this triathlete was hatched. I did not actually start triathlon until 1986. The delay was my own doing—I knew that triathlon would be an all-consuming pursuit for me, so I finished my education first.

—Sue Latshaw, from Boulder, Colorado, is a U.S. top-ranked long-course female triathlete and the 1998 XTERRA Champion. She won her first Ironman victory at the 1997 Ironman Europe. ■

meeting new friends, living in the moment, working toward a goal—are yours. It's more robust than simple exercise.

Blasting off from here is up to you. I'm not going to be out there on the bike or in the pool or on the track with you, although I'd like to be. You'll have to apply yourself and decide how to best live in the world of triathlon. Each of us is different, and each of us can, over time, figure out our place in triathlon. Whatever you decide, I'd like to be the little voice in your head encouraging you to explore a bit more of the extraordinary world of triathlon.

Welcome to the new universe about you!

How the Triathlon Bug First Bit Me

I happened to pass a triathlon field while riding my bike. When I saw, a little later, Dave Scott finish first with ease and without shenanigans, I was hooked by the logic of this sport: three different kinds of straight-line movement without sudden changes in speed and direction; no collisions with strong bodies led by weak minds. Having seen so many patients crippled by the unthinking traditions of ball games, and so forth, the total contrast struck me with a great force. It has lost none of its impact now, eighteen years of triathloning later. No wonder there are so many bright and educated people in this sport.

—Frank Cokan, M.D., who lives in Bellevue, Washington, has the most age-group wins in the Ironman Hawaii among males and has first-place age-group wins in Ironman Canada, Ironman Europe, and Ironman New Zealand. He is board certified in internal medicine and is the author of One Life Won't Do. ■

chapter 2

Why You Don't Have to Be a Pro to Be a Triathlete

Triathlon started as a participatory sport, and it still is one. Even though it seems that every triathlon magazine cover is devoted to the professional triathlete, these elite men and women represent only 1 percent of the people entering triathlons of any distance. Sure there's prize money to be had for the pros. You can even earn a good living by it, although it's not quite as much as professional athletes in many other sports earn. However, the majority of triathlon products, gear, and races are for amateurs. So choosing to participate in triathlon is choosing to be the focus of the entire triathlon industry.

Everybody Goes the Distance

When you enter a triathlon, you stand at the same starting line as the elites. They probably begin three minutes before you start with the rest of your age group or alphabetical group or race number order group (depending on how the race is set up), but ordinary folks and professionals alike will cover exactly the same swim, bike, and run course. In contrast, how likely is it that your tennis game will ever see center court at Wimbledon? How about a touch football game during half-time at the Super Bowl? Only in your dreams. When you work out, you're going to rub elbows with some of the sport's stars while you sweat. Don't think it isn't hard for them, too, or that they don't work as hard as you do. The professionals just go faster.

Open Door Policy: Everybody Plays, Everybody Wins

You train and enter one triathlon, and presto! You're a triathlete. Sounds easy, but finding time to train can be the biggest hurdle to becoming a triathlete. Still, you'll be surprised at how much time you can find when your heart is set on completing a triathlon. Get up ten minutes earlier so you can get in your sit-ups or push-ups. Take a thirty-minute run at lunch. Put a bike on a wind trainer in front of the TV for that average of two hours a day we Americans watch. It's about balance and persistence. Triathletes come from many different walks of life. They're every gender, age, weight, and speed. Even in the toughest race—the Ironman—physically challenged athletes compete successfully.

Skills Available for the Asking

When was the last time you learned a new skill? Most participants in a triathlon have picked up at least one new skill. Swimmers have to learn biking, bikers have to learn swimming, and everyone could stand to learn to run a little faster. Remember, you'll be running across the finish line in triathlon. Triathlons are designed to challenge athletes in all three sports.

Water, Water Everywhere!

We're born to run, but it's been a long time since we crawled out of the sea. We can't fly without an apparatus of some kind, but

> **Sheila Taormina**
>
> Olympic swimmer Sheila Taormina finished the swim portion of the 2000 Olympic Triathlon in Sydney, Australia, way ahead of the pack, but she couldn't maintain a solo lead on the bike course. She rode her bike out ahead rather than in the pack–not a good biking strategy in a triathlon that allows wind blocking or drafting. The bike pack riders conserved up to 20 percent of their energy on the same course by riding together, using each other's draft in turns. That energy savings paid off in the run portion.

How Long Is a Triathlon

In the beginning, triathlons were something lifeguards and runners did around Mission Bay in San Diego. The distances and the relations between the distances were not an issue. Like Phidippedes and the distance between Athens and Marathon, a triathlon was as long as it took to get around Fiesta Island and across the bay, a bunch of times, three different ways. The determination of the Ironman distances was similar: Put the three toughest events on Oahu together in one day and drink beer at the end. The only controversy was over whether the beer should constitute an official leg.

In the 1980s, there was a great proliferation of triathlons. If an event's validity of distance wasn't based on being a fraction of the Ironman, it was the subject of hot debate among athletes, race directors, and sponsors. By 1983, the following formulas were each being strenuously argued as the basis for worldwide growth and Olympic acceptance. Each leg should be:

we can enjoy a sensation of weightlessness in the water once we've mastered the basics. Swimming is the number one new skill that most triathletes have to learn. It's true that world champion swimmers like Sheila Taormina and Amy Van Dyken are being drawn to triathlon, but you'll find that almost 90 percent of triathletes don't come from a swimming background. (Also, just because Amy and Sheila are great swimmers, doesn't mean they didn't have to learn biking and running skills.) So you'll be in good company if you're learning to swim as an adult. Swimming is one of the best ways to improve health and body tone. It's also an inexpensive sport, requiring only a swimsuit, swim cap, and goggles. With a race that starts with swimming, you'll find the impetus to sign up for swimming at the pool you drive by every day. Even if your swim stroke is a little rusty or you're just now learning how to swim, don't worry—enjoy picking up a new skill. If you want to be there, triathlon is still the place for you.

1. equal in length of time, based on elite testing
2. equal in the time distance between an elite in that sport and an average age-group competitor
3. whatever would benefit Scott Tinley most
4. just plain equal in distance

This controversy summed up the state of confusion that was about to be resolved by the many races being planned for the U.S. Triathlon Series.

—Jim Curl created, or was at least involved in, every significant triathlon series held since the sport began in the 1970s. He has produced hundreds of single triathlons, both domestically and internationally. He also cofounded the U.S. Triathlon Federation, which became USAT, and the International Triathlon Federation, which became the ITU. A member of the Triathlon Hall of Fame, Jim is presently involved in helping organize the first international marathon in Jamaica, W.I.: The Reggae Marathon. ■

Biking in Triathlon: A License to Speed

You don't have to be accomplished at bike racing to compete in a triathlon. As long as you can ride your bike and follow the rules of the road (stay to the right, point out road obstacles to other riders, hold your line when cornering, wear a helmet, and so on), you should have no problem. Unlike in the Olympics, most races in which amateurs compete, from the Danskin Women's Triathlon sprint series to the Ironman series, don't allow drafting. Therefore, you don't need professional cyclist skills to be a triathlete. Just go as fast as you can!

Until recently, the move from the world of biking to the world of triathlon was a big leap. Most triathlons didn't allow drafting, which is a major part of professional and championship bike races. With the advent of triathlon in the 2000 Olympic Games, however, this has started to change. Now world cup races and Olympic points races allow drafting, because it's allowed in the Olympics.

Lance Armstrong

Professional cyclist and three-time Tour de France winner Lance Armstrong actually got his start in triathlon. It's funny to think of a world-class cyclist coming from a triathlon background. It is usually the other way around: Triathlon usually attracts athletes from other sports and doesn't often serve as a testing ground for single-sport athletes. Especially athletes who go from triathlon to such accomplishments as Lance Armstrong has achieved.

There are pros and cons about drafting in triathlons, and the dust has not completely settled on this issue. Maybe it never will, and maybe there will always be some races that allow drafting and some races that don't. Since most of us are looking at triathlon from an age-group perspective rather than from an Olympic hopeful perspective, it doesn't matter—just enjoy going as fast as you can!

Swim, Bike, RUN!

You also don't need to be a fast runner to complete a triathlon. Even the pros sometimes walk during the Ironman. I know I have. You simply need to be able to cover the course on your feet, however quickly or slowly. During your training, you can use Heart Zone Training and speed work to improve your running skills and ability, but you don't have to run an 8-minute mile to finish a triathlon. But it is nice to run to the finish, if only for the finish line photo to look good.

Now for Something Completely Different, NOT!

What a boring life it would be if it were lived in one dimension. Just living in our heads (conversation, work, media input) isn't all we humans are about. We also like spiritual gatherings, outdoor recreation, gardening, and cooking. We prefer the fabric of our lives to be multicolored. We like a full and hectic pace. Unfortunately, we can often overpromise and underdeliver to our friends, family, work, and ourselves. Then people get impatient, deadlines get missed, and personal time gets skipped.

Triathlon, too, is full of competing priorities. You'll want to swim, bike, run, lift weights, stretch, and cross train on aerobic machines to achieve some success, as well as a comfortable finish. Doesn't that sound like your life? You have to juggle family, friends, job, home, personal time, significant others, and health issues to achieve a measure of comfort, fun, and security. You see, you're already doing a multisport event every day.

Plan the Work, Work the Plan

Planning your triathlon training makes goal setting and commitment important. Training for a triathlon is not a subtraction from your time bank. It adds something to your life that will change your relationship to time. You'll gain energy from being more fit, and your capacity for more output will increase. The questions you'll ask yourself are how much is too much, how little is too relaxed, how much time do I really need to take care of the basics of my life? You'll have to assess where you spend your time and then decide if you're spending it where you really want it to be. So make a plan for working out, and then work at making that plan stick.

Busy Bees and Harvester Ants

If you feel you haven't got enough time in life, then triathlon is definitely for you. Time management skills are the key to triathlon training. And watch out—that skill of planning the work and then working the plan will spill over into other arenas. Believe me, you have exactly the same amount of time in the day as a professional athlete has. Each day has only 24 hours no matter who you are and where you live on this planet. Allow yourself the opportunity to rethink your relationship to your time and your priorities. You'll reap the benefits of more time, not less, and certainly more energy from adding consistent workouts to your life in pursuit of triathlon training.

How the Olympics Got Their Distance

In 1982, the United States Triathlon Series (USTS) suffered from the distance/relation identity crisis suffered by all triathlons not tied to Ironman. The USTS distances were 2K swim, 35K bike, and 15K run, based largely on the "selfless" recommendations of Scott Tinley. Tinkering changed the distances to 2K/40K/15K in 1983, but this change had no basis other than it felt right and deflected some complaints. The controversy raged in the winter of 1983. The Olympic year was upon us, and the sport wanted to begin pressing its claims to Olympic membership. But at what distances? Every day brought more inflamed rhetoric and more outlandish schemes, such as the "Equilateral Triathlon." Taking "equal" seriously, it boasted a 3-mile run, a 3-mile bike, and a 3-mile swim. Someone had to act.

Perhaps because the Los Angeles Olympics were the talk of the country, or maybe because it just made good business sense, Carl Thomas called his partner in CAT Sports, Jim Curl, with a solution: Pick three well-known Olympic distances (1.5K swim, 40K bike, 10K run), put them into practice in USTS in 1984, and stop arguing.

It did not have the physio-caloric backing to be right. It too much favored the strong biker to be right. It was too different from the Ironman to be right. It was too simple to be right.

1.5K/40K/10K debuted at the Sydney Olympics in 2000. It was right.

—Jim Curl

chapter 3

WHY CHOOSE TRIATHLON?

Imagine yourself at the starting line of a triathlon. At that moment, you might be thinking of getting to the finish line. But it takes greater courage and commitment to get to the starting line than to get to the finish line. Once the starting gun sounds, your body goes into autopilot. That's what you trained it to do, and it happens. As you will see, the test is not getting to the finish line; it's getting to the starting line.

What's in It for Me? Everything and Nothing

In training for triathlon, you have everything to gain (health, peace of mind, less stress to use the same volume of your cardiovascular system, fun, to name a few), but there's nothing for you if you put nothing out. You also have nothing to lose by training for a triathlon. There's no downside to swimming, biking, or running. They are just plain fun at any fitness level, especially when you feel your body responding to the workouts and you can gradually achieve better results in weight management, speed, endurance, or all three.

Triathlon gives you the framework on which to hang your fun. It's something like a picnic, where you have three-legged races, sack races, and egg-on-a-spoon races. Triathlon is an outdoor circus of swimming, biking, and running. When the day arrives for you to walk up to the starting line of your first triathlon, it will be one of life's moments that you'll always remember, and you're going to replay that moment as you go through the rest of your life.

Medicine for Mind and Body

According to the American Psychology Association, exercise can improve mental health by helping the brain cope better with stress. Research has shown that active people have lower rates of anxiety and depression than sedentary people do. Reasoning, vocabulary, memory, and reaction time can all improve through exercise. A mind is a terrible thing to waste.

Since 1968, when he published his landmark book *Aerobics,* Dr. Ken Cooper has been an advocate of using aerobic exercise to prevent disease and the negative effects of aging. According to his latest research at www.cooperfitness.com, even brisk walking for 30 minutes three times a week can reduce the risk of diabetes, heart disease, cancer, and strokes by 50 percent and increase your life by six years. You can't afford not to exercise.

Where's My Motivation?

Many people today are weary. Our fast-paced age of information has placed greater emotional and physical demands on us. Even during this time of prosperity and modern conveniences, the average person feels more overwhelmed, more depressed, and more like he or she is getting less out of life. Physical and emotional stresses have infected our culture with fatigue and depression, robbing us of the simple pleasures of everyday life. But there is a way to live a high-energy lifestyle.

You want it. You know you do. All of us want to be fitter, happier, and healthier, with more energy and less stress in our lives. Have you had it with stress and low energy taking a big bite out of your life? Are you concerned about your health and fitness? Are you concerned about the health and fitness of a loved one? The World Health Organization calls a low-energy, overstressed lifestyle a global epidemic. I have a promise for you: Living the life of a triathlete will help you find the sizzle and eliminate those things that fry your life. You'll learn, through the process of focusing on fitness, to shrink the stress in your life and enlarge the joy.

Working Toward a Goal: Train vs. Exercise

What does it take to toe the starting line of a triathlon, even long ones like the Ironman? By dividing the journey into small steps, it's possible for most individuals to finish an Ironman-distance triathlon (2.4-mile swim, 112-mile bike, 26.2-mile run). It involves following a few simple rules and commitments that you make to yourself.

The first step in any change process is to learn. That's probably why you're reading this book, because it's one of the support systems to taking that first step. As you learn to live like a triathlete, you will change. And as you change, all things around you change.

How Much Do I Have to Change My Lifestyle?

Not so many years ago, participatory sports were only available to students. When you were in elementary, junior high, high school, or college, you could easily participate on a game field or sports court with your friends. Even if we didn't participate in team sports, many of us would hop on a bike to take a ride around the neighborhood or to a friend's house. The fitness opportunities were all around us, even though we never called it "working out."

Then one day, suddenly, boom! We blast out of school to Planet Work, and all those moments with bikes, hoops, and balls seemed to be less and less interesting. Staff meetings, memo and report writing, financial forecasts, clocking in, and restocking held our attention. Wow, a paycheck for reading, writing, and arithmetic! We just did this in school for free! So we put in our time in the working world to be noticed and rewarded: a worthy adult goal.

Tips from the Pros

Many people in our society would rather be somewhere else in their lives. They remain in the "cannot's" and the "should not's" and the "what if's" of everyday life, until one day they wake up and realize that they've lived in that "cannot" world for 40 years.

These same people dream of being "doers." They fantasize about actualizing their goals and dreams. They look to and live vicariously through role models to actualize what they haven't been able to make happen for themselves. Often those role models are athletes. That's because athletes and sports represent the dream world we all seek: goal reaching, money, fame, fantasy, extreme experiences, adrenaline highs, being in the great outdoors. These "should not" people choose to remain in the stands rather than play on the field in the stadium of life.

—Terri Schneider raced with Team SCAR for the past 7 years, including five Eco-Challenges, two Mild Seven Outdoor Quests, the Raid Gauloises, and many other one-day adventure races. She previously raced triathlon professionally for 10 years and has completed 22 Ironman Triathlons. ■

Unlike sports, Planet Work has elusive, unwritten rules. We put forth a great deal of effort trying to figure out how to play in the work world. We move from city to city and from job to job. We find new challenges as we go. It can be very satisfying and certainly all consuming.

In the process of our relocation to the working world, most of us lost the thread of recreation. Only 10 percent of us Planet Workazoids belong to a health club, and only 5 percent of that 10 percent run marathons. Exercise stops being part of our world. But it doesn't have to be that way. In fact, your chance of professional success greatly increases if you're a fit person. By taking care of your physical self, you can put out the extra energy when the proverbial stuff hits the business fan. So let's explore how to get to triathlon, where you can become that recreation- and game-playing person you want to be and still be a decent citizen of Planet Work.

The Triathlon Lifestyle

Through the process of change, you'll find yourself at the starting line, probably of a triathlon. This is really just the starting point of the circle of expansive living that follows your vision of what your life with physical activity can be. After you go around the circle the first time, you'll notice that the circle enlarges. The process of the health and fitness lifestyle becomes a habit, a way of living, as it grows larger and larger (see figure 3.1). As you continue along the path of the triathlon lifestyle, you return to a new starting point that takes into account how far you've traveled.

The triathlon lifestyle is the same as the fitness and health lifestyle. It is a paradigm, a way of looking at one's inner and outer well-being. It's a way of living, of breathing, of believing in yourself, of learning about the outside and inside world. It's not a religion. It's not a cult. It's not a solution to personal problems. It's not nirvana. Rather, living like a triathlete is living in har-

Figure 3.1

The Triathlon Lifestyle Circle

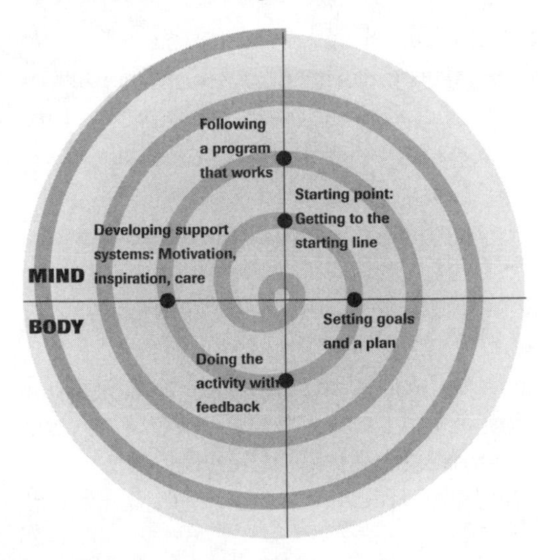

mony with your body. The benefits of a calm heart and cool head show up in every cell in my body and every part of my life. That's what I want for you.

The human body is a physiological organism that gives off energy. Living a day in the life of a triathlete is living a day filled with high energy—it's giving and taking emotional, physical, spiritual, social, psychological, and other types of energy. But what happens in a typical day of a triathlete? What do triathletes eat, think, do, act, and breathe?

You begin by setting priorities. Most people who have stayed with the triathlon lifestyle put their emotional and physical health first. Your health is the most important thing in your life. This health and fitness priority means that you ensure that your body receives proper rest, nutrition, challenges, and aerobic training. It also means that you take care of your emotional heart through, for example, proper personal time, joy, solid relationships, and relief from stress. Spend but one day without good health and you'll know why personal health is your first priority.

Now imagine yourself adopting a triathlon lifestyle. What would you do for just one day? Here's an example. You wake after eight hours of peaceful sleep. You snack lightly and slip on your running or walking shoes and take your body out for a 30- to 45-minute steady-state training session in heart zone 3. After a shower, you eat a balanced breakfast of nutrient-dense foods. You communicate with and give attention and love to those with whom you share your home and life. After taking care of your responsibilities to those individuals, you venture forth in a day of high productivity, which might include professional work, working at home, or a day of leisure activities.

Best Ways to Gain Back Time

- Videotape all TV shows, including the news, so you can fast forward through the commercials.
- Set time limits on phone calls, e-mail, and Internet surfing.
- Get up one hour earlier.

How the Triathlon Bug First Bit Us

We felt as though we were soul mates from our first date. It didn't take long for us to decide to spend our lives together. We had already realized that triathlon would only afford us this fairy-tale existence for a short while, so we quickly made plans to start a family and get "real" jobs soon. We worked well as a team from the beginning, although our day-to-day method of getting the job done was quite different. Erin likes to be organized and needs to have plenty of structure. I like to leave more scope to improvise and let my whims dictate my day a bit more. She always wants to get things done as early and as quickly as possible. I often let things linger. I've always been a bit of a procrastinator, and she hates that! But each week, we both make sure to get done all the training and other jobs one must do to get through a life and have a career. There were travel arrangements and sponsor liaising. There were bikes to take care of and meals to be prepared, laundry and bills, interviews and taxes—all the normal stuff that people do. But mostly we trained a lot.

If we didn't have to travel or race, a typical week for us included six runs of about an hour on average, five to six bike rides of an average of three hours each, six swims of just over an hour, three weight sessions, two massages, twenty minutes per day of stretching, two hours of eating, and nine hours of sleeping. I slept a lot! Many days would include a nap of about an hour during the day.

To us, pain, fatigue, overuse injuries, bad weather, and so on were just things you dealt with when they came. We expected the challenge to be very tough. We relished it. It was the opportunity of a lifetime, the chance to put together every skill we had acquired with every training session we had ever done to race a triathlon.

One of the wonderful aspects of this sport for us was the renewed sensation of taking on that challenge every time we lined up for an event we hadn't done before. Some events had heat or mountains or cold water or currents. Some had trails or big waves.

The opportunity to travel was a huge plus for us. We're both small-town people, so seeing the world on foot or from the seat of a bike afforded us a rare opportunity to see places and meet people we never could have imagined. Even now we find it hard to pass up invitations to locales we've never visited.

One important part of the equation that makes us who we are and perhaps explains why we were good at this sport is the fact that we did it for the challenge. There wasn't a dime to be made when we began. It actually cost us a ton if you add up the time spent training instead of working, the bikes, the travel, the entry fees, and so on. In that respect, we have a lot in common with everyone else who does it. Even though that aspect of our motivation changed over the years as money became available, the underlying reason to pursue excellence in the sport was that it was a terrific challenge and it brought out the best aspects of our characters.

—Scott Molina has won virtually every major triathlon in the world, including the Hawaii Ironman. Currently he is a coach, gym manager, and writer. In 1990, Scott married professional triathlete Erin Baker, who has won 107 professional triathlons and duathlons. Currently, she serves as a council member in Christchurch, New Zealand, and organizes a triathlon series for kids with 10,000 children participating. ■

Toward the middle or latter part of the day, if it's in your training plans, you dedicate time to stretching, strength training, or a sport-specific activity, such as indoor or outdoor cycling or a swim workout. Throughout the day, you're conscious, noticing the present moment and living in it, because it's the only moment you have available to you. As you pass through your day, you need to remember the philosophy of finding joy in your life and not causing pain or suffering to others. In addition, you eat small amounts of food regularly to keep your energy level high. It's well documented that eating processed foods results in negative energy, so you periodically eat small amounts of quality foods to maintain a high level of energy.

As you progress through your day, you're presented with challenges that may take many different forms: You may not have enough time in your day; you may not have completed an important transaction; you may have experienced a negative event. As you ride through these daily highs and lows, you handle each one like an endurance athlete might. Rather than getting depressed, you accept these events for what they are: challenges. Life is an endurance event. It requires each of us to be patient, to stay on the road to health and fitness.

Toward the end of the day, you unwind. You've taken care of your daily responsibilities to your family, your tasks, your training, your friends, and most of all, to yourself. Now you select a favorite activity (possibly including those people you share your life with) that results in positive energy, such as reading, playing, writing, listening to music, or talking. In your personal log or triathlon training log (on a scale from 1 to 10, with 10 being the best), give your day a good solid score of 10. Triathletes who are in balance and working their life plan will have 10 days in a row with scores of 10. That's what living like a triathlete is—it's living life as a series of 10s.

Why choose triathlon? Triathlon takes us to a place of high energy, low stress, and more joy. It takes us to a place where we are healthy, strong, and fit. It takes us to the place that we've always wanted to go.

chapter 4

assess your current fitness level

Improvement of your health and fitness is an endless journey; there's no final destination. The journey continues as long as you live. You'll be traveling over many bumps, and there are many twists and turns in the fitness road of your life. It's personal and intimate, and it requires a road map of sorts that you draw for yourself. Some of the days of your journey will be effortless, as simple to remember as brushing your teeth. You won't give it a moment's thought. Other days will be like pulling teeth—hard to get a grasp on it and exert the effort because you know there's a bit of pain involved. But in the end, you'll see a definite result. If you view your life as a long journey—the longest journey you can possibly make—then you'll want to know exactly where you are today on the fitness road.

Even if you're a professional athlete, your fitness level will rise and fall. That's the nature of the journey. How far and how fast you go up or down will be up to you, your lifestyle, and, in the case of some circumstances, plain luck. How long you stay below your desired fitness level may be up to you. Like any journey, you start with a single step, so let's see where you are today so you can get going down the road.

Pre-Workout Guide

"To boldly go where no one has gone before" may sound like a stirring rally to action and a great opener for a TV series, but even the most primitive adventurer had to figure out a few details before beginning a journey. Take a moment to review the following progressive statements of fitness involvement. Where do you fall in the list?

Ten Fitness Program Beginnings

I'm wondering about exercise benefits.

I'm new to fitness activity.

Weight management is my primary goal.

I used to be fit but not right now.

I work out at fitness center or club sometimes.

I work out regularly.

I participate in one of the three tri sports already.

I participate in two of the three tri sports already.

I've done all three tri sports.

I've done one triathlon.

If you're new to fitness, you probably most closely identified with one or more of the first five items on the list. If you're already active, you may find yourself on the last five levels. If you don't fit any category, don't worry. Guidelines are broad generalizations at best, and this is only one way to rate your level of activity.

Now that you've placed yourself on an activity scale of fitness programs, let's see where you place on another questionnaire, the PAR-Q (physical activity readiness questionnaire). The PAR-Q is designed to identify those people for whom certain physical activities might be inappropriate or who should receive medical advice about the kind of activity most suitable for them. If you answer "yes" to any of the questions in figure 4.1, you should not start an exercise program until you get clearance from your medical doctor.

Before you start any exercise program, you'll want to follow the prudent guidelines of the American College of Sports Medicine. The following is a synopsis of those recommendations.

Apparently healthy men over age 40 and apparently healthy women over age 50 should have a medical examination and diagnostic exercise test before starting a vigorous exercise program, as should symptomatic men and women of any age. However,

Figure 4.1

PAR-Q Form

The Physical Activity Readiness Questionnaire (PAR-Q)

Becoming more active is very safe for most people, but if you're in doubt, please complete the questionnaire below.

Some people should check with their doctor before they start becoming much more physically active. Start by answering the seven questions below. If you are between the ages of 15 and 69, the PAR-Q will tell you if you should check with your doctor before you start. If you are over 69 years of age, and are not used to being very active, definitely check with your doctor first.

YES NO

❑ ❑ 1. Has your doctor ever said that you have a heart condition and that you should only do physical activity recommended by a doctor?

❑ ❑ 2. Do you feel pain in your chest when you do physical activity?

❑ ❑ 3. In the past month, have you had chest pain when you were not doing physical activity?

❑ ❑ 4. Do you lose your balance because of dizziness or do you ever lose consciousness?

❑ ❑ 5. Do you have a bone or joint problem that could be made worse by a change in your physical activity?

❑ ❑ 6. Is your doctor currently prescribing drugs (for example, water pills) for your blood pressure or heart condition?

❑ ❑ 7. Do you know of any other reason why you should not do physical activity?

If you answered YES to one or more questions, talk with your doctor before you start becoming much more physically active.

If you answered NO to all questions, you can be reasonably sure that you can start becoming more physically active right now. Be sure to start slowly and progress gradually—this is the safest and easiest way to go.

Delay becoming much more active if:

- You are not feeling well because of a temporary illness such as a cold or a fever—wait until you feel better; or
- You are or may be pregnant—talk to your doctor before you start becoming much more active.

Note: If your health changes so that you then answer YES to any of the above questions, ask for advice from your fitness or health professional.

these procedures are not essential when such persons begin a moderate-intensity exercise regimen.

This is one of the reasons I always advise people who are new to training to start in zone 1, the Healthy Heart Zone (see chapter 5, "Heart Zone Training")—it simply poses less of a medical risk than the higher zones. With low-intensity exercise, there is less need for medical evaluation and program supervision or monitoring.

Getting an annual checkup from your health care professional is one of the best assessment tools you have. Find a doctor who stays fit, who swims, bikes, runs—all three is best. Keep all the paperwork and test results right next to your training details. Figure 4.2 shows the kinds of questions your health care professional may ask you to answer. Table 4.1 (on page 31) provides the scorecard that goes with the risk appraisal.

If you score above 25 on this lifestyle test, then maybe this book will serve as a wake-up call. You can change to a healthier lifestyle while pursuing a training program. I guarantee that you'll think twice about that cigarette or cheeseburger once you begin to feel the benefits of healthier choices. Thinking twice is a great first step. Keep in mind the long journey of your life and the fitness road you are on. Don't wallow in your past choices, and you'll be trucking in no time.

Incremental changes are the most easily sustained. Planning to improve gradually is not the same thing as seeking perfection. Why overload your own expectations to the point where you've made the goal unattainable and given yourself yet another excuse to quit looking for improvement? Whipping yourself into a frenzy of activity is a sure way to burn out. So rather than working with an idea of the perfect life that may be unattainable, take it slow and be kind to yourself as you journey toward a lifestyle change. Every little bit does help, and you'll stay on the fitness and health path, one step at a time.

Kaizen

The Japanese word for small, constant improvement is *kaizen*. First used by the Japanese business community to express a way of

Figure 4.2

Measuring Your Risk for Heart Disease: Your Lifestyle Test

Age	10–20 1	21–30 2	31–40 3	41–50 4	51–60 6	61–70+ 8
Exercise	Intensive exertion at work and in recreation 1	Moderate exertion at work and in recreation 2	Sedentary at work and intense exertion in recreation 3	Sedentary at work and moderate exertion in recreation 5	Sedentary at work and light exertion in recreation 6	Complete lack of exercise 8
Heredity	No known history of heart disease in family 1	One relative over 60 with cardiovascular disease 2	More than one relative over 60 with cardiovascular disease 3	One relative under 60 with cardiovascular disease 4	Two relatives under 60 with cardiovascular disease 5	Three or more relatives under 60 with cardiovascular disease 7
Weight	More than 5 lb. under standard weight 0	Between 5 lb. under or over standard weight 1	6 to 20 lb. over standard weight 2	21 to 35 lb. over standard weight 3	36 to 50 lb. over standard weight 5	More than 50 lb. over standard weight 7
Tobacco Use	Nonsmoker 0	Cigar or pipe smoker 1	Smokes 10 or less cigarettes daily 2	Smokes 20 cigarettes daily 4	Smokes 30 cigarettes daily 6	Smokes 40 or more cigarettes daily 10
Cholesterol or Fat % in Diet	Cholesterol below 180 mg/dl Diet with no animal or solid fats 1	Cholesterol between 181 and 205 mg/dl Diet with 10% animal or solid fats 2	Cholesterol between 206 and 230 mg/dl Diet with 20% animal or solid fats 3	Cholesterol between 231 and 255 mg/dl Diet with 30% animal or solid fats 4	Cholesterol between 256 and 280 mg/dl Diet with 40% animal or solid fats 5	Cholesterol between 281 and 300 mg/dl Diet with 50% or more animal or solid fats 7
Blood Pressure	Upper reading between 100 and 119 1	Upper reading between 120 and 139 2	Upper reading between 140 and 159 3	Upper reading between 160 and 179 4	Upper reading between 180 and 199 6	Upper reading over 200 8
Gender	Female under 40 years old 1	Female between 40 and 50 years old 2	Female over 50 years old 3	Male 4	Stocky male 6	Bald stocky male 7

The Coronary Heart Disease Risk Appraisal (RISKO), adapted from the Michigan Heart Association improving quality control (the era of TQC, or total quality control, espoused by Deming), it has now spread to other disciplines, in this case, triathlon.

The principle of kaizen is to improve in small ways frequently. The idea is that it's better to improve 1 percent a hundred small times than try to improve 100 percent all at once. In triathlon training, this idea fits with physiological fitness changes that take place during training. The human body doesn't respond to one large dose of exercise, resulting in one large improvement. Rather, constant, small, continuous, contiguous, progressive changes can lead to a measurable and substantial improvement in fitness.

In most cases, the results of reaching for a one-time, enormous change can range from havoc to damage. For example, if you start with little to no fitness background and you immediately decide to spend half of your work week exercising because you read that Lori Bowden trains 20 hours a week to prepare for the Ironman, the cost could be significant—overtraining, muscle soreness, and potential injury.

If you use the system of kaizen, however, you would increase your training dosage in a regular and progressive manner, resulting

Table 4.1

RISKO Score Table

Score	Level of Risk	Training Recommendation
6–11	Risk well below average	You are probably already on an exercise program. Keep it up!
12–17	Risk below average	Begin your program today!
18–24	Average risk	Start slowly and progress.
25–31	Moderate risk	Stay in Healthy Heart Zones for at least the first month (see chapter 5).
32–40	High risk	Stay in Healthy Heart Zones for the first 2 months and get a medical checkup.
41–62	Very high risk, see your physician	Don't begin until you have clearance from your physician.

in positive cardio, strength, endurance, and flexibility improvements. Kaizen is the smart way to train. It will keep you on your training program, help you realize the benefits, and ensure that you get the results you want.

Self-Testing for Your Individual Physiology

Controversy: Fit or Fat?

While you are on the path of assessing your fitness journey, I hope you have taken a good look in the mirror, both metaphorically and literally. The mirror can be one way to see physical changes in our body that result from physical activity. If, for you, looking good is part of feeling good and being healthy, then your journey is well planned. However, if your idea of health is tied only to what you see in the mirror, take another look. Appearances can be deceiving.

It used to be assumed that if you were thin, you were healthy. Research is now showing that someone who is overweight and trains regularly is healthier than someone who is thin and doesn't train. This is a happy boon to many overweight or large-sized people who worry about their weight as a main indicator of their health. Rather than using the term "overweight," say "over fat." This shifts the emphasis from overall weight to percentage of body fat, which can be a better indicator of fitness and health.

When it comes to watching what you eat, you never want to cut your caloric intake to the point that you aren't getting enough fuel to sustain your activity. If you do so, then you are mistaking the goal of fitness to be fat loss. It really is okay to be larger than the "ideal" size. And whose ideal is it anyway? If you're training and eating well, you're on the right track. Fitness is its own reward. Appearances are no indication of performance, nor does high performance guarantee a healthy lifestyle. They now have Clydesdale/Athena divisions at many triathlons for those athletes who don't fall into the "skinny" category.

Not everyone can or should aim to be slim. When Olympic swimmer Dara Torres returned to competitive swimming after years of Tae Bo and modeling, she found she had to put on weight to get back her prowess as a swimmer. Professional beach volleyballer Gabrielle Reece found that when she was at the "ideal" weight of 145 pounds at over 6 feet tall, she was weak and got injured and sick more often.

Remember that those height/weight charts you see at the doctor's office were created for people who don't train, and the charts haven't been adapted for the modern athlete. It's not about your body weight, it's about your physical activity.

Body Mass Indexing: Why It Is Meaningless to Individuals

In addition to the height/weight chart in doctor's offices and elsewhere, another popular measure of your lean mass and fat is expressed in a mathematical formula. You plug in a couple of height/weight numbers and bingo, you generate a Body Mass Index number. It sounds simple, and it is. However, body mass indexing (BMI) was created as an anthropological tool to study the effects of dietary change in ethnic populations. BMI was not intended to be applied to individuals, only to populations. Thus if everyone in a tribe started eating coconuts for breakfast, the effect of that additional food or eating behavior could be measured with a formula that statistically proves a change in total group weight (a loss or a gain) from a dietary change. Unfortunately, BMI has now become a popular way to gauge an individual's fitness, and there are plenty of personal trainers, Web sites, and magazine articles that offer to calculate your BMI and then sell you some training to improve your score. You can use the BMI if you want, but remember that the way it's used in popular media is not necessarily accurate or helpful to your training.

So if you can't use a height/weight chart and BMI doesn't relate to you as an individual, how do you assess your physique? Looking in the mirror is a good start. You know what you want to see and you know what you don't. After looking in the mirror, see where you fall in table 4.2.

Table 4.2

Fit or Fat: Quadrants of Concern

	Fat	Not fat
Fit	**** worthy pursuit	***** most desirable
Not fit	** least preferred	*** less preferred

An even better way to track your fitness is through body fat monitoring and Heart Zone Training. Both of these give you individual facts and concrete data that you can use to gauge your personal improvement. We'll discuss body fat monitoring in chapter 9 and Heart Zone Training in chapter 5.

Heart Rate Information and Tests

Heart rate monitors (covered in detail in chapter 5) are powerful feedback tools that also provide baseline assessments so you know where you stand. Athletes know that heart rate, or beats per minute (bpm), can tell a great deal about fitness over time if the information is recorded during different sport-specific activities. Heart rate information also serves as a physiological benchmark—keeping track of your heart rate during stationary conditions helps when planning an increase in activity. As you record the different heart rates (ambient, resting, and recovery) over time, you'll find data about your response to an activity and make adjustments to your training as necessary. Following are the terms to get you started.

Ambient Heart Rate

Your *ambient heart rate* is the number of beats per minute that your heart contracts when you're awake but in a sedentary and stationary position. In conditions of stress, such as a performance review at work, you might see this ambient number rise, even though you're motionless. Change in moment-to-moment ambient heart rate is normal and healthy. An average ambient heart rate above 80 beats per minute indicates a lack of fitness.

Resting Heart Rate

Resting heart rate is the number of beats your heart contracts in 60 seconds when you first wake up, before you get out of bed. If you're training appropriately, you'll most likely see this rate drop over time. Very fit people see numbers in the low 50s. You can get an average resting heart rate by writing down the number you see for a week or so and dividing by the number of days you've tracked it. If your training volume is high, your resting heart rate might be higher than your average. Sometimes a higher resting heart rate is to be expected (perhaps due to a planned increase in workload), so it's not necessarily a cause for worry or concern. But it is still a good indicator of what's going on with your physical and emotional stress.

Recovery Heart Rate

Your *recovery heart rate* is the number of beats per minute that your heart drops after exercise, usually measured after 1 or 2 minutes of rest. Some heart rate monitors collect this information for you and give you either the time it takes your heart to reach a certain heart rate number you have selected or tells you how many beats your heart rate has dropped in a given amount of time. This is an important indicator of your current fitness level.

You can use the heart rate monitor to give yourself several different kinds of tests that will help you track and assess your fitness level. One of these tests, the delta heart rate test, tells you on a daily basis where you're overtraining.

Delta Heart Rate

One of the basic physical activities we all do is to stand up. *Delta heart rate* is the difference in heart rate response between lying down and standing. Looking at what happens to your heart rate in the simple act of standing up is an indicator of the current health and stress condition of an individual. Less than ten beats difference is great; do any workout you want. A difference from ten to nineteen beats is okay; you can do what you had in mind.

A difference of more than twenty beats is a yellow light of caution—you might consider taking a rest day.

Self-Scoring for Your Sport-Specific Fitness

Beyond activity, health, and lifestyle, you also have to have the equipment and facilities to train well. Here's a quick list of the

Delta Heart Rate Test

Lie down and remain still for about 2 minutes. Note the lowest number on your heart rate monitor in this position.

As you slowly stand, there is a spike in your heart rate, which gradually drops to a standing heart rate number after about 2 minutes. Ignore the spike.

After waiting 2 minutes, measure your heart rate while standing. Subtract the prone heart rate number from the standing heart rate number, and you have your delta heart rate.

The higher the number, the more stressed your body is.

Example:

Lying down heart rate:	75 bpm
Standing heart rate:	– 55 bpm
Delta heart rate:	20 bpm

Sample Delta Heart Rate Chart

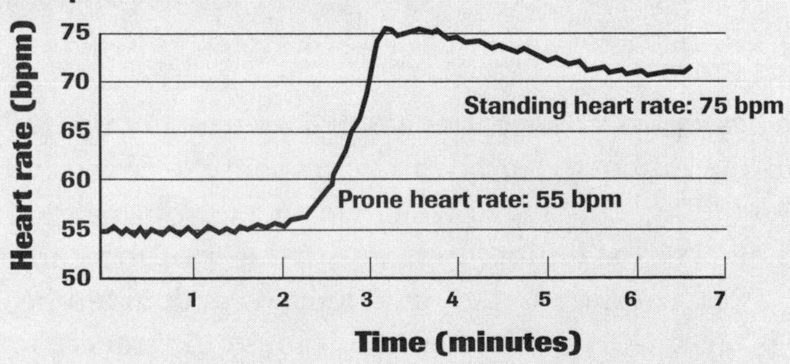

basics that you'll need. Design a plan for finding and accessing these resources. If you find it's difficult to answer these questions, then get some help to find the solutions.

Logistics and Gear at the Ready

Where can I swim?

Where can I bike safely inside (with a stationary bike) and outside?

Where do I get a heart rate monitor?

Where is my bike? Where is the bike shop for tune-ups?

Is my helmet safe?

What about apparel?

Now that you've thought about lifestyle and health, taken a few heart rate measurements, and searched in the garage or elsewhere for the necessary gear, let's see where you rank on a couple of benchmark activities. Remember where you fell on the Ten Fitness Program Beginnings? If you fell somewhere in the first five on that metric, try this New to Fitness scorecard (table 4.3). Do the activities to find out where you rank.

What does it mean to be level 1, 2, or 3? This number indicates your beginning place. A wise person once said that a journey of a thousand miles begins with one step. With your assessment in hand, you can take that step easily, knowing where you are heading—off this scorecard and on to the next one.

If you list yourself on the bottom half of the Ten Fitness Program Beginnings, you may need a slightly more progressive scorecard. Try the activities in table 4.4 to find out where your

Table 4.3

New to Fitness Scorecard

	Swim	**Bike**	**Walk/Run**
	2 min.	10 min.	5 min.
Level 3	100 yards (4 lengths)	2.5 miles (15 mph)	½ mile (2 laps)
Level 2	75 yards (3 lengths)	2.0 miles (12 mph)	⅜ mile (1.5 laps)
Level 1	50 yards (2 lengths)	1.5 miles (9 mph)	¼ mile (1 lap)

performance falls. You can do the test with full-out or moderate effort—it's your choice. Just be sure to do the same effort when you retest yourself on these scorecards.

Refer to these scorecards as a benchmark for your progress as you work toward your training plan. Watch your numbers improve as you get fitter.

Table 4.4

Active Scorecard

Fitness	**1½-mile Run**		**400-yard Swim**		**3-mile Bike Ride**	
categories	Time	Score	Time	Score	Time	Score
High	<7:05	20.0	<5:01	20.0	<5:53	20.0
	7:20	19.5	5:07	19.5	6:00	19.5
	7:35	19.0	5:13	19.0	6:08	19.0
	7:55	18.5	5:20	18.5	6:17	18.5
	8:05	18.0	5:27	18.0	6:26	18.0
	8:20	17.5	5:34	17.5	6:35	17.5
	8:35	17.0	5:41	17.0	6:45	17.0
	8:55	16.5	5:49	16.5	6:55	16.5
	9:10	16.0	5:57	16.0	7:05	16.0
	9:31	15.5	6:05	15.5	7:17	15.5
	9:50	15.0	6:14	15.0	7:29	15.0
	10:16	14.5	6:23	14.5	7:41	14.5
Medium	10:35	14.0	6:32	14.0	7:54	14.0
	11:01	13.5	6:42	13.5	8:08	13.5
	11:31	13.0	6:53	13.0	8:23	13.0
	12:01	12.5	7:04	12.5	8:39	12.5
	12:35	12.0	7:16	12.0	8:56	12.0
	13:10	11.5	7:28	11.5	9:14	11.5
	13:50	11.0	7:41	11.0	9:33	11.0
	14:31	10.5	7:55	10.5	9:54	10.5
	15:20	10.0	8:10	10.0	10:16	10.0
	16:10	9.5	8:26	9.5	10:40	9.5
Low	17:00	9.0	8:43	9.0	11:05	9.0
	18:00	8.5	9:01	8.5	11:33	8.5
	19:00	8.0	9:20	8.0	12:04	8.0
	21:00	7.5	9:41	7.5	12:37	7.5
	23:00	7.0	10:03	7.0	13:13	7.0
	25:00	6.5	10:27	6.5	13:53	6.5
	30:00	6.0	10:53	6.0	14:37	6.0
	32:00	5.5	11:21	5.5	15:26	5.5
	34:00	5.0	11:52	5.0	16:21	5.0
	36:00	4.5	12:25	4.5	17:07	4.5
	>37:00	4.0	>13:02	4.0	>18:00	4.0

chapter 5

Heart Zone Training

Heart Zone Training is the key to training and performance. Using one simple tool, a heart rate monitor, will give you important information about you and your workouts on a regular basis. A heart rate monitor helps you track your progress as you train.

Summary of Goals

This chapter will help you

- ✔ Know the five training zones.
- ✔ Learn the functions of your monitor.
- ✔ Learn your maximum and resting heart rates.
- ✔ Track your daily heart rate.
- ✔ Track approximately how much time you spend in each zone when you're training.

Why Heart Zone Training?

Heart Zone Training, with the help of a heart rate monitor, is a smart way of keeping track of your training and fitness across many different types of activity. Have you ever wondered who is more fit—a basketball player or a football player? What would happen if you took all the rackets away from tennis players and replaced them with baseball bats? The Ironman triathlon event was actually conceived around the same kind of endless hypothetical discussion as to who was the better athlete—a swimmer, a biker, or a runner—which was the toughest sport, and which created the fittest person. The argument was somewhat settled by triathlon, as a combination of all three certainly makes for a compromise answer of sorts.

At any rate, each sport and physical activity requires a different combination of muscles and skills, but there is only one pump, your heart, driving them all. Heart Zone Training does for your physical activity what triathlon does for the argument about separate swim, bike, or run events: It's the great equalizer.

A heart rate monitor also gives you immediate feedback on your performance, which can be highly motivating. Heart Zone Training is much more accurate than the rate of perceived exertion (RPE) scale, in which you decide where your effort falls on a scale from 1 to 10 based on how hard you feel you're working. The numbers on your monitor tell you exactly how hard your heart is working, measuring relative exercise intensity.

If you use such benchmarks as steady state heart rate test (see page 50), you'll see how much stronger and faster you get. If you track your progress via your heart rate, you'll know when you're ready to go to the next level and increase your training. You'll also know when to take it easy.

Gear

When you're ready to buy a heart rate monitor, you'll have many options. You may see two types of monitors: pulse monitors and heart rate monitors. The first measures your pulse (the biochemical blood flow), and the latter, your electric heartbeat. What you need is a heart rate monitor that is at least waterproof and has a chest strap (see figure 5.1). You no longer have to spend $300 for a monitor with all the bells and whistles. You can find a simple, starter monitor for as little as $50, or you can buy one that's downloadable with software and a port to your computer for greater versatility in tracking. I like zone monitors, which allow you to program in one or several training zones. It's also nice to have a stopwatch and a clock on your receiver (the wrist piece), but it's up to you. Buy what fits your budget. You can always upgrade later and give that starter monitor to a friend.

Get a heart rate monitor. Go ahead. I'll wait until you get back.

Figure 5.1
Heart Rate Monitor

Starting Your Heart Zone Training

Heart Zone Training is a system for getting the most out of your training. Rather than following the faulty and outdated information on the age-adjusted heart rate charts you find in the gym, you train according to a plan that you tailor for yourself. There are five zones in Heart Zone Training, and you need to spend time in each one, according to your fitness level and training goal. Each zone is described later in this chapter. Zones are represented as a range of percentages of the maximum rate at which your heart can beat. There is a very different feeling between activity that brings you close to your maximum heart rate and your activity that uses only 50 percent of the maximum capacity of your heart in terms of beats per minute. Knowing different heart rate zones is the key to making an easy day easy and a hard day a true workout, regardless of the activity you choose.

Let's take a look at how to test to get the highest number of heartbeats per minute so you can set your Heart Zone Training to your individual physiology.

Find Your Maximum Heart Rate

There are many ways to find your maximum heart rate (max HR). One of the easiest is to use the highest number you see on your monitor, particularly at the end of a fast workout or a race. You can also take a max HR test under the supervision of a doctor or exercise specialist. For those who haven't entered any races yet and don't have the wherewithal to visit a lab for a test, here's another way to do it.

Take a 3-minute step test: Step on and off an 8- to 12-inch step 30 times a minute for 3 minutes. Stay as relaxed as you can for those 3 minutes, maintaining a steady pace and then record the highest number you see on your monitor. To that highest number, add your fitness factor number to estimate your maximum heart rate. Add 55 bpm if you are recently returned to fitness, add 65 bpm if you are engaged in physical activity, and add 75 bpm if you are already training consistently.

Next, though not as accurate, use the formula:

210 − ½ your age − 5% of your body weight + 4 (male)
or 0 (female) = predicted max HR

This is called the Math Max Heart Rate method.

Average the two results and use the resulting number as your "estimated" max HR. If you later see a higher number on your monitor, don't be alarmed. Just use that higher number as your new max HR and calculate your zones according to figure 5.2.

Because of the physiological differences in the different types of training, you may find that you have sport-specific max HRs. For example, your maximum heart rate swimming is lower than that for running. When you're swimming, you are both prone

Figure 5.2

Heart Zone Training (HZT) Chart

Training Zone (% maximum heart rate)	Fuel Burning															
		Max HR	Max HR	Max HR	Max HR	Max HR	Max HR	Max HR	Max HR	Max HR	Max HR	Max HR	Max HR	Max HR	Max HR	Max HR
Z5 Red Line 90%–100%	Glycogen Burning	150 ↑ 135	155 ↑ 140	160 ↑ 144	165 ↑ 149	170 ↑ 153	175 ↑ 158	180 ↑ 162	185 ↑ 167	190 ↑ 171	195 ↑ 176	200 ↑ 180	205 ↑ 185	210 ↑ 189	215 ↑ 194	220 ↑ 198
Z4 Threshold 80%–90%		135 ↑ 120	140 ↑ 124	144 ↑ 128	149 ↑ 132	153 ↑ 136	158 ↑ 140	162 ↑ 144	167 ↑ 148	171 ↑ 152	176 ↑ 156	180 ↑ 160	185 ↑ 164	189 ↑ 168	194 ↑ 172	198 ↑ 176
Z3 Aerobic 70%–80%		120 ↑ 105	124 ↑ 109	128 ↑ 112	132 ↑ 116	136 ↑ 119	140 ↑ 123	144 ↑ 126	148 ↑ 130	152 ↑ 133	156 ↑ 137	160 ↑ 140	164 ↑ 144	168 ↑ 147	172 ↑ 151	176 ↑ 154
Z2 Temperate 60%–70%		105 ↑ 90	109 ↑ 93	112 ↑ 96	116 ↑ 99	119 ↑ 102	123 ↑ 105	126 ↑ 108	130 ↑ 111	133 ↑ 114	137 ↑ 117	140 ↑ 120	144 ↑ 123	147 ↑ 126	151 ↑ 129	154 ↑ 132
Z1 Healthy Heart 50%–60%	Fat Burning	90 ↑ 75	93 ↑ 78	96 ↑ 80	99 ↑ 83	102 ↑ 85	105 ↑ 88	108 ↑ 90	111 ↑ 93	114 ↑ 95	117 ↑ 98	120 ↑ 100	123 ↑ 103	126 ↑ 105	129 ↑ 108	132 ↑ 110

and supported by the water. Both of these factors could affect your max HR number for swimming. If possible, use your sport-specific max HR for each sport to personalize your Heart Zone Training.

Healthy Heart Zone: Zone 1

When you exercise at 50 to 60 percent of your maximum heart rate, you are in the Healthy Heart Zone. This is the zone in which you're burning mostly fat calories and working on making your heart healthier. When you first start training, you'll spend a lot of time in zones 1 to 3 building up your base fitness level.

Temperate Zone: Zone 2

In this zone, you're exercising at 60 to 70 percent of your max HR. Training in zone 2 helps you raise your fitness level by increasing your muscle mass and aerobic capacity. The more muscle mass you have, the more calories you burn, even at rest. In this way, you can raise your metabolism and burn fat more efficiently. You also train in zone 2 on your recovery days, or between hard training days, to avoid burnout and injury.

Aerobic Zone: Zone 3

In zone 3, you work your aerobic system—the efficiency of the body in using oxygen intake (from breathing). You are in this zone when you reach 70 to 80 percent of your max HR. A fit person training for a triathlon or other longer event trains frequently in this zone to increase endurance. This is the zone in which most fitness enthusiasts spend the bulk of their time, because it's comfortable and sustainable.

Threshold Zone: Zone 4

In zone 4, at 80 to 90 percent of your max HR, your body reaches its anaerobic threshold—the point at which you cross over to a different energy system. The anaerobic threshold can be changed through smart training using all the different heart zones to get you to your fittest.

Train in zone 4, at or near your maximum sustainable heart rate, to increase your strength and speed. Your anaerobic threshold, unlike your max HR, is changeable. As you become more fit, your anaerobic threshold will increase, up to a point. People who are not fit might have an anaerobic threshold in zone 3, but with training they will increase their fitness and thus increase their anaerobic threshold. Triathletes tend to train near this level frequently, because our races are long and we want to be able to sustain a high heart rate for most of the race.

Red Line Zone: Zone 5

At 90 to 100 percent of your max HR, you're in the Red Line Zone. I call it this because it's like a danger flag. No matter what your level of fitness, you won't be able to stay in zone 5 for very long. And you shouldn't try. Visits to this zone generally occur at the end of a race. You can also take trips to the Red Line Zone to increase your speed, but you want to avoid spending more than 10 percent or so of your total training time in zone 5.

Zone 5 is both challenging and dangerous and, to some people, a scary place. When you see your heart rate moving up toward your max, know that you're working yourself toward exhaustion and you'll soon have to stop. You also build up lactates in your muscles and bloodstream when training in zone 5, which may lead to stiffness and soreness within 24 to 48 hours as your body recovers and adapts to increased training stress.

The benefits of zone 5 training are increased speed, improvement in your anaerobic threshold, and an enlargement of your fat-burning range. When you are fit, you do want to spend some time here but just not as much as you spend in other zones.

Why Train in Different Zones?

In each zone, different adaptations and positive stresses occur. The effects of training in the different zones are not cumulative, so you need to spend time in most of them. Zone 1 is beneficial to your heart, energy, and self-esteem. Zone 2 helps you increase muscle and burn fat. In zone 3, you're increasing your aerobic capacity and burning more carbohydrates. Training in zone 4 helps increase your anaerobic threshold, which will increase your speed and enlarge your fat-burning range. And training in zone 5 will help you reach your peak fitness. Mix up the zones in your training according to your fitness level and goals to reap the benefits of each.

A training tree is a conceptual way of representing the different training periods (see figure 5.3). The left side of the tree shows the aerobic side and the right shows the anaerobic side. To climb up the tree in the Heart Zone Training method (see figure 5.3), you can track your heart zone points (5 minutes in zone 1 = 5 points, 5 minutes in zone 2 = 10 points, etc.) to give you a total value for a training period.

Safety

Remember, Heart Zone Training is not a license to speed. If your workouts are only about seeing high heart rate numbers, then you'll

Figure 5.3
Training Tree

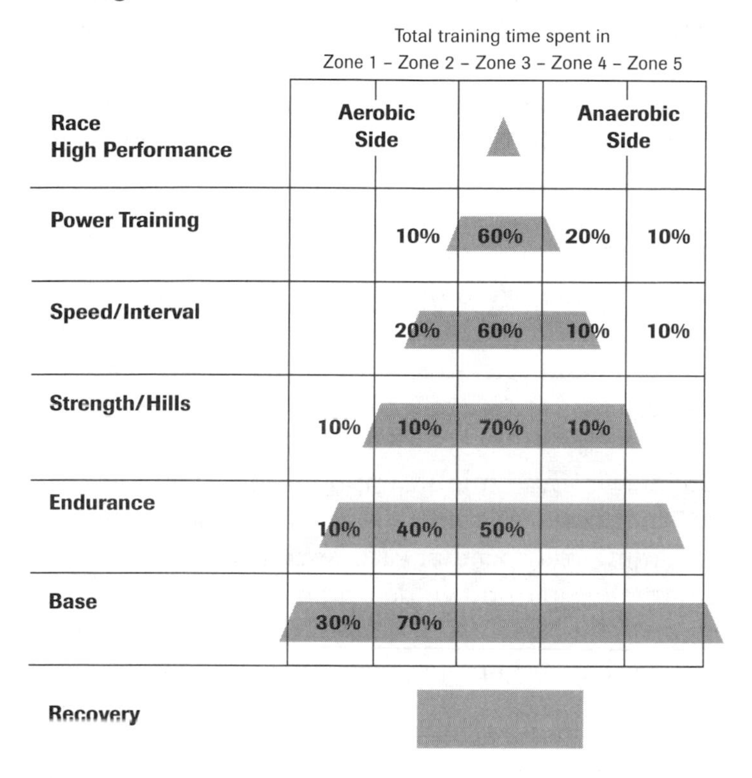

miss out on the overall benefits of a comprehensive Heart Zone Training plan. You need to spend time in the lower zones as well as the upper zones. Training exclusively in zone 3 and above is an invitation for overtraining and injury. Even after you've reached your fitness and training goals, spend time in zones 1 and 2 to reap the benefits of a healthy heart and cardio improvement.

Workouts

This section provides some examples of how to use your heart rate monitor in training.

The Ladder Workout

This workout can be adapted for any of the three triathlon sports, as well as to fit other activities. After your warm-up, increase your pace until you're at the bottom of your zone 3 (the aerobic zone, 70 to 80 percent of your maximum heart rate). Stay at that heart rate for 5 minutes and then increase your pace until you're in the middle of zone 3. Stay at that pace for another 5 minutes and then increase again until you reach the top of zone 3. Stay at the top of zone 3 for 5 minutes and then ease your pace until your heart rate drops back down to the middle of the zone, which is 75 percent of your maximum heart rate. Stay in the middle of the zone for 5 minutes and then drop your pace again to reach the bottom of zone 3. Stay at that pace for 5 minutes and then begin your cool-down.

This workout, with a 10-minute warm-up and 10-minute cool-down, lasts 45 minutes (see figure 5.4). You can increase or decrease the amount of time you spend at each level, and you can adjust your goal heart rates up or down depending on your fitness and your training goals for the day. You can also go up and down more frequently, rather than just up once and then back down.

Figure 5.4
Graph Profile for the Ladder Workout

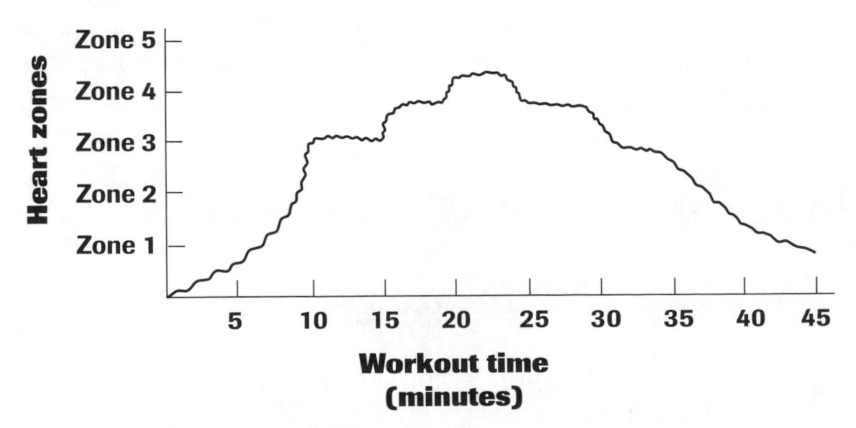

The Criss Cross Workout

In this workout, you cross two zones. You go from being very comfortable to slightly uncomfortable. This workout allows you the chance to experience two of the most enjoyable zones, and at the end you will feel invigorated and refreshed. Warm up for 10 minutes, then increase your pace until you are in the middle of zone 3. Immediately recover until your heart rate drops to the middle of zone 2. Repeat the sequence for 25 minutes and then warm down for 10 minutes. (See figure 5.5.)

The Steady State Workout

Warm up for 10 minutes and then increase your pace until you're at the target heart rate you planned for the workout. This target can be anywhere in zone 2 or 3, but it's only a good workout for zone 4 if you are very, very fit. Keep your heart rate at the same level—within three to five beats per minute if possible, but definitely within the same zone—for half an hour to an hour. Then cool down. (See figure 5.6.)

The purpose of this workout is to train yourself in pacing and maintaining a specific heart rate. It's also known as a "Tempo Workout." It's good training for the steady state heart rate test (see page 50).

Figure 5.5

Graph Profile for the Criss Cross Workout

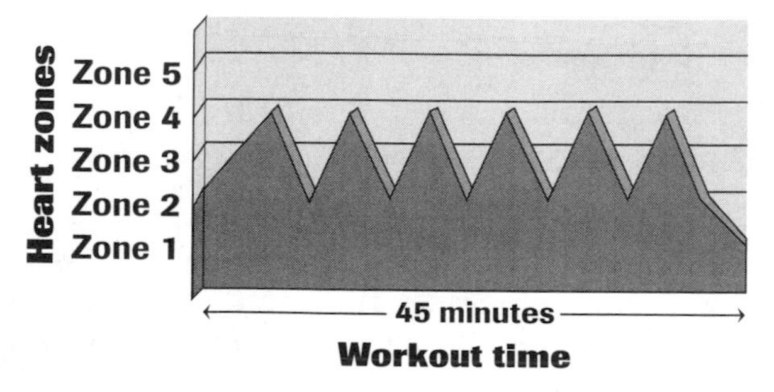

Figure 5.6
Graph Profile for the Steady State Workout

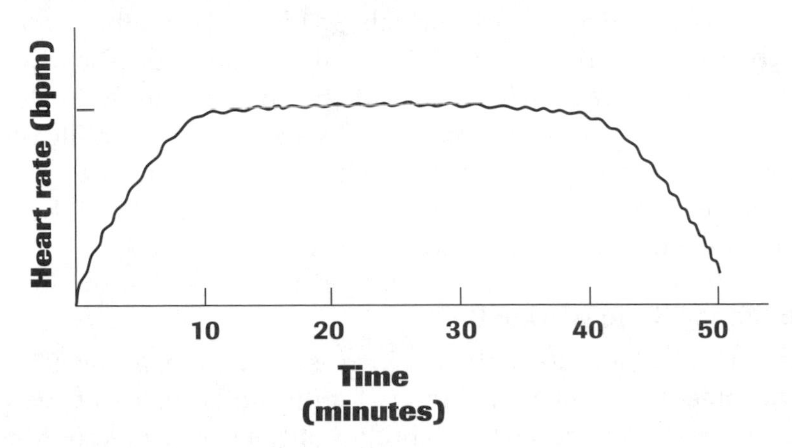

Skills Checklist

When training with your heart rate monitor, can you

✔ Adjust your intensity by watching your monitor during exercise (up and down; you need to be able to do both)?

✔ Plan a week of training that includes all five zones, appropriate to your available time, goals, and fitness level?

✔ Program your monitor (do you know the functions and how to use them)?

Charting Your Progress

Steady State Heart Rate Test

The purpose of this assessment is to set a benchmark and then measure your fitness improvement by retesting yourself. For this test, you need a set distance. It's helpful to do this at a track so you know exactly how far you're going. If you don't have access to a track, then pick a safe route, measure and mark the distances (1–2 miles) that you can visit over time (you need to do this test regularly to track your training).

Run 1 mile (or whatever your set distance is) at a steady heart rate. This can be the middle of your aerobic zone or below it if you're not yet capable of maintaining that heart rate for a mile. Time yourself and write down your time, distance, and heart rate. Once a month or so, as you continue your training, repeat this test using exactly the same course and heart rate. You should see an improvement in your time as your fitness level increases. If you don't, then either you've reached your goal level of fitness or you need to adjust your training to increase your fitness.

Know the State of Your Fitness by Your Training Heart Rate

If you're new or returning to fitness, you may find that you can't reach your max HR or train above zones 2 or 3 for any length of time. That's okay. The whole point is to continue with your training so that you reach the point of maintaining a higher heart rate. You may be able to reach higher levels when you're unfit, but you won't be able to sustain them. That's the point of training: increasing your fitness to sustain a higher heart rate for the duration of your workout or race. Heart Zone Training helps you know when you're there.

Heart Rate Is Relative

Your heart rate, both resting and training, can vary from day to day, depending on a number of factors. Whether you got enough sleep the night before or ate and drank enough, what the weather is like (particularly temperature), whether you're training inside or outside, and dozens of other variables can affect how your heart

Sport Equivalencies

The effort it takes to run a mile is not the same as the effort it takes to swim a mile or bike a mile. Dr. Kenneth Cooper, who more than 30 years ago wrote *Aerobics*, which changed the fitness world, worked out some equivalencies to help us allocate our training time.

6-mile run = 1.5-mile swim = 30-mile bike = 15-mile walk

performs. So don't obsess about the numbers. Keep a log and record your training and resting heart rates as well as external factors. Eventually, over time, you'll see patterns emerge. This will help you customize your training to fit your personal lifestyle as well as help keep you motivated when you're having a bad training day.

Spending More Money Isn't Always Better

I'll say it again: You don't need to spend a lot of money on a fancy heart rate monitor. Get the most you can for the least amount of money. If you like all the bells and whistles or crave the greater details you get from fancier monitors, by all means get one. But it isn't necessary for fitness. Visit www.heartzones.com for comparisons of different monitors.

When You're Ready for More: Resources

This is too complex a subject to cover in one chapter, but I hope I've given you enough information to get started. If you'd like to know more, check out my other books on the subject:

The Heart Rate Monitor Book, Polar Electro Oy (Finland), 1993.

The Heart Rate Monitor Book for Outdoor and Indoor Cyclists, Velo Press, 2000.

The Heart Rate Monitor Guidebook to Heart Zone Training, Heart Zone Publishing, 1997.

The Heart Rate Monitor Logbook, Heart Zone Publishing, 1999.

The Heart Rate Monitor Logbook for Outdoor and Indoor Cyclists, Velo Press, 2000.

The Heart Rate Monitor Workout Book for Indoor Cyclists, Velo Press, 2000.

Heart Zone Training, Adams Media Corporation, 1996.

Or you can take a step-by-step online training program, plus sign up for a free newsletter, at www.heartzones.com.

chapter 6

swim skills

In the United States, more than half of all adults are afraid of deep water in lakes or the ocean. Almost half of all adults also fear being in water over their heads in a pool. And plenty of people fear putting their head under the water. If you're part of this vast majority, you have some homework to do. But there are many resources that can help you overcome the fear of water in a practical way. Because you are not alone in this fear, feel free to ask for a referral to a swim coach who specializes in making folks feel more natural in the water. Before signing up for swim lessons, work on getting comfortable in a pool.

You can learn to prevent panic, stay in control, and be relaxed in any type of water. From this position of strength, you can learn to swim or swim better. Even if you can gut it out through the swim but never really get past nervous thoughts about water to enjoy swimming, consider finding a coach with a teaching method that addresses the anxiety factor.

Swim Training Goals

Before you get to the start line of your first triathlon, you should

✔ Be able to cover the distance of the race in the pool.

✔ Swim in open water at least once following safety guidelines.

✔ Know how your equipment works.

- How to get your wet suit on and off
- How to adjust your goggles so they don't leak
- How to fit the cap to your head as you like it, over or above your ears, for example

Swim Equipment

In comparison with other sports, swimmers get by pretty cheaply (except for their pool fees). In a small gear bag, you can stash almost everything you'll need to train for the water-sport leg of a triathlon.

Swimmers use training devices to help them improve their technique or their strength. These devices include hand paddles for resistance training, kickboards for strength, and fins for speed and for building strength in your legs. It's a good idea to invest in these devices, as they will hasten your improvement dramatically. Most pools have kickboards and pull buoys available, and some will have paddles. Check before you buy. Some swimmers train at least half of their laps using these swim toys, because this can help break up the monotony of swimming distances in a workout.

Insider Tip

Flotation devices are not permitted in the race. Rubber ducky stays home!

You might have seen some full-body or pant-length swim apparel at the Sydney 2000 Olympics. Perhaps you have been involved in swimming events, and you wonder if that professional-looking gear might help you place higher in your age group. An "age grouper" is someone who races to become one of the top finishers in an age category. According to Brent S. Rushall, Ph.D., R.Psy., a noted expert on swimming efficiency, it's unlikely that for age-group swimmers an investment in a high-priced new suit would be wise. Age groupers can gain much more by swimming with good technique and by training with sensible volume. Dr. Rushall says, "Any minuscule assistance from a new-fabric bodysuit would be a short-lived, transient advantage."

Only the first two items in the following essential equipment list are required for swimming. As a triathlete, however, you'll want to count four pieces of essential equipment, with the cap being the third and a wetsuit being the fourth. Usually when you race a triathlon, you must wear a cap (preferably a brightly colored one), because it helps safety officials see you in the water. You might also want to wear a cap for your training to protect your hair and to get accustomed to wearing it because of the race regulation. A wetsuit provides buoyancy, safety, and speed. But, for training, whether you use any gear beyond a swimsuit and a pair of goggles is up to you.

Swimming Gear

Essential Equipment

- Racing suit.
- Goggles that fit your face. You should take them out of the package in the store and make sure they'll stick to your eyes without the strap. Try them on to see if they're comfortable.
- Gear bag. Get the kind made for swimming so you can air out your suit.
- Cap (brightly colored). Protects your hair from damage and keeps you visible in the water.
- Wetsuit. Make sure it fits and practice using it before the race.

Optional Equipment

- Kickboard
- Swim fins
- Hand paddles
- Pull buoys
- Plugs (ear and nose), if necessary
- Goggle defogger
- Deck sandals (for at the pool)

Why Freestyle?

Triathletes use the freestyle stroke (otherwise known as the Australian or front crawl) because it's the fastest way to swim. Try not to use the breaststroke or any stroke other than the freestyle. Unfortunately, if you don't like the freestyle, you'll still need to learn it because it's much superior to other strokes. For example, swimming with the backstroke can get you far off course, since you can't see where you're going, and the breaststroke is much slower than the freestyle (which is why the world long-course record for 100 meters freestyle is just over 46 seconds, but the 60-second mark hasn't yet been broken in 100 meters of breaststroke long course).

There are many theories on the fastest way to swim. The old theory was to remain as flat as possible in the water, with your body parallel to the surface. More recent thinking involves rotating your body with your shoulders, keeping your hips and legs in line with the shoulders so that your body is fishlike, and gliding somewhat on your side with your arm stretched forward. Whichever way you swim, the idea is to reduce drag, or water resistance, in the water so you reach your destination as quickly and efficiently as possible.

Basic Stroke Mechanics

A successful freestyle stroke has five different components: (1) arm stroke, (2) kick, (3) timing of arms and legs, (4) body position, and (5) breathing. Each of these can affect the amount of drag that retards the forward motion of a swimmer. If you want to swim well and quickly, you must reduce your drag by learning to streamline your body's motions.

With the advent of underwater photography, the visual analysis of the efficient swim stroke dramatically changed the theories of stroke mechanics. Words like "push and pull" for the arm stroke were replaced with "sweep." The former suggested that the hands and feet were operating like paddles. Sweep, on the

Top 5 Things Not to Do in a Race

1. Don't line up in the swim with a group that is way faster than you or way bigger than you. Going 10 seconds later to avoid the elbows won't make a difference in a 2-hour race, but getting a fist in the nose will.
2. Don't start the race without either running the ins and outs of the transition area or having a perfect mental picture of the flow of the transition. I guarantee if you don't know the flow of the transition area before the race, in the heat of the battle you will surely be lost. And so will your bike.
3. Don't forget to smile at bystanders and fans. If you make racing and doing triathlon look like fun, then maybe the next year the bystanders will be next to you at the start line. Grimacing in pain just makes them think you are crazy.
4. Don't forget to spend 5 minutes sometime race morning saying a prayer with your husband's arms around you. This puts racing all in perspective. Pray for safety of all athletes and for a fair race. And, hey, it's okay to pray that you kick butt!
5. Of course, the most obvious thing not to do in a race is try something new as far as gear and/or eating and drinking go. Sometimes even the most minute adjustments of the helmet, shoelaces, half a scoop more of drink mix, 2mm raising of the seat, one more bagel for breakfast can ruin months of training.

—Barb Linquist, from Jackson Hole, Wyoming, lists triathlon as her third priority; first is her faith, and second is her marriage. Her elite career results include first place at Wildflower Half Ironman 2001 and second place at ITU World Toronto and Japan 2001. Barb attended Stanford University and is a former member of the U.S. National Swim Team.

other hand, describes the lift, the propulsion, and the propeller action of the limbs.

Let's look at each of the five components of the freestyle.

The Arm Stroke

The arm stroke can be broken into five different, smoothly connected, sweeping motions: (1) the entry, (2) the stretch, (3) the catch, (4) the sweep, and (5) the recovery.

THE ENTRY With a slightly flexed elbow, your hand enters the water at or near a full elbow extension. Keeping your elbow higher than your hand, your fingertips will touch the water first. The "hole" that your hand enters is forward of your head, midway between the outside of your shoulder and your head. Your hand slices through the water with the palms facing outward, 30 to 40 degrees from the prone or face-downward position. Your pinky finger should be higher than your thumb.

THE STRETCH The arm stretches as you glide—the arm is always moving forward. Your wrist is straight, with the arm relaxed from

Figure 6.1

Correct Hand Entry and Angle of Hand and Elbow

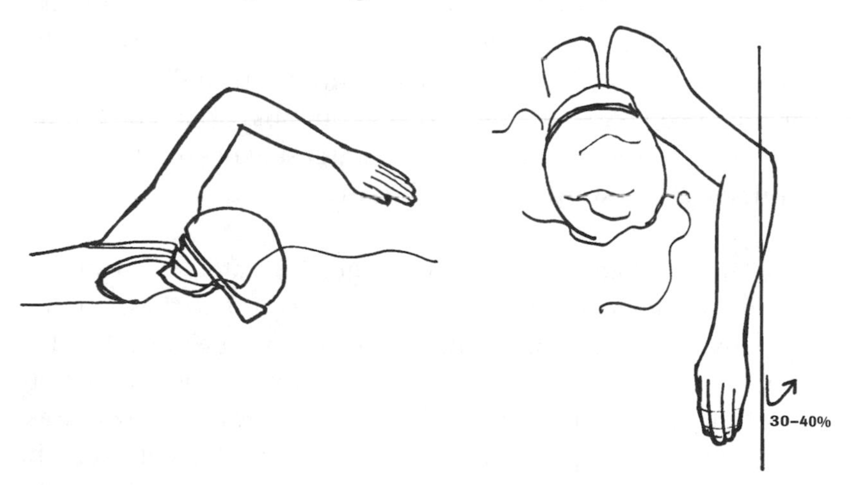

Figure 6.2
The Stretch with Body Roll

elbow to fingertips. Your body rolls somewhat down on the side of the arm that is stretched forward at an angle of about 45 degrees to the bottom of the pool.

THE CATCH The catch begins as the opposite arm finishes its sweep. Your wrist bends downward (40 degrees) and rolls outward. The elbow bends, and the sweep starts. You'll feel your head and shoulders surge forward over your bent arm. You can actually feel the catch, and you should. This is the start of the first propulsive phase of the arm stroke.

You should feel like your arm is not moving, but rather like your body is gliding over your arm. This is why it's called the catch: You catch a piece of water and hold it to pull your body over, using your core strength (from your abs, back, and shoulders). Practice this until you feel the water stay in your hand and your body slip forward through the sweep.

THE SWEEP When you sweep through the water, you can feel three phases: down, in, and up. As you move through these phases, your body's forward velocity will increase—you'll be moving faster. As your body rolls, with your shoulder pointing toward the bottom of the pool, you start the down sweep. Your elbow bends, and your hand sweeps downward and outward in a curved path.

Figure 6.3
The Catch

You sweep down, not just back. The palm of your hand rolls downward, then the palm pushes away from your torso, then it rolls inward and finally backward as you lift to take another stroke. This is called hand pitch. Your hand is slightly cupped, fingers together, and your elbow remains high.

In the next phase, the in-sweep, your hand and arm sweep backward, as they pass under your body and toward your midline (the line drawn from your nose through your belly button). Don't cross the midline, but continue to sweep backward past your waist and hips.

The sweep up begins as your hand passes your hips toward the outside of your thigh. Your hand is pitched outward and upward as you finish the sweep phase. Your palm is facing inward, and again your pinky finger is high.

THE RECOVERY At the point of the recovery, you're preparing for the next arm stroke. Some swimmers have a high elbow recovery; others recover with their hand leading in front of the elbow. Your elbow breaks through the surface first and moves forward in a bent position. Your elbow will be higher than your hand through the entire arm stroke portion of recovery. Your hand slides out of the water, little fingers first. Reach forward, almost dragging your fingers across the surface of the water, and the entry phase begins.

Figure 6.4
The Sweep

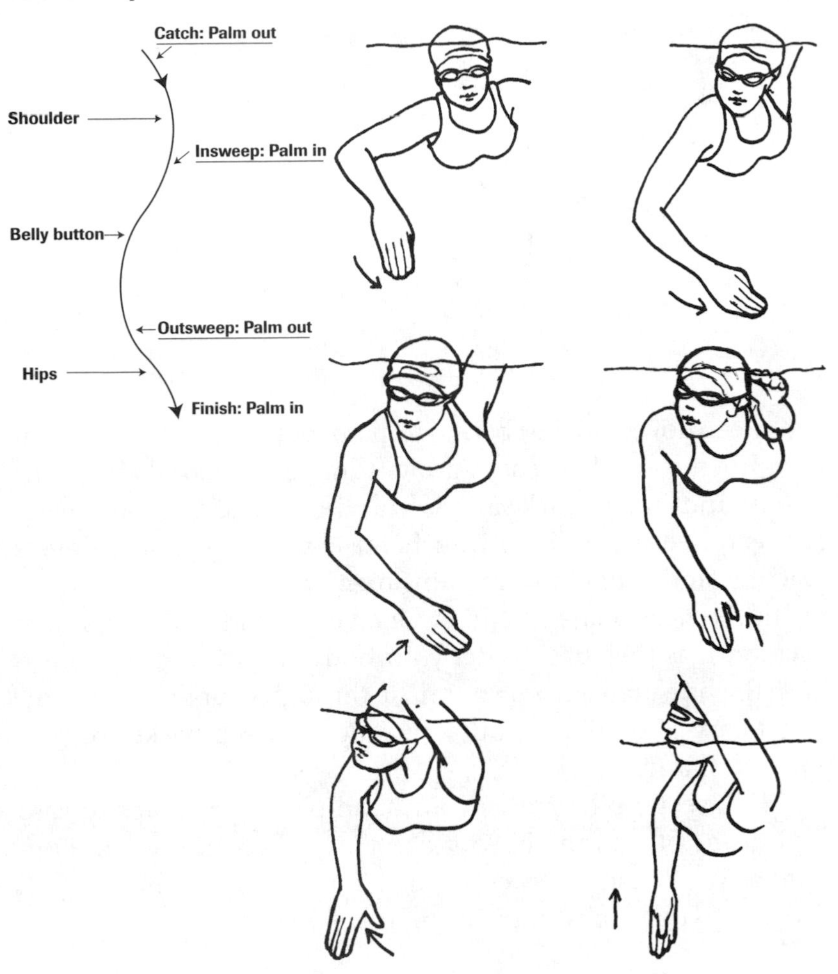

A key point on the recovery is to keep your hands as low and as close to your side as possible. Think about dragging your thumb along your armpit while you drag it through the water!

The Kick

The flutter kick mechanism consists of a downbeat and an upbeat. You kick sideways, or laterally with the roll of your body, as the legs move up and down. The downbeat starts with the flexion

Figure 6.5
The Recovery

from the hip joint, the knee passive, ankles and feet relaxed. The bottoms of your feet are pitched inward, and your toes are pointed. When your knees are about 10 inches deep, or chest deep, extend the knee joint. Your lower leg sweeps downward until your foot is 12 to 14 inches deep—the end of the downbeat.

The upbeat begins as the downbeat of the opposite leg begins. Your lower leg and ankle are relaxed in a natural position. The upbeat ends when your foot almost cracks the surface of the water. Simultaneously, both legs are moving sideways, as well as up and down, as your body rolls from side to side. As the right arm sweeps downward, the right leg kicks down. The left leg kicks up to coincide with the left arm as it's recovering.

Ankle flexibility is important to the kick in swimming. Swimmers don't point their toes rigidly, as divers and gymnasts do. Rather, the toes are pointed in a relaxed manner so that the foot doesn't cause drag, but the movement of the leg from knee to toes is one long line. If your toes point downward rather than straight behind you while you swim, your feet will cause drag and slow you down. If your ankles aren't flexible enough, you can stretch them by sitting on the bottoms of your feet and rolling backward, lifting the knees off the ground.

Timing the Arms and Legs

The number of kicks per stroke varies from swimmer to swimmer. Because the swim distance in triathlon is long, and when you're done you have two more leg-focused events to complete, the two-

Figure 6.6
The Downbeat and the Upbeat of the Flutter Kick

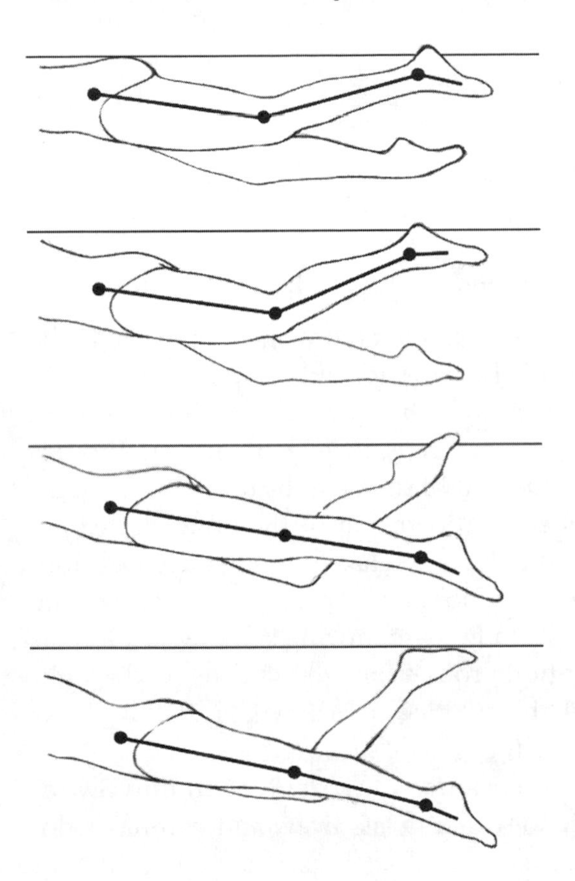

beat kick is most frequently chosen by triathletes. The rhythm consists of one downbeat of each leg per arm stroke. Each downbeat ends with the finish of the sweep of that arm. Relax your legs as your arm stroke recovers. Use the kick as much for body positioning or to stabilize you in the water as for propulsion.

The recent advances in swim technique involve holding your position longer when each arm is at the stretch position. You should be at an angle on your side, arm stretched straight toward the direction you're headed (in a pool, this would be toward the wall ahead). The idea is to glide along in your most hydrodynamic position, lessening the amount of energy you expend.

Swim one length of the pool, counting the number of arm strokes it takes to get there. The idea is to lower that number as you grow stronger and more efficient. Practice gliding when you're stretched out and then test yourself again. If you continue to practice gliding, you should eventually take fewer strokes per length. This will allow you to save energy for the bike and the run later in the race.

To learn more about this technique, I suggest you read *Total Immersion* by Terry Laughlin and *Fitness Swimming* by Emmett Hines. You could also hire a trainer or coach, join a masters swim team, or take a workshop if one is offered in your area.

Insider Tip

If you're a slower swimmer, stay to the back or sides of the pack where there are fewer people when you start the swim.

Body Position

The key here is to streamline your body position so that you create as little drag as possible. There are two components to body position: the horizontal and lateral positions.

In the horizontal position, the body lies flat in the water, parallel to the surface, and rolls to either side as you stroke and breathe. This is a natural position and doesn't require arching the back. Kicking too forcefully will cause the legs and feet to drop. Kicking too shallowly results in a lack of the stabilizing effect, and propulsive force, or forward motion, is lost. And kicking too strenuously will leave you little energy for the bike and the run to follow.

Think of swimming as a way to take up very little space in the water. If your lateral alignment is correct, your feet and legs are within the width of the body. You can lose lateral alignment

Figure 6.7

Streamline Position (top) and Legs Out of Position, Causing Drag (bottom)

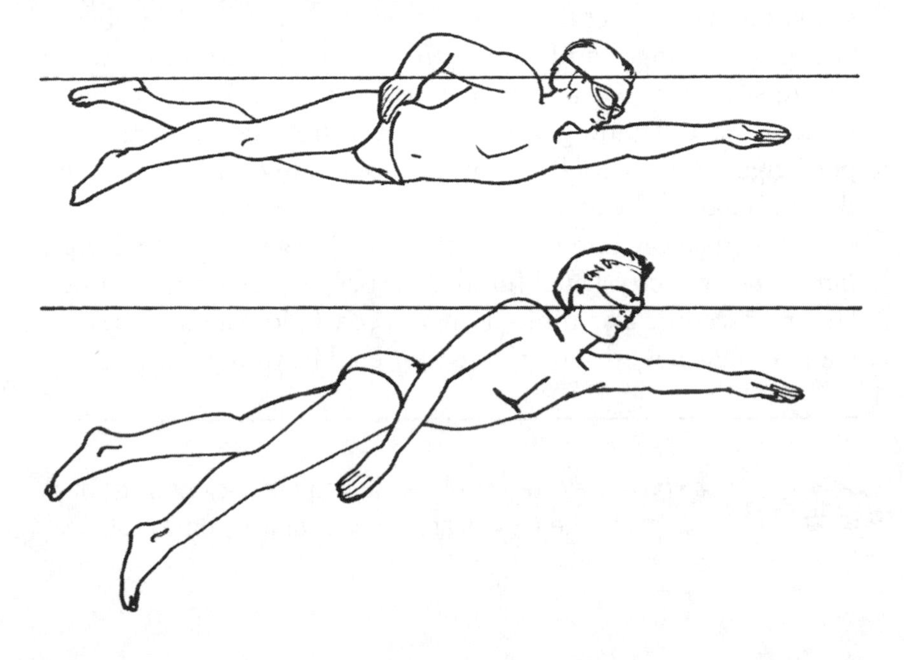

by overreaching, which causes you to "fishtail," or by pulling your head backward (up) while breathing, which causes you to drop your feet and hips toward the bottom. You'll want to look down most of the time, except when you look up to sight (see chapter 14).

As you maintain your body position, you also rotate your body around the longitudinal axis, that is, around a line centered along the length of your body. You constantly roll on your axis as you swim, actually spending more time on your side than in a flat position. The amount of roll is important—you should roll 45 degrees on each side, with the roll coinciding with the sweep of the arm on that side. Just remember not to swivel at the waist as you roll; your hips should stay in line with your shoulders so that you minimize drag. When your hips initiate the roll, it's easier to keep the shoulders aligned. So let the hips lead this dance!

Figure 6.8

Correct (left) and Incorrect Lateral Positioning

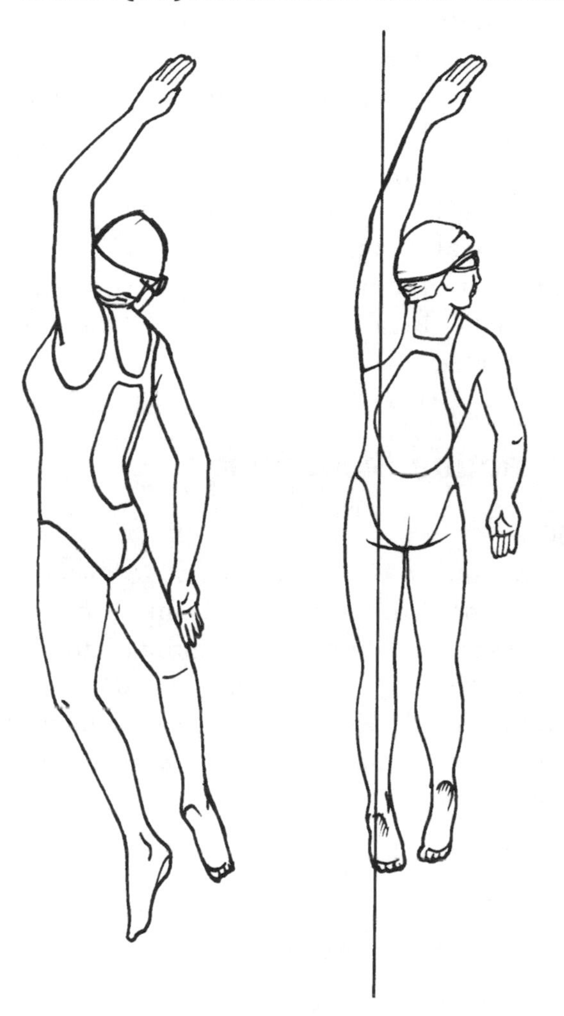

Breathing

Just as you reach that 45-degree roll position, you breathe. Your face turns sideward, as if you were going to look over your shoulder, and the head rolls to the side along with your body. Just as the arm on the opposite side enters the water, breathe. Your head doesn't lift. Rather, a bow wave is formed next to your mouth by the forward motion of your body, which makes a hole in the water in which you can breathe. After you breathe, your face rolls back into the water in coordination with the body roll. Breathe out in the water, breathe in out of the water. There should not be a pause in your arm recovery when you breathe.

Many triathletes, as well as competitive swimmers, employ alternate breathing, or bilateral breathing, in which they breath on alternating sides with the uneven numbered strokes, such as three or five. I breathe that way because it feels natural to me, my body positioning feels better, and in the event I need to breathe on a particular side because of wind or wave action, I'm comfortable doing so. Try to get used to breathing on both sides, but use whichever technique you prefer.

Let's Practice Swimming

Swim Workout Design

Most swimming pools are built in either 25 yards or 25 meters. It's great to find a 50-meter pool that isn't divided into two 25-meter segments so you can get a good long swim. A sprint triathlon swim is generally 750 meters, and an international distance triathlon swim is 1,500 meters. Be sure that you feel confident swimming that distance. Since so many pools are measured in yards, here are the equivalents:

25 yards equals 22.86 meters

25 meters equals 27.34 yards

50 yards equals 45.72 meters

50 meters equals 54.68 yards

If you're following a workout that's been written for yards but your pool is in meters, there will be some differences in total distance at the workout finish. You will swim more total distance. If you follow a workout written for meters but your pool is built in yards, you will swim less total distance. But most swim workouts are about both total distance swum and the type of workout—

steady state, intervals, ladders, or over-distance. For example, a workout might be oriented around a wind sprint style or it might have you swim progressively faster. So ultimately, it doesn't matter whether the workout is written for a 25-meter pool or a 25-yard pool—just follow the parts of it that help you benefit from the workout. We've referred to yards in our workouts, but you can use meters instead. Also, remember that times given for a workout in yards might be too fast if you do the workout in meters. Give yourself extra time for the send-off (more below).

Insider Tip

If you need help, the universal signal to catch the attention of the nearest lifeguard is to raise a hand.

A typical workout is designed around four phases: the warm-up, the preset, the main set, and the cool-down.

The warm-up is usually the same for each workout. It serves just that purpose: to warm up the muscle groups in preparation for the more intense swimming that follows. Swim the warm-up steadily and slowly. How far you go in your warm-up depends on your level of swimming ability. In a competitive swimmer's workout, the warm-up is usually about 500 yards. If you're new to swimming, warm-up can be 50 yards. It's up to you (or your coach, if you're on a swim team).

Following the warm-up is the preset, which usually consists of drill work. Drills are swim mechanics that are used to improve swim technique and are something all swimmers should do. Later in this chapter, I'll describe some specific drills for you to try.

The main set is the focus of the workout. It's designed to train swimmers for their specific event. Distance swimmers train by swimming shorter than race distances but at a faster pace.

The cool-down is a short distance set that allows the swimmer to adequately loosen up and recover. It should be done at a slow pace and can be as few as 25 or 50 yards.

What Master Swimmers Already Know

A note about laps in swimming. There is a lot of confusion about laps versus lengths, and some folks refer to laps when they mean lengths. Technically, swimming a lap is a full up and back (like a lap on a track) in which you start off and touch both ends of the pool before you stop. If you're only swimming down to the other end, that's technically considered one length. It's just better to use numbers: 50 yards in a 25-yard pool is down and back. If you join a master swim team, much of this mysterious lingo will become second nature to you. If you want to be swimmer cool, just refer to "a fast 50" and leave off mention of yards or meters.

To swim laps, most group swimming practices have the individual swimmers follow each other in counterclockwise rotation in a lane. It's known as "circle swimming." The lane marker is always on your right, and the stripe painted down the middle of the lane on the pool bottom helps you stay on your side of the lane and avoid oncoming swimmers. In swimming practice, you only stop at one end of the pool so the coach or drill instructor knows where to find you if they want to talk to you about stroke refinements. The other end is used primarily for flip turns, so hanging out there isn't a good idea.

If you really want to impress the swimmers at your local lap pool, know about lane etiquette. In a crowded lane, when swimmers faster than you come up behind you and tap you on the foot, you should let them pass. If the lane isn't crowded, they can go around you but still tap your foot to let you know they're there. The same sort of courtesy applies at the end of the pool. When other swimmers are approaching the wall, don't push off for your next set just as they're about to flip. Let them go first and then follow. You can always pass them later if you need to.

Insider Tip

Don't break into the breaststroke when someone is trying to pass you; you might kick them and hurt your toe.

Set Directions

A swim workout is broken down further into swim intervals. A swim interval consists of a specified number of repeats (or intervals) at a prescribed speed, with a specified rest period between swims. The formula is the number of swims multiplied by the distance of each swim, along with the length of time until the swimmer leaves for the next interval.

10 × 50 yards @ 55 sec., or in abbreviated form: (10 × 50 @ :55)

In other words, you would say number times distance on send-off.

All time interval numbers are written with a colon, like so—:50—which means 50 seconds. The "@" stands for "on" and means the send-off time, or the time on the pace clock when you swim again after a rest.

There are other workouts that are written with the exact amount of time that you can rest, called a rest interval (RI), when you finish the swim interval. Still other rest intervals can be set based on heart rate. "HR 20" means that swimmers rest until their heart rates drop to 20 beats in a 10-second count.

Safety Tip

During the triathlon, do not swim from boat to boat or from paddle board to paddle board. The lifeguards or swim safety people need to be able to move their flotation devices around in case someone is in trouble.

The use of parentheses ( ) denotes an interval. Therefore 2 (2 × 50 + 4 × 25) means 50 yards two times and then 25 yards four times. The number 2 preceding the formula stands for the number of times you repeat the interval or the workout within the parentheses.

The plus sign (+) is used to connect different segments, one after another. The lines that follow the lead statement on a white board are for additional instructions that can modify the top line of the workout list.

If there isn't a pace clock on the wall, swim with a waterproof wristwatch that has a second hand so you can accurately complete your timed intervals.

Insider Tip

If you're about to pass someone, lightly tap him or her on the foot so the person knows you're there.

Let's Work Out at the Pool

A workout could look like this:

Freestyle 4 × (2 × 50 + 4 × 25 + 4 × 50) @ :60/:45/:60

50s = even pace

25s = fast with alternate breathing

What this formula means is "Swim freestyle four sets of the same interval. The workout interval is composed of three different parts. Twice you swim 50 yards, then four times you swim 25 yards, then four times you swim 50 yards. Swim the interval every time the clock reads 60 seconds for the 50 yards, 45 seconds for the 25 yards, and 60 seconds for the 50 yards."

The next line—"50s = even pace"—means that you should swim each of the 50-yard repeats at the same time split. The next line—"25s = fast with alternate breathing"—means that you should swim each of the 25-yard laps as fast as you can swim, breathing every third stroke.

Sample Workouts

Let's put it all together. Here's an intermediate workout:

1,500 yards total

Warm-up: 200 easy any stroke

Preset: Kick with board 4 × 25

Pull with paddles 1 × 100

Main set: 2 × (2 × 100 + 2 × 75 + 2 × 50) @ 2:00/1:45/1:00

100 = out easy, back hard

75 = even pace

50 = hard

Cool-down: 100 to 200 mixed strokes

If you wanted this explained in a phrase, it would be, "The total workout is 1,500 yards in distance. It is divided into the following: a warm-up of 200 yards, easy intensity (zone 1–2), using any stroke of your choice. Next, complete the preset, consisting of four different repetitions of 25 yards, with a kickboard, resting at each end. Then get your hand paddles and do four lengths for a total of 100 yards of pull (arms only). The paddles make it harder. The main set is comprised of three parts, swim 100 yards, out easy and back hard, on a 2-minute send off. That means if you get the 100 yards done in 1:30 minutes, you get a 30-second rest. Do this twice. Then swim 75 yards at an even pace on a 1:45 send off (twice) and then do a 50s on a minute, twice. For the cool-down, swim 200 yards at an easy pace, mixing up your strokes (freestyle, backstroke, breaststroke).

Workout Levels

You might want to think about these levels when choosing swim workouts:

- Novice workouts: 25 to 500 yards
- Beginner workouts: 200 to 1,000 yards
- Intermediate workouts: 500 to 1,500 yards
- Advanced workouts: 1,500 to 5,000 yards
- Competitor workouts: 2,000 to 5,000 yards

Advanced Workout

Warm-Up: 400 + 4 × 100 + 4 × 50

Preset:

10-minute kick: Speed Play (alternate moderate and sprint kicking)

10-minute swim: Speed Play (alternate moderate and sprint swimming: 0–30 strokes moderate; 10 strokes fast)

Main Set:

8 × 100 @ :20 R.I.: 25 free; 50 choice @ 80%; 25 free; 200 kick hard to easy

Cool-Down:

2 × 100 EZ

Total: approximately 3,600 yards

Insider Tip

If you see someone in difficulty, always stop to help. Would you rather win the race or save a life?

Pacing

In the early 1960s, competitive swimmers maintained one philosophy about pacing during a race—get out in front and stay there.

Today the strategy used by the fastest swimmers is to pace the entire race. In physiological terms, pacing prevents the early accumulation of lactates (by-products of exercise) in the muscles and the subsequent acidosis that contributes to muscle fatigue. This strategy is essential in distance swimming.

If you study the swim splits by every 100 meters for the world record holders in the 1,500 meters, you'll see that they swim evenly paced until the last 100 to 150 meters, when they sprint to the finish.

Pacing is a learned technique. The best method for learning pacing is to practice using under-distance repeats, that is, using 200- or 400-yard time trials. You should train with intervals one-quarter the distance of the swim by timing them and setting a time goal that is one-quarter of what you would like to achieve for the full distance of the course. As with running or biking, you don't want to go all out at the beginning or you'll run out of steam before you finish. This is especially important to remember in a triathlon, because the swim is the first leg of the event and you need to save some energy for the bike and the run.

We'll discuss how much swim training you need in relation to biking and running in chapter 11, "Putting It All Together."

Swim Skills Checklist

If you can complete most of this list, you're ready for your event. If not, this checklist will help you see which areas you need to work on. Can you

- ✔ Swim with your face in the water?
- ✔ Swim the freestyle (Australian crawl) stroke?
- ✔ Breathe on both sides (alternate breathing)?
- ✔ Complete the race distance without stopping?
- ✔ Swim with even pacing?
- ✔ Swim comfortably without hyperventilation or anxiety?

Extra Credit for Better Workouts

- ✔ Watch a swim mechanics video or have your stroke technique analyzed.
- ✔ For pool swimming, can you
    - Circle swim (remember, always counterclockwise)?
    - Flip turn?
    - Do timed repeats using the pace clock?
    - Count your laps as you swim?
    - Do swim technique drills?

Charting Your Progress

This is the steady state heart rate test described in previous chapters. Be sure to keep your heart rate the same, within five beats, for each test. With fitness improvement, you are looking to decrease the time it takes you to go the same distance.

Swim 100 yards (4 lengths of your pool) freestyle as fast as you can and record the following:

Month						
Time						
Average HR						

When You're Ready for More: Resources

Books/Magazines

Fitness Swimming (Fitness Spectrum Series) by Emmett W. Hines, Human Kinetics, 1998.

The Fit Swimmer: 120 Workouts and Training Tips by Marianne Brems, NTC Publishing, 1984.

Swim, the official magazine of U.S. Masters Swimming

Swim Techniques magazine

Total Immersion: The Revolutionary Way to Swim Better, Faster, and Easier by Terry Laughlin, with John Delvesn, Fireside, 1996.

Video

The Miracle Swimmer: How to Overcome Fear and Discomfort in Water, Shallow and Deep. Available from www.conquerfear.com (1-800-658-8805 in the U.S. and outside Northern California; 1-510-526-6000 in Northern California)

Web Sites

FINA (La Federation Internationale de Natation): www.fina.org

Swim News Online: www.swimnews.com

United States Masters Swimming: www.usms.org

USA Swimming.Org: www.usa-swimming.org or www.usswim.org

chapter 7

Bike Skills

We're all familiar with the bike. You probably got one as a child. Once you learn how to ride a bike, you never forget, right? So what's the big deal about bikes?

Here's the big deal: For the average racer, the bike portion of a triathlon *of any distance* takes twice the time and energy of the run portion and up to five times that of the swim portion. It's the most gear-intensive leg, covers the most distance, and, unlike swimming and running, requires more up-front preparation and mechanical skills. If you want to maximize enjoyment and performance in triathlon, most of your money and time will be spent on bikes, bike gear, and bike skills.

Learning to ride or improving your cycling is essential to your triathlon success. Even if your priority isn't to race well, basic biking skills, such as pedaling, require proper gear, because skills and gear are linked in biking. For your first triathlon, it's okay to borrow any bike or use your old bike. However, bike gear does affect bike technique.

Bike Training Goals

This chapter will help you

- ✔ Increase your comfort on your bike
- ✔ Be able to ride the race distance
- ✔ Learn how to ride safely with others
- ✔ Improve your bike biomechanics
- ✔ Improve your bike handling skills
- ✔ Go faster on the bike

Gearing Up the Biking Machine

Why is there so much mumbo jumbo about the bike and its assorted gear? It is, in large part, all about drag. In swimming, you streamline your body's position to reduce drag. When cycling, you do the same because resistance, whether from air or water, is significant and costly.

In the air, drag starts to make an impact at speeds greater than 5 miles per hour. Add to this the resistance from ground movement and machinery friction, and you realize that your biking speed depends on more than your raw physical talent. Though the power available to beat the drag is limited to your muscles, streamlined positioning and a well-designed bike help cut down the problem at its source. So at the root of all the mumbo jumbo are four simple principles:

1. The better the bike fits, the more comfortable you are.
2. The more comfortable you are, the more you ride your bike.
3. The more you ride your bike, the better trained you are.
4. The better trained you are, the faster you go.

Should I Buy a New Bike?

Whether you should buy a new bike depends on your current bike and your attitude. If you want to enjoy the event, you will do so on a comfortable bike. Thoughts about cycling have changed over the past 20 years, but many people still think that the more expensive the bicycle, the better they'll race. The truth is, however, the more comfortable the bike, the more you will train on it, and the better you will race.

Remember, the bike portion is much longer than any other leg in the triathlon. In a half-mile swim, improving your swimming may net you a 5-minute lead time out of the water. But on the bike leg, you could take 20 minutes off your time by riding a road bike rather than a cross or mountain bike. In addition, with the proper bike, you could go up to 3 minutes per mile faster, a savings of 36 minutes over a sprint distance bike leg.

Ask yourself these questions:

- How important is your bike split time?
- Is your bike comfortable?

- Does your bike need mechanical work? If so, how much will that cost? If it costs $400 to fix up your current bike, should you just buy a new one?
- Is your bike mechanically able to cover the terrain? Did you buy your bike in flat Florida and now you live in hilly Hawaii and need a triple chain ring?
- How heavy is your bike? Is that important to you?
- Did you buy your bike 20 years ago and now your physical ability is different?

If you decide to buy a new bike, first look briefly at how to go about purchasing one.

Choosing the Bike Shop

Getting a new bicycle, figuring out all the components you want, and being excited about the whole process is good plain fun. If you've recently returned to a fitness lifestyle, a new toy can definitely help get you out on the road. If you're a first-time bike buyer, read up on the subject. Bike and triathlon shops have free literature from bike manufacturers that they want to give you. Be sure you buy your bike from a specialty bike shop rather than a sporting goods store, because general sporting goods stores don't usually employ bike experts. The specialty bike shop will be your ally in helping you select a bike that works best for your budget and to figure out where it makes sense to compromise.

Finding the right bike shop is imperative. You want personnel who listen to your needs and are knowledgeable. It's also important that the shop know competent mechanics or, better yet, that it has competent mechanics in the store to help you.

If you have a friend who recently bought a bike, ask if the bike shop personnel spent a lot of time measuring and fitting him or her to the bike. Did the people in the bike shop ask questions about the riding plans of the potential customer? Bike shops that measure you and talk with you about your plans are a valuable resource.

Fit Tips for Women

Prime candidates for *custom* bikes are women who are 5' 3" and under or who have a short torso. Few off-the-shelf bikes are manufactured for this consumer. If you're in this category, you might as well buy any old bike, because the majority of bikes will be uncomfortable for you.

Fit is about frame size, frame geometry, and parts. If you are a woman, no matter what brand of bike you buy, most brake levers will be big for your hands. However, the levers can be adjusted.

If your butt is still sore after a month of riding, it's the bike fit. On the other hand, if your back hurts, it could be your technique. It could be that you are bending too far forward, or overextending. However, it could be bike fit. Perhaps the top tube length, the stem length, or the handlebar height is too long. If riding is uncomfortable, go to a bike shop for help.

Insider Tip

Petroleum jelly is a must for prevention of chafing

Whether you upgrade your current bike or buy a new one, there's going to be a compromise among budget, bike fit, and top speed. I believe that putting bike fit first will maximize your muscle power and comfort and minimize training injury. So, if you can, make sure your bike fits you. This may mean getting a custom bike that costs more than $100 per pound, but it's worth it. A bike that fits you can cost anywhere from $1,000 to $3,000. Unless you plan to train to win your races, it is probably not economically prudent to spend more than $3,000.

How to Buy a Bike

The most important thing about a bicycle is fit. You can always get a new derailleur or tires, but if the bike itself is a bad fit, you'll have to live with that as long as you own the bike. Go to a bike shop that actually measures you and asks some questions. Sometimes the smaller shops can offer more personalized service than the large ones with all the glitz.

If you are buying a new bike but you already have a bike, bring the old one with you so the bike shop can see what you are used to. Let them know if you are comfortable on your current bike. Then have them measure it. If you were comfortable on the old bike, that will help determine the size and style of your new bike. If you weren't, then it's time to find something new.

Be leery of a bike shop that fits you by having you lift the bike up from under you. Most bike shops use the Fit Kit, a method of measuring your body so that you know what size frame and components to purchase. Make sure they spend a lot of time working with the reach to the bars. Ask how much reach you need from the top of the seat to the pedals? How much reach from the seat to the bars? What is the relative position between the seat and the bars? Are the bars level with, higher than, or lower than the seat and by how much? Once you know these numbers, you'll be able to look at a bike and determine if it can be adjusted to fit what your body needs.

Once you sort out the fit, try out the different shifting systems. The three basic systems are Campagnolo, Shimano,

Bike technology is changing rapidly. In frame materials alone there are tremendous differences between the materials currently available—aluminum, composites (plastic moldings like carbon fiber), steel, titanium, or combinations of these—and those of just ten years ago. Or consider frame geometry (the angles in which the different frame tubes are constructed). The days of the standard and bar end shifters. You may not think you'll be able to tell the difference, but you will. The different systems feel differently in your hands. Some require more hand strength; others require thumb action. Once you narrow down which you like, that will pretty much determine the brand of parts you'll be looking for.

In addition to fit and ease of use, budget is a big determining factor in the type of bike you will buy. Just because a bike comes equipped as is, you can make changes to fit your needs. For example, if you like a bike but the saddle is uncomfortable, upgrade or change to a different seat. Consider a bike's gearing. You may want higher or lower gears, depending on the terrain you ride and your fitness level. If a bike comes with clipless pedals, be sure they are the brand and model you want. Don't use a clipless system just because the pedals came with the bike. Try the various brands, and make a conscious decision.

You may also wish to have a different or a second pair of wheels. If you are not sure how important this is to you, ask to demo or test a pair of high-tech wheels. Now is also the time to accessorize: Get a computer installed. Pick out a pump for training rides and a CO_2 cartridge for racing. Get an inner tube and a small seat pack to keep it in. Walk out of the store with everything you need, and nothing you don't need.

—Estelle Gray holds the women's tandem record for Ride Across America and owns R+E Cycles in Seattle, Washington. ■

triangle-shaped frame may be limited. With the advent of wind study tests and high-speed photographic measurement techniques, designers have come up with the most radically shaped frames, which are now some of the best. With the use of composite materials, wheel design is also experiencing a technological revolution. Disc and composite wheels are making firm advances in the triathlon marketplace.

You need to know a lot before you buy, but remember that the time spent on research and making a careful choice equals both money and race-time saved.

What Kind of Bike to Buy

The answer to the following three questions can help you make the best decision of which kind of bike to buy.

1. Are you able to dedicate a bike to triathlons only, not for touring or for bike racing?
2. How do you feel when other cyclists pass you on a ride because their bike is better, even though they themselves may not be?
3. What do you like in shifters—using your wrist for a grip shifter or using your thumb and fingers for a shifting system that is integrated into the brake levers?

In response to triathletes' needs, bike manufacturers have established a new category of bikes—triathlon bikes. If you are going to do an Ironman, then buy a triathlon bike. Triathlon bikes are made for triathlon. They are not comfortable to ride all the time. In fact, most triathletes train on a more comfortable road bike for the bulk of their miles.

If you already have a good bike but you are thinking about a newer bike, you might consider buying a triathlon bike specifically for racing. Triathlon bikes vary dramatically from standard road-racing bikes, touring bikes, track bikes, and sport bikes (a combination of the racing and touring bikes) in that they are designed specifically for a solo cyclist who wishes to go as quickly as possible. In their design, they have smaller front wheels, clipless pedals, aerobars, and gear shift systems that work from an aerodynamic body position. These bikes are committed to aerodynamics in everything—the wheels, the tubes, the geometry.

A triathlon bike is tight, which means that the top tube (the tube that is parallel to the ground) is shorter than the top tube on a road bike. The front forks are more vertical and less curved. The down tube (the tube running from handlebars to pedals) is at a steeper angle. The wheels are also tight, having minimal clearance to the frame. Altogether, this means that the wheelbase (the distance from the center of one wheel to the center of the other wheel) is short. The tightness of the triathlon bike also means it's not as comfortable as regular road bikes. This is why so many triathletes do most of their training on something other than their triathlon bike.

Insider Tip

Basic design of the bike hasn't changed since it was invented. It's not what you have, it's how much it's ridden.

Also, with front forks and head tubes (the short tube from the handlebars to the front forks) that are less curved and at steeper angles, your hands and arms absorb more shock from the road vibrations. This is one of the prices triathletes pay beyond the sticker price. In return, they go faster.

You may have watched a traditional bike race, such as the Tour de France, and noticed a few bike race characteristics. For example, cyclists position themselves in a pack of other cyclists. They maneuver around, making little surges and feints to intimidate or

Figure 7.1

Parts of the Frame of a Racing Bike

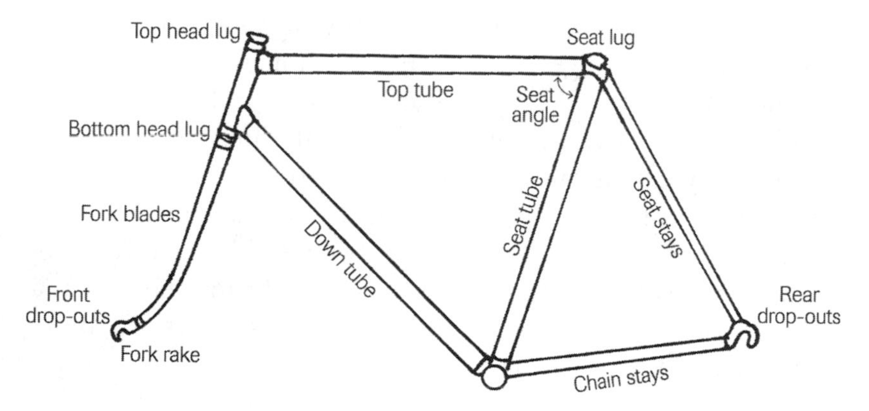

challenge the pack (also known as the peleton) into thinking they're ready to break away and finish first. The winning strategy uses drafting, team tactics, blocking, and other techniques specific to the sport of bicycle road racing. However, the bike leg of a triathlon hasn't typically followed these bike race characteristics. Although drafting on the bike leg was allowed in the Sydney 2000 Olympics (where women's triathlon was chosen as the opening event for the games) and the rules are changing, most triathlons remain a time-trial format, or a contest of the fittest, in which individuals are left to gut it out with their own private headwind. Aerodynamic equipment thus plays a big part in a winning strategy for the bike leg.

Is It the Bike or Just Me?

Get your bike checked out to see if there are improvements you can make. If you are less fit and you are riding a 40-pound not a 20-pound bike, your source of discomfort could be the bike. If the bike fits, there should be no discomfort.

Setting Up the Bike

The better the bike, the better you will feel on the run. The better the components (which include everything but the frame), the faster you will go. In general, it's easiest to buy a complete bike, focusing your choice on frame suitability, and then upgrade the components as you figure out what you want.

The most important upgrades are pedals, wheels, saddles, and handlebars. When you want to go faster, the first things to buy are clipless pedals, if you don't have them already. Use the wheels that came with the bike for your training wheels. Then buy a set of racing wheels. Research different types of saddles. Do you prefer the hard seats or those with cushioning? Having aerobars is a must. As with saddles, there are many types of aerobars, and more are being designed every day.

Next purchase a cyclometer that measures speed, elapsed time, distance, and total mileage, all of which are quite helpful for training. A bike computer that measures cadence can be more important to a beginner cyclist than even a heart rate monitor. Add a high-pressure pump, under-the-saddle tool bag (with a few tools), and a water bottle, and you're set with the basic component and tools.

Getting the Gear

Bike Pedals and Bike Shoes

Whether to put your foot into or onto the pedal is a decision you must make. Your bike is probably equipped with toe clips and straps that tightly secure you to the pedal. The clipless pedals are safer, faster in transition, and lighter weight. It's definitely worth upgrading from toe-clip straps to clipless pedals. You'll appreciate the additional peace of mind while riding.

When you change pedals, you'll also need to change to bike shoes. You'll never go back. Bike shoes are narrower, lighter weight, and ventilated, with thin, reinforced, rigid soles to keep your feet from flexing. This allows energy to be efficiently transmitted through the foot to the machine. Regardless of the type, bike shoes hold your foot in a relatively fixed position, which helps you maintain

Essential Tri Biker Gear

The Essential Tri Biker has helmet, aerobars, fast wheels, clipless pedals and shoes, a heart rate/bike monitor, and sunglasses with multiple color changeable lenses. The cycling world is traditionally conservative in what is allowed, but the triathlon world allows for more freedom in terms of bike geometry and accessories. Do some research and find out what's available and work your bike budget around what you need, want, and can afford.
—*Estelle Gray* ■

proper alignment with the pedal. Remember to buy shoes for road cycling, not mountain biking. There is a difference.

Adjust the pedal plate on your bike shoes if necessary. Some shoes have premounted plates, and when you ride, you may notice that they just aren't right. If you don't watch out for this, it could result in an injured knee. There is no foolproof method of determining where to mount your pedal plates on your bike shoes. Check with your bike shop. Using the trial-and-error method and asking other riders for their solutions are other good bets.

Helmet

Cyclists must wear helmets. In some places, it's the law, and in triathlon, you will not be allowed on the bike course unless you're wearing a helmet. But any old helmet won't do. It must fit your head.

Everyone's head is shaped differently, so don't be surprised if finding the right cycle helmet takes as long as finding the right shoes. Your helmet should be worn just over the brow, with the straps going around your ears and snug under your chin. When you put on the helmet and walk into a wall, the helmet should touch the wall before your face does. You shouldn't be able to get more than one finger between the strap and your chin. Trying on helmets is the only way to make sure that your helmet will protect your head in case of a crash. Your salesperson should spend 5 to 15 minutes fine-tuning the adjustments. Only buy a helmet if it has a sticker inside that reads "ANSI Approved."

Insider Tip

Write your name, phone number, and address on an adhesive label and secure it inside your helmet.

Helmets come with Velcro foam pads that can be added and taken out to fix small adjustments. Once you fit your helmet to your head, cut off those extra lengths of chinstrap, or else they'll flap in your face as you speed along. You can burn the edges of the excess straps to prevent them from fraying. If your helmet hits the pavement in a crash even one time, you need to replace it. Be careful not to drop your helmet many times, because that can cause invisible fractures in the material and weaken it over time. Inspect your helmet often. Helmets should be replaced every three to five years.

Apparel

Wear what is comfortable and what works for you. If you wear padded shorts, skip underwear. It's an additional bunch of fabric that you don't need and can cause friction or irritation. I wear tank tops with wicking properties in the summer and long-sleeved shirts made from Dupont Supplex or other synthetic fabrics to keep me warm in the winter—not necessarily cyclists' jerseys. Sometimes I ride in running gear, sometimes in my swimsuit. The point is that you should ride in what fits and is comfortable for you, not what you think other cyclists think you should wear.

Insider Tip

Bike shirts have pockets for a reason: Stuff them with food.

Look for cross-training activewear. Today, apparel manufacturers realize that multifitness athletes want versatility in their workout wardrobe. Companies like Danskin and Pearl Izumi make high-quality cross-training wear in which you can run and bike. They also make one-piece suits that you can wear for all three sports. And bright colors are not only high fashion, they are a safety must—triathletes need to be visible as they float, coast, and stroll.

Bike Maintenance

Your bike deserves fine care, not only because it is a major investment deserving of maintenance, but also for your own health and safety. Not much maintenance is required, but you will need to put some effort into the machine on a regular basis. It'll take less than 5 minutes a week, on average, to practice the following bike maintenance procedures:

- Listen for sounds of rattling.
- Always keep the tires inflated to the proper pressure.
- Inspect bike tires for cuts.
- Clean chain and lube it.

Figure 7.2 shows the different parts of the bike that you should check on a regular basis.

- Seat post and clamp: Twist and rock the seat. It should not move. If it does move, tighten the binder bolt and saddle clamp.
- Brake cables: Check for fraying or tightness.
- Handlebars and stem: Check tightness. Adjust bolt if loose.
- Brake levers: If you have to pull either brake lever more than an inch to stop the wheel, the brake needs adjusting.

Figure 7.2
Basic Bike Parts to Check

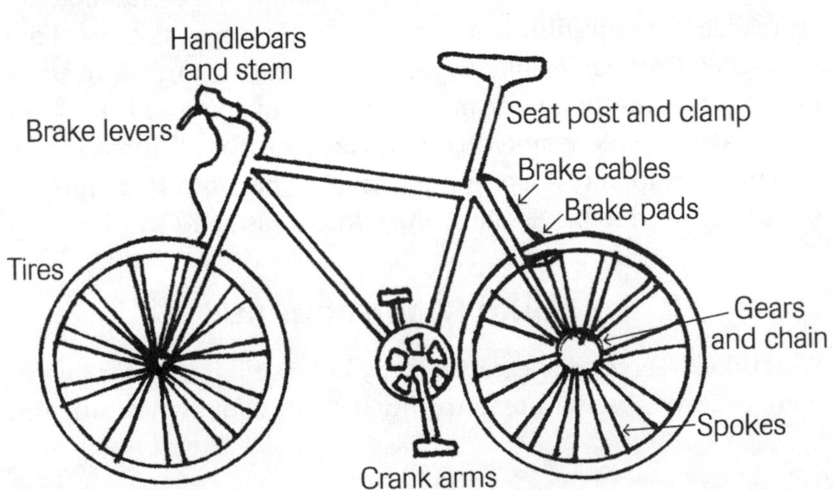

- Brake pads: Check for cracking. Pads should hit the rims squarely.
- Spokes: Check for broken or bent spokes.
- Tires: Push tires against a curb. If they flatten, they need more air. Inflate to the pressure shown on the tire sidewall. Check treads for wear or puncture dangers, such as glass fragments.
- Crank arms: Rock them from side to side. If there is any give, the bearings inside the bottom bracket shell need tightening.
- Gears and chain: Does the bike shift into all gears? Check the chain for excessive grease or dirt, dryness or rust.

Changing Tubes

When riding, you should at all times have a spare tube that fits your wheel size. The side of your rubber tread tire usually has a marking that indicates the tube size for your wheel. Tubes cost about five dollars each. Carrying a spare tube is even more important than remembering your frame pumps, because there's a much better chance that some other biker riding by will have a pump. The chances of someone having the exact tube size you need are not very high. Also, be sure to carry a glueless patch kit that you can use as a back-up for that second flat.

After a little practice, you'll be able to change a tire tube in less than 5 minutes. Recently, one of my training partners, a seasoned triathlete, flatted. She had finished the Ironman in Canada the year before, and we were out training for the Ironman Hawaii when it happened. "I have never had a flat," she said in an incredulous voice. Nor did she know how to repair one. It was my turn to be incredulous. Flats will happen, so be prepared.

Practice changing flats, both front and back, at least three or four times at home before you actually get a flat on the road. You'll need a set of tire irons and a replacement tube (see figure 7.3). Ask your bike shop to show you a Speed Lever-type tire iron, a really good improvement over the older irons. The basic steps to changing a tire tube follow.

Figure 7.3

Tire Changing Tool

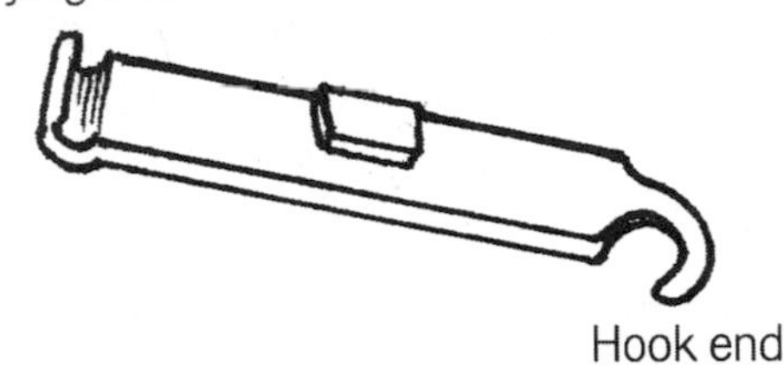

1. If it's the front tire that is flat, release the brakes, if necessary, and take the wheel off the frame, hopefully by using the quick release skewers. If it's the back tire, you may need to do some additional fussing, such as having your bike shifted to both of the low chain rings. Be sure to find out what your bike's individual quirks are, especially where the back tires are concerned.
2. If it's not already completely flat, let all the air out of the tube by pressing on the rod in the middle of the valve with your finger. The flatter the tube, the easier the tire comes off the rim. If you have a Presta valve (most road bikes do), you'll need to unscrew the round metal washer so it's loose. This will let the air escape. For a mountain bike or cross bike, you may have a Schraeder valve, which doesn't have this extra part. If you don't see any metal on your tube valve, you may have a plastic cap on your valve.
3. Pull back the hard rubber tire. Insert the tire irons or Speed Lever between the edge of the rubber tire and the wheel rim. Be sure to hook the top of the tool under the edge of the tire so the tip of the tool is inside the tire rubber. To keep this part of the tire from slipping back into place, hook the other end of the tire iron around a spoke. (See figure 7.4.)

Figure 7.4

Insert prying end of tire iron between tire and rim. Hook other end of tire iron around a spoke to free up your hands.

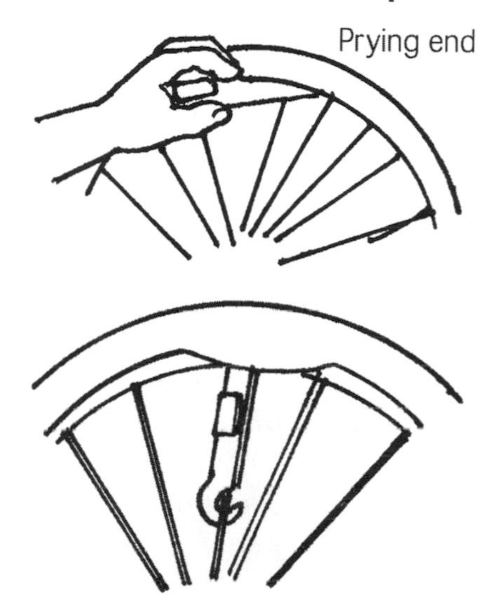

4. Use another tire iron to pry the rubber tire off the wheel rim using the leverage provided by the tools. It will be difficult at first, but as you work around the tire, you'll find it gets easier as you go. (See figure 7.5.)
5. Find the valve on the inflatable tube inside the tire and pull the tube out of the tire.

Figure 7.5

Use a second tire iron to pull the rest of the tire off the rim.

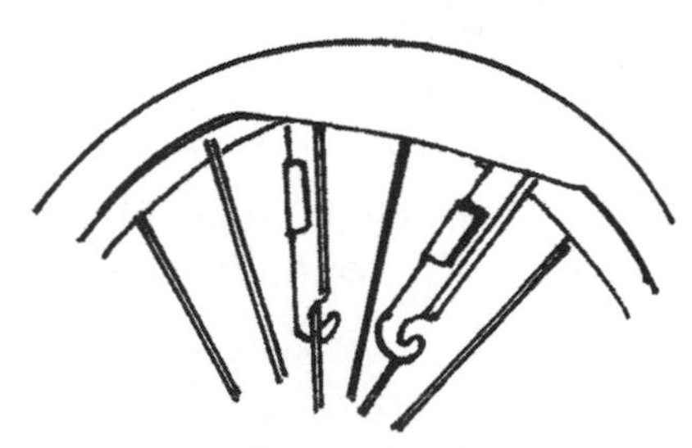

6. If you're on the road, rub your finger carefully around the inside of the tire, looking for the sharp bit sticking in the rubber of the tire that gave your tube the hole. Even a pine needle can work its way into a tire and eventually puncture a tube.
7. Put the flattened tube back in your pack for recycling or patching at home.
8. Pump a little air into the new tube so it's not flopping all over the place.
9. Tuck the tube into the rubber tire. The valve goes back in the hole.
10. Position the rubber tire with the tube back on the wheel rim, manipulating the tire iron to seat the tire back on the rim. It'll get more difficult as the rubber tire goes back on. Avoid pinching the new tube between the lever and the rim or even pinching the tube between the rubber edge of the tire and the rim. Either of these pinch points will result in a blowout when you start to refill the air in your tube.
11. Check the seating of the tube in the tire for these pinch points with your fingers pressing back on the tire rubber, looking for pinches before you inflate the tube.

Even though changing a tire is easy, with a little practice, it's a good idea to bring your cell phone or carry change for a phone call in case you get stranded.

Patching Tubes

If you want to patch your tire tube, do it after the ride. Don't waste time looking for that hole to patch when you're flat. You carry the glueless patch kit for that potential second flat on your ride. If you do get a second flat, remove the tire and tube, using that expertise you developed during your first flat. Find the puncture by inflating the tube and listening for the sound of hissing air. Follow the instructions on your patch kit.

Changing a Flat

Well, it had to happen. I have gone over in my mind a million times how to fix a flat but never found the time to do a "dry run" at home to be sure I could do it on the road. I left my house at 6 A.M. and was about 3 miles away when I hit a rock. I was thanking my lucky stars I didn't fall when I realized that my flat fear was now a reality. I became mosquito food at the side of the road while I first tried my Fix a Flat in a can. No luck. I took everything apart and could not get my pump to work. I knew I had to use an adapter on the valve, but I had no idea that I had to unscrew the little thingy at the end of the Presta valve. I ended up walking my bike to the house of an acquaintance. All's well that ends well. I got to work on time, and my friend's son walked me through my first tube replacement. I sure could use a hands-on bike-repair class. Reading about it just isn't the same.

—Anne Q. Coloma, first-time Danskin triathlete 2001. ■

Tires

Tires eventually wear out after about 1,000 miles of riding. They can also wear out on the sides from improperly seated brakes. There are many different kinds of tire treads and widths, and they have many uses. Some bike commuters use special rain tread tires wherever daily city riding can be slippery from motor oil. A mountain bike tire tread, or knobby, is specifically designed to grab on and hold to the riding surface. The knobby tires have indents that are a great help to keep from slipping on the trail. Whichever tire you use, you want to ride using the full surface of the tire. The inflation for a knobby is 40 to 50 pounds per square inch (psi), whereas a road tire is 110 psi. The lower inflation for a knobby means that when you go over rocks, sticks, and uneven softer ground, the tire still contacts the uneven surface. Bumpy tread for bumpy ground. On the other hand, the smoothness of a road tire matches the smooth asphalt surface conditions, so you can keep more rubber on the road. More rubber, more contact, less slipping, and, therefore, more speed.

If you use a mountain bike in a triathlon with a course mainly of asphalt, change the tires of the mountain bike to a tread that maximizes your effort, such as slicks. Although I have seen the behinds of many faster bikers on road bikes, I have rarely been passed by anyone riding a mountain bike in a triathlon and certainly never by anyone on a mountain bike with knobbies. Tires cost about $60 each, top range, on down to $12.50.

Cleaning Your Chain

Clean your chain as needed. How often depends on the conditions where you ride your bike. It's easy to see when the chain is dirty. Clean it once, and you'll know what it looks like clean. Eventually, with enough miles, you're going to need to replace your chain and freewheel.

Brakes

Brakes are life-or-death components, so keeping them properly adjusted deserves your attention. If your brakes loosen, you'll notice it; they'll twist to the side or pull forward when you stop. Brakes must be centered over the rims. If they aren't, you might hear a rubbing noise or whistle during the ride. If the brakes are rubbing and they have never rubbed before, try to reposition the wheel. If they still rub, take your bike to the shop.

Seasonal Service

It's a good idea to have your bike overhauled each year. The bottom brackets and headsets need to be repacked, cables adjusted, and new chains installed. You can buy the tools and a book on how to overhaul your bike and do it all yourself. Even with the book, it's a good idea to take a class from a bike shop. If you are used to working on machines, beware: This kind of equipment is different. You can torque out the bike, because nuts and bolts on bicycles are much different from motorcycles and cars. Take the class. If you decide to do your own repair, do not touch anything the night before a race!

Personally, I let the shop have the privilege of the repairs.

Insider Tip

Learn the name of your bike mechanics and treat them as you would your auto mechanics.

Riding the Machine

Getting good at cycling requires falling in love with your bike—a love affair that seems endless in miles and hours. Bike techies like to talk about bikes. They use all the cycling jargon, have the right equipment, and know all the bike stories and celebrities. But putting in time on the bike is a dedication that far exceeds the talk.

Pedaling Mechanics

To pedal efficiently, you must develop a smooth and circular stroke, applying even pressure throughout the large part of the stroke circle. This is not a down-then-up, piston-like stroke; think circle, not piston.

The maximum force starts just forward of the top of the stroke—the 12 o'clock position. The rotational force is divided between three major muscle groups, as shown in table 7.1.

From the 7 o'clock to the 11 o'clock position is the "rest," or minimum exertion phase, because here the opposite leg is exerting maximum torque on the opposite pedal. During this phase,

Table 7.1

Rotational Force of Pedaling

Phase	Muscle Group	Muscle Description
From 1 to 4 o'clock	Gluteals	Hip muscles
From 4 to 7 o'clock	Hamstrings	Back of the thigh
From 11 to 3 o'clock	Quadriceps	Front of the leg

the muscles are allowed to relax from their tensed state, and since blood flow is minimal when muscles are tense, this is the point at which blood flow increases and recovery can occur.

You should keep your foot at a position parallel to the ground, with the heel at the same level as the toe, throughout the entire pedal revolution. You might think of scraping the mud off your heel as you pedal. You'll want to minimize the flat spot in the pedal stroke and also stay loose. It is difficult to have a smooth pedal stroke with a locked or stiff ankle.

Pedal cadence, the number of revolutions completed per minute, is usually optimized at 70 to 90 strokes per minute. This technique of pedaling rapidly in low gears is called spinning. Though competitive cyclists may spin at rates as high as 120 strokes per minute, if your pedal stroke is optimized at a different rate, you may be sacrificing efficiency for your efforts. Pedaling cadence varies with the individual. Lance Armstrong and Marty Nothstein are incredibly efficient at very high cadences. (At a bike summit, I saw Olympic medal cyclist Connie Carpenter Phinney wearing a t-shirt that said "Blessed Are the Genetic Freaks.") The important thing is to experiment for yourself at different cadences and see what works for you. You can measure cadence with a cyclometer or a wristwatch. After properly warming up, time the number of revolutions in 1 minute. Your proper cadence is an instinct—with time, it becomes second nature.

Body Position on the Bike

How you position yourself on the bike affects your aerodynamics as well as the mechanical leverages of your leg muscles. Adjustments of your seat position can make a major difference in reaching your optimal joint angle, the point at which your leg and hip muscles can exert the greatest contractile force. Try riding in a number of different seat positions. Adjust your seat by loosening the nut directly under the saddle and pushing the seat forward or backward until you find where you can exert the greatest force. Don't make your seat adjustments all at once, however. It's important to make a series of minor adjustments, one at a time, to avoid injury.

Adjusting the saddle height can affect your performance as well—even just a few millimeters' difference can noticeably reduce or enhance efficiency. Likewise, the horizontal angle of the seat is another variable you must toy with. (I like my saddle at a position about 5 degrees downward from the horizontal.) If you have discomfort in the front of your knees when you ride, the seat is most likely too low. If there's discomfort in the back of your knees or your hamstring origin points, your seat might be too high.

The next riding position variables are your upper body and hand positions. With standard handlebars, there are three possibilities: hands on the tops of the bars, gripping the brake hoods, or in the dropped position. Use the dropped and the top-of-the-bars positions the least often. On a twisty descent, the drops work well for control. With aerobars, the preferred position is with the forearms resting on the pads and the lower arms extended forward.

Riding Hills

When you hit an uphill, it's best to downshift when your heart rate increases by 5 to 10 beats. Stay seated in the saddle, lower your upper body, and use your hip extensors. If you stand on the pedals, you can use more of your body weight, but the position itself requires more energy. Still, climbing out of the saddle can serve as a relief, allowing you to stretch tired muscles. If you do stand in the pedals, place your hands on the brake hoods or bars, let the bike sway slightly from side to side, and remember to maintain a straight line in the direction of the uphill. Keep your arms and shoulders relaxed.

Riding the downhills is a thrill worth the effort of the uphill. Get down in your drops for best control, fingers on your brakes. Move quickly to a high gear, assume a tight aerodynamic profile, and spin. If you top out of your cadence, clutch the top tube with your knees, tuck, and enjoy the ride.

Pacing

Maintaining an even pace results in an even heart rate, which in turn produces the highest state of fuel efficiency, allowing you to eke out the most miles per calorie expended. When you ride uneven terrain, continually adjust your rate of pedaling (cadence) and shift your gearing according to your heart rate. This allows you to ride at an even pace, whether on an uphill or downhill.

Insider Tip

Expect a "road tattoo" of chain grease on your leg. But try to avoid this since roadies call them "rookie marks."

Rules of the Road

Ride a Straight Line

In some races, as I pass my competitors, I yell, "Ride a straight line," even more than, "On your left." That's because I've gone down more often from collisions with other cyclists than from anything else. Maybe the unpredictability of riders braking rather than riding through turns or changing their line unexpectedly is what gets me, but for both our sakes, once you've taken a straight line, stay on it.

You'll also save yourself some energy by riding a straight line. When you run a race, you wouldn't dream of running an S pattern, because it just takes extra steps. It's the same idea when you bike. Consider the 12-mile bike leg in a sprint triathlon; how much farther do you want to bike than everyone else?

Practice riding a straight line by finding a vacant lot that has a long, straight, painted stripe. Work on holding a straight line by keeping both wheels within 3 inches of the stripe. Pick a point a ways in front of you. Don't look directly in front of the front wheel.

- Hold your line when you shift gears.
- Hold your line when you reach for your water bottle or drink.
- Hold your line as best you can when you encounter bumpy roads.
- Hold your line through a turn, and choose it before you enter the corner.
- Hold your line, please.

Other Rules of the Road

It's good to know some other common courtesies of the biking world before you head out for some riding:

- Always let other bikers know you're there when you come up behind them. Call out, "On your left!" before you pass so they know not to move toward you and possibly cause a collision. A bell is a commonly used substitute for calling out.
- Ride single file when you're on the road or trails. This will help keep you from obstructing traffic or having close encounters with cars sneaking up behind you.
- When you hear a car coming behind, call out, "Car back!" to the other riders in your group. This lets everyone know to stay right to allow the car to pass.
- If you see potential flat-causing debris or potholes in the road, point it out to other riders. You can say what it is or just point where it is so riders know to avoid that spot.
- It's also very smart to use hand signals for stopping and turns so riders and drivers behind you can anticipate your movements.

Safety Rules of the Road

- Know hand signals for stop, left, right, and slow to indicate to cars or other bicycles behind you what you're doing.
- Slow down on wet or damp pavement.
- Always carry tools, cell phone (phone card, quarters), an extra tube, patch kit, tire levers.
- Know how to change a flat tire with a new tube.
- Always, always, always wear a helmet.
- Use any or all for riding at dusk, dawn, or dark: reflective clothing, reflective tape, reflectors on the bike, lights.

Bike Workouts

One piece of equipment that I recommend for your triathlon training is a track stand or wind trainer for your bike. This stationary stand holds the back wheel off the ground and ensures that you go nowhere fast. As interval training methods for cycling, track stands and a heart rate monitor are hard to beat. I've written a whole book about how to train on a stationary bike called *The Heart Rate Monitor Book for Outdoor and Indoor Cyclists*. Remember, the bike portion of a triathlon takes longer to complete than either the swim or the run, regardless of your ability or fitness, so spend extra training time in this discipline. The following are a couple of bike workouts for you to try at home on your bike.

Bike Interval

Warm up for 10 minutes at 50 to 60 percent of your max HR. Pick up the cadence, load to 85 percent of your max HR, and hold it for 4 minutes. Then drop back to 70 percent for 4 minutes. Do this 8-minute repeat two to four times. Cool-down by spinning or noodling at 60 percent until you're back where you began.

5 × 5 Ladder Workout

This is a fun workout. You can change the range of your ladder to start and finish depending on your training goals for the day. This workout will allow you to work on speed, strength, and power. Warm up for 15 to 20 minutes and begin at the bottom rung of your ladder (bottom of zone 2, or 50 bpm below your max HR). Try to get at least a 20-beat ladder or 30-beat ladder to the top and then back down again. You'll increase either your cadence or workload (through gearing) every 5 minutes as you work your way up the ladder 5 bpm every 5 minutes until you've reached the top, then 5 bpm down every 5 minutes until you've reached the bottom. You may also do 5 bpm every 1, 2, or 3 minutes. It's your choice.

Skill Checklists

Can you

✔ Turn, corner, and brake?

✔ Cycle safely in a group of other riders?

✔ Ride fast and safely downhill?

✔ Ride efficiently and strongly using uphill climbing technique?

✔ Shift comfortably through all your gears even on a hill?

✔ Maintain a pedal stroke rate (cadence) of sixty, seventy, eighty, or more?

✔ Cycle comfortably on any terrain at any speed for 60 minutes continuously?

✔ Stop suddenly, using proper hand signals, without falling over?

✔ Drink from a water bottle and replace it in the water bottle cage while riding?

Charting Your Progress

This is the steady state heart rate test described in previous chapters. Be sure to keep your heart rate the same, within five beats, for each test. You're looking to decrease the time it takes you to go the distance. Ride a stationary bike for 2 miles and record the following:

Month						
Time						
Average HR						

When You're Ready for More: Resources

Magazines

Bicycling (www.bicycling.com): Maintenance, fitness, and training forums

The Journal of Competitive Cycling (www.velonews.com): Includes tech talk and training tips

Mountainbike (www.mountainbike.com)

Videos

American Flyers (Warner Bros.)

Breaking Away (20th Century Fox)

Web Sites

Bicylopedia (www.bicylopedia.org)

Centric BicycleLink (www.bicyclelink.com): An Internet bicycling hub

Cyber Cyclery (www.cyclery.com): An Internet bicycling hub

Cycling Organizations

Union Cycliste International (www.uci.ch): The international governing body including World Cup and World Championship race information

USA Cycling (www.usacycling.org): USA national governing body of cycling

chapter 8

RUNNING SKILLS

When it comes right down to it, triathlon is a runner's race. The last leg is the run. Each person you pass on the run course is potentially another person listed after you on the overall results list. You can be the fastest swimmer that day and the fastest cyclist that day, but if you aren't the first at the end of the run, you don't finish first. Strong running legs can help overcome poor swim or bike times.

According to the USA Triathlon Association, about 54 percent of triathletes come from a running background. That still leaves 46 percent who hadn't taken up running prior to their participation in triathlon. So if you're one of the 46 percent, I encourage you to start running for the overall health benefits as well as the advantage to you as a triathlete. Fall in love with running.

Years ago, there was a TV commercial that impressed me. It showed a dark, cold, rainy day. Olympic gold medal marathoner Joan Benoit Samuelson awakens and looks at the alarm clock; it says 5:30 A.M. She looks out the window; it's pitch dark, and you hear the sound of rainfall. She experiences prolonged hesitation. You can tell that she's listening to her mind's negative chatter trying to dissuade her from her morning run.

How many times have you felt that way about working out? I do, regularly. So do most of us. And for Joan Benoit Samuelson, like us, it's a struggle. But she puts on her shoes, dresses in rain gear, and heads out the door.

Samuelson is the first women's Olympic gold medalist in the marathon, a champion runner, and a former world record holder, yet she experiences the same hesitations that you do, and she began from the same point in her running career as you will—the beginning.

Run Training Goals

- ✔ Improve your running efficiency.
- ✔ Get faster running.
- ✔ Run continuously for 30 minutes or more.
- ✔ Assemble your gear to cover a variety of outdoor conditions and seasons.
- ✔ Set up running partners or a run support group.
- ✔ Try a running event.
- ✔ Know your personal best time for the distance you'll run in your triathlon. Match or exceed that time in the triathlon.

Your Running Identity

Defining your running identity can help you see yourself in relation to others as they evolved through the growth cycle of a runner.

Stage 1. The Beginner

You're making the break from an old lifestyle to a new one, and it may not be easy. You might have started a walking or running program before and not stuck with it—this could be your tenth or fifteenth attempt. You are starting the program at this point to lose a few pounds. You hope for quick results, but you know that it doesn't work that way. After a couple weeks, however, running starts to get easier; you look forward to the next run. This means you're making the transition into the next stage.

Time in stage 1: 2 to 10 weeks, before moving on.

Insider Tip

If you've never run a race before, stay to the back of the pack.

Stage 2. The Slogger

You know you've reached stage 2 when you can run continuously for 1 to 3 miles, and it doesn't hurt like it used to. It's also not quite as boring, but maybe that's because you've realized that running is only boring if you're boring. Your friends are more supportive, and you're feeling comfortable with yourself—the sense that people are looking at you while you run has dissipated. You run now to feel good about yourself, and you notice that the same distance is taking less time (the training effect).

Time in stage 2: 2 to 4 weeks.

Insider Tip

Know what the pace placards at the start of a running race are for, and pick the one nearest your actual ability.

Stage 3. The Jogger

You feel secure about running. At the end of the run, you feel a glow of pride, because it just feels so good. You've noticed some physical changes in yourself, such as increased muscle definition in your quadriceps, and you like it. You run for the "health" of it, and you feel proud of your accomplishment and wonder if you might continue to be a jogger for the rest of your life.

Time in stage 3: 4 weeks to a lifetime.

Stage 4. The Fun Runner

There's a change—you now care how fast you run, and you're keeping track of your mileage because it's valuable to you. You run for "fitness," and you are starting to set some goals, such as entering a fun run event. You now understand when other runners tell you they're addicted, because if you miss a scheduled run, you really do feel unwell, maybe even guilty. You've read a book or two on running and have asked friends for a few tips. In terms of your health, there's no need to transition out of this stage, although you may find yourself doing so. You can stay here for the rest of your life.

Stage 5. The Racer

You're competitive. You keep a training log and regularly enter local road races. You shop at runner's stores and buy the top-of-the-line goods at full price, because you want the best. You've experienced your first injury, returned to the beginner stage for reconditioning, and have recovered. You plan your running around racing goals—finishing times. You've tried fartleks (putting out a burst of speed on the run when you feel like it) and LSD (long slow distance) training. You may find yourself transitioning to the next stage before you quite know that it's happening.

Insider Tip

Remember, you're not alone out there. Treat other racers with the courtesy you would expect, and enjoy being part of the racing community.

Stage 6. The Runner

You're committed to working out by running, for a lifetime. It doesn't matter which stage of development you're currently in, because you now know the comfort that comes from realizing that the answer to "Who are you?" is summed up in two words—*a runner*. You're no longer obsessed with finishing in the top percentage of your age group, because running, like life, is a game where pacing counts. You may not be as fast as you once were, but you know that you're the best you can be. Perhaps most important, you've balanced running with the other parts of your life: family, profession, finances, and friends.

Running Gear

The only thing you really need for running is a pair of shoes. Make sure you get shoes that fit your feet and your running style. The clothing you wear will depend on the climate and the season. Some runners want to carry water bottles and maybe gel packs, but that depends on both your needs and how long you're training.

Essential Gear

- ✔ Shoes
- ✔ Lace locks
- ✔ Shorts or tights
- ✔ Tank top, t-shirt, or long-sleeved shirt
- ✔ Sports bra (women only)
- ✔ Socks
- ✔ Heart rate monitor
- ✔ Stopwatch
- ✔ Water bottle
- ✔ Energy food (gel, bar, etc.)

Throughout my career, I've gained a great deal of respect for the technology behind running gear—from the fabrics in the activewear to the incredible changes in the midsoles of training shoes.

Running Shoes

People who write about the current status of either shoes or apparel know that their comments are immediately dated. For example, as I write this, running shoes are available for stability, cushioning, pronation, heavier runners, the heel striker, the rigid foot, and the floppy foot. But very few people have any idea what styles and concepts will be on the market one year from now. Running shoes are being designed for all the individual styles of running—that is why it's important for you to identify your own style and proceed from there.

Insider Tip

Don't bring your dog or the baby jogger to a race unless they're explicitly permitted (some races have a stroller category). These can be hazardous to other runners.

There are no secrets to shoes. There is no perfect pair of shoes for everyone; what works for one person won't work for the next. The wisest advice I can give you is to buy the best shoe you can; it's cheaper to spend $100 on running flats than to visit the doctor once. If you already have a pair of running shoes, take them with you to a specialty running store and show the salesperson the wear pattern on your shoe. The salesperson you want will have enough technical knowledge to steer you to the right shoe. When you're running more than 5 miles at a time, invest in a second pair of shoes and alternate their usage. If you wear the same pair of shoes every day, you'll have a higher incidence of injury than if you alternate.

If shoe fit is an issue, and you don't feel you've gotten all you need from the choices available at the specialty running store, you might consider orthodics—a piece of material, such as plastic or rubber, that replaces the foot bed of a shoe. Orthodics are designed specifically for your feet with the help of a podiatrist. They aren't just for severe cases of foot or stride defects. Check with a qualified foot doctor to see if you might be able to improve your enjoyment and performance with orthodic inserts for your shoes.

Activewear

Just as there are no secrets to shoes, so, too, are there no secrets to running apparel. With the innovative developments from today's textile manufacturers, the fabrics, styling, and cuts of functional activewear change more quickly than books can be reprinted. The latest entries are the cross-training apparel lines, which are primarily carried by specialty shops that cater to you, the fitness triathlete.

Beyond style, it is important that you dress properly for your environment. In cold weather (around 50 degrees Fahrenheit or less), layers are suitable—you just strip as you warm up and tie the extras around your waist. In really cold weather, wear a scarf or muffler over your mouth to warm your inhaled breath; breathing below-freezing air can damage your lungs and is painful. In hot weather, light and loose clothes are in. Finally, if you run at night, wear a reflective shirt or vest, whatever the season.

Remember, too, that 99 out of 100 times, the weather is no reason to keep you from training, as long as you're sufficiently prepared. Joan Benoit Samuelson may hesitate when faced with a gray, chilly morning, but she doesn't let the weather stop her from carrying out her goals and dreams. And neither should you.

Insider Tip

Stay to the right so that runners coming up behind you can pass.

Running Technique

We all run differently. When my training partners run ahead of me or toward me, I know who they are from their running style long before I see their faces.

Accept that you were born with a certain natural style. Then accept that there are a few mechanical changes that can make you more efficient and result in more enjoyment and fewer injuries. You must also realize, however, that change for change's sake doesn't work; you must allow your body to run essentially the way it wants. Given these guidelines, the "ideal" running style toward which you can strive follows.

Foot Plant

- ✔ Strike softly and quietly, on your heel.
- ✔ Roll forward onto the ball of your foot.

- ✔ Push off with your toes.
- ✔ Check the bottoms of your shoes and look at your wear pattern to see if your foot plant is out of balance. You might need to talk with a podiatrist about how your foot strikes the ground and how it can be corrected.

Stride

- ✔ Do not lift your knees high.
- ✔ Do not kick your feet high behind you.
- ✔ Bend your knees slightly as your feet contact the ground.
- ✔ If an object you see on the horizon bounces as you run, you're overstriding. Shorten your stride length.
- ✔ Hold your line; any sideways motion lowers efficiency.

Posture

- ✔ Stand up straight; do not lean forward.
- ✔ Push your shoulders back and keep your chest flat.
- ✔ Tuck your buttocks in; tip your pelvis back.
- ✔ Hold your head up straight.
- ✔ Think of the shape of the number 1, not the number 9.

Arms and hands

- ✔ Keep your elbows at a 90-degree angle, close to your waist.
- ✔ Swing your arms forward and back in a straight line.
- ✔ Don't let your hands cross your midline. Always keep them the width of your body apart.
- ✔ When running slowly, swing your arms slightly; when running quickly, pump your arms.
- ✔ Cup your hands loosely; don't make a fist.
- ✔ Keep your wrists firm.
- ✔ Move your lower arms substantially but not your upper arms.

Figure 8.1

Correct (top) and Incorrect Running Form

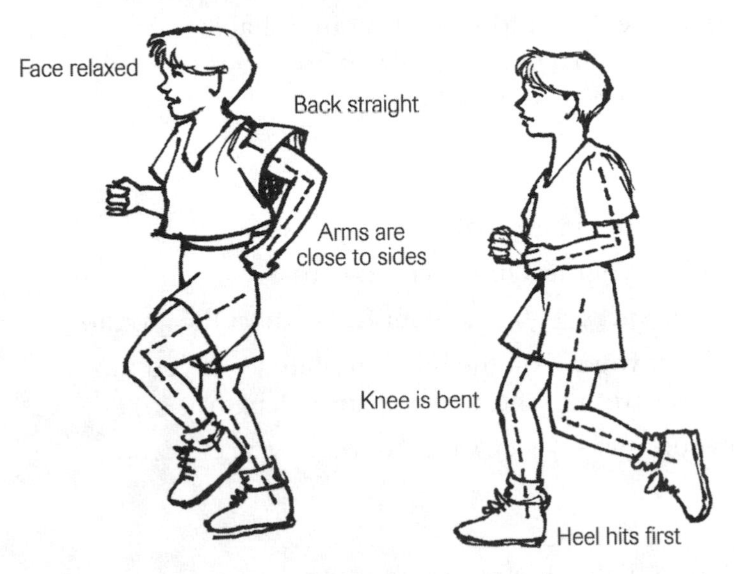

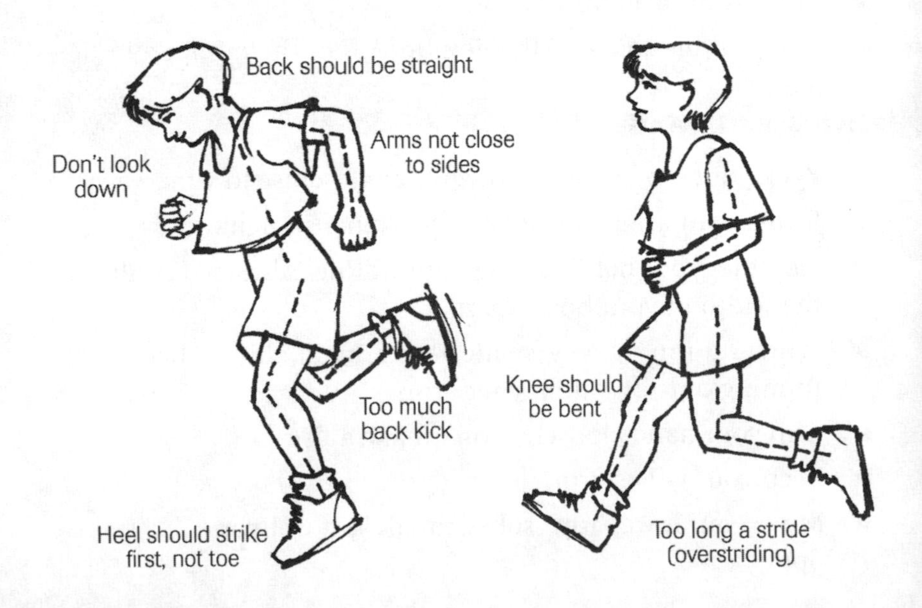

Head and Shoulders

- ✔ Relax your neck, shoulder, and jaw muscles.
- ✔ Keep your eyes up, looking at least 6 feet forward.
- ✔ Keep your head up.

Breathing

- ✔ Breathing out fully is more important than breathing in.
- ✔ The abdomen should move *outward* when you breathe *in*.
- ✔ Breathe deeply and smoothly, not shallowly or with gasps.
- ✔ Make sure that when training, you can always pass the talk test, which means you're able to talk continuously while training. If you can, it means that you have enough wind to do both and you aren't overexerting.

If you find that your abdominal muscles feel strained and sore when you run or after a long run, you need to increase your core body strength. This will happen somewhat naturally as you train, but you also need to do some form of sit-ups or other abdominal exercise. Strength training (we'll get to that in chapter 10) is also very helpful.

Insider Tip

Don't run more than two abreast. You can gab, but be conscious of others in the race.

Everyone has a unique style. Some of us are bouncers, some float, some are short and choppy, some waddle (mostly women because of our wider hips), some are gazelle-like, and so on. I am a shuffler, and I trip a lot because of it. There are some poor running styles that affect your training, however, so make sure your style isn't listed in table 8.1.

Pacing

The idea behind pacing is to cruise, smoothly and efficiently. Just as you sweep in the swim and spin on the bike, you can cruise on

Table 8.1

The Quick Six Symptoms of Poor Running Styles

Error	Effect
1. Feet slapping loudly on the ground	Leg, ankle, and foot stress
2. Shrugged shoulders	Upper-body tension
3. Arms and hands high, clenched fists	Tension, wasted energy
4. Flapping arms and hands	Wasted energy
5. Tilting forward	Excessive impact
6. Bouncing high with each stride	Wasted energy, muscle strain

the run. However, the cruise mode is not for gaining speed or for running down hills. Cruising is for when you want to maximize your energy output over long, steady miles.

Insider Tip

Be courteous and aware of those around you. Don't stop or slow down in the middle of the road—move to the right to tie your shoe or adjust your clothing.

Pacing yourself, following a steady, nonvarying rhythm, is a learned skill. One of my favorite workouts is a pacing run. I run with two others, and we play the Guess the Mile Split game by running a mile at varying paces without looking at our watches. Once we come to the 1-mile post, we take turns guessing how long the run has taken, and the one who guesses our pace to within five seconds wins. This little exercise allows us all to develop our internal time clocks, which we can then use to set our pace when we wish to run at an even rate and cruise.

Remain Injury Free

Recognize that, like a bicycle accident, athletic injury is probably inevitable in running. It comes with the turf. Here are a few sage words on the subject:

- Listen to your body.
- Don't try to do too much too soon.

- If there's a problem, get a diagnosis—don't be one of the walking wounded.
- Follow the RICE (rest, ice, compression, elevation) plan.

Insider Tip

If you must stop, check behind you and then move off the racecourse so people don't have to go around you.

All runners experience some common problems: blisters, heel injuries (like bone bruises or inflammations), shin splints, muscle soreness, tight muscles, dehydration, side aches, tendonitis, chafing, diarrhea, and support problems (hernia-like pains for men and sore breasts for women).

When these happen, react. Take a couple of days completely off training. Try self-care first, then seek medical advice from a sports medicine physician or clinic, if necessary. Learning as much as you can about injuries is a wise idea, and trying over-the-counter remedies can sometimes help. If you have to train, don't strain. Run in a pool or cross train on a rowing or cycling machine.

The rule of recovery is that you must double the number of days that you were forced to rest in order to find the length of time you must train to return to your conditioning level prior to injury. See table 8.2 for rules of recovery.

You can benefit from your loss of conditioning by understanding what went wrong and adding some preventive measures to your training program so the same injury doesn't occur again.

Table 8.2
Rules of Recovery

Rest Time Without Exercise	Number of Training Days to Return to Your Former Level
2 days	4 days
1 week	2 weeks
1 month	Start from scratch

When you return to training, start slowly and plan your training according to the recovery time required. If you have to start at the beginning, then do so.

Insider Tip

Don't zigzag through and around people or make sudden dashes. Slow and steady wins the race, and anything else will cause a collision.

Run Safety Checklist

- ✔ Always be aware of what's going on around you. It's wise to run without headphones when outdoors.
- ✔ In case of an emergency, carry change for a phone call or carry your cell phone.
- ✔ Carry identification of some kind.
- ✔ Don't run alone in dangerous (or dark) locations. If you're visiting an area, ask around for safe places to run.
- ✔ To ensure a comfortable run, make sure your shoes and clothing fit well and are in good condition.
- ✔ Keep an eye on the ground ahead, to avoid debris or potholes that could cause you injury.

Let's Practice Running

Following is a running pyramid workout for those easy days or if you're just beginning to run.

Easy Run Workout

Warm up by walking 10 minutes easy. Run 1 minute at a comfortable pace. Walk briskly, swinging your arms for 2 minutes. Run 2 minutes at a comfortable pace. Walk briskly 3 minutes. Run 3 minutes, then walk 4 and run 4. Continue in this pattern until the run minutes start to feel fairly hard. Then back down the pyramid you go. Be sure to cool down by walking, and remember to stretch. If you find yourself progressing beyond this workout, try jogging instead of walking and pick up the pace on the run minutes slightly.

Insider Tip

If you see someone in difficulty, ask if they need help.

Favorite Run Workout

90-SECOND HILL REPEATS The steps to becoming a better runner include adding hill running to your repertoire of workouts. Hill repeats develop not only your running-specific muscles but also simultaneously improve your aerobic capacity. Find a slight to medium grade that takes at least 90 seconds from the bottom to the top. Running repeat hills on soft surfaces is always better for your joints and muscles, but you can do this workout on hard surfaces as well. Warm up adequately. Time yourself running up the hill at about a 70 percent perceived effort level and note your heart rate. Do one to five repeats. Increase your speed and your perceived effort by 5 percent with each repeat, and note the peak heart rate when you crest the hill. As you get stronger, try to add a few additional repeats or take an active rest and do sets of three at a time up and recovery jog back down to the bottom of the hill. For the recovery and return to the bottom of the hill, your heart rate should be in zone 2 or zone 3. It should be in zone 4 or kiss the floor of zone 5 when you reach the top of the hill; note the peak number on your heart rate monitor.

PYRAMID RUNS Your profile, or the graphic representation of your heart rate during a pyramid run, should resemble the shape of an Egyptian pyramid. Start with a long warm up in zone 1 and zone 2, which is at least 10 percent of your total running time. Start at the floor of zone 3 and hold this heart rate number (70 percent of your maximum heart rate) for 5 minutes. Accelerate to the midpoint of zone 3 for 5 minutes and then increase your speed and heart rate to the floor of zone 4 for 5 minutes. Finally do one last acceleration to the midpoint of zone 4 for a total of 2 minutes before you drop off the pace and head back down the other side of the pyramid (by holding the floor of zone 4 for 5 minutes, the midpoint of zone 3 for 5 minutes, and the floor of zone 3 for the last 5 minutes). This is a 40-minute run/walk, including the warm-up and cool-down. Pyramid runs improve stamina and push you into your threshold zone, which leads to improved running economy.

Insider Tip

Never wear headphones in a race.

STEADY EDDY Tempo runs, or Steady Eddy, are workouts that are at, about, or around your race pace. If you don't have a race pace, then use 80 percent of your maximum heart rate as your Steady Eddy heart rate number. After a gentle and easy intensity warm-up, pick up your speed until you reach your tempo pace and hold it for 20 to 45 minutes, depending on your current running fitness level. Slow down for a 5-minute cool-down. Enter this training session into your log and collect a big training load because it equates to 90 to 165 heart zone training points. The more points you earn, the more calories you burn, so work toward that top point count if you are training for weight management purposes.

Run Skills You'll Want

Can you

- ✔ Run for a mile without stopping?
- ✔ Run the distance of your race without stopping? Run farther than that?

- ✔ Keep your heart rate at a comfortable and safe level for the distance of your race?
- ✔ Maintain a steady pace?

Charting Your Progress

Following is the steady state heart rate test described in previous chapters. Be sure to keep your heart rate the same, within five beats, for each test. You're looking to decrease the time it takes you to go the same distance.

Run 1 mile and record the following:

Month						
Time						
Average HR						

When You're Ready for More: Resources

Books

The Competitive Runner's Handbook by Bob Glover and Shelly-Lynn Florence Glover, Penguin Books (1999).

The Complete Book of Running for Women by Clare Kowalchik, Pocket Books (1999).

Magazines

Runner's World

Videos

Chariots of Fire (Warner Bros.)

Prefontaine (Buena Vista Pictures)

Running Brave (Buena Vista Pictures)

Without Limits (Warner Bros.)

Web Sites

Road Runners Club of America: www.rrca.org

Runner's World: www.runnnersworld.com

chapter 9

tracking tools for triathlon training

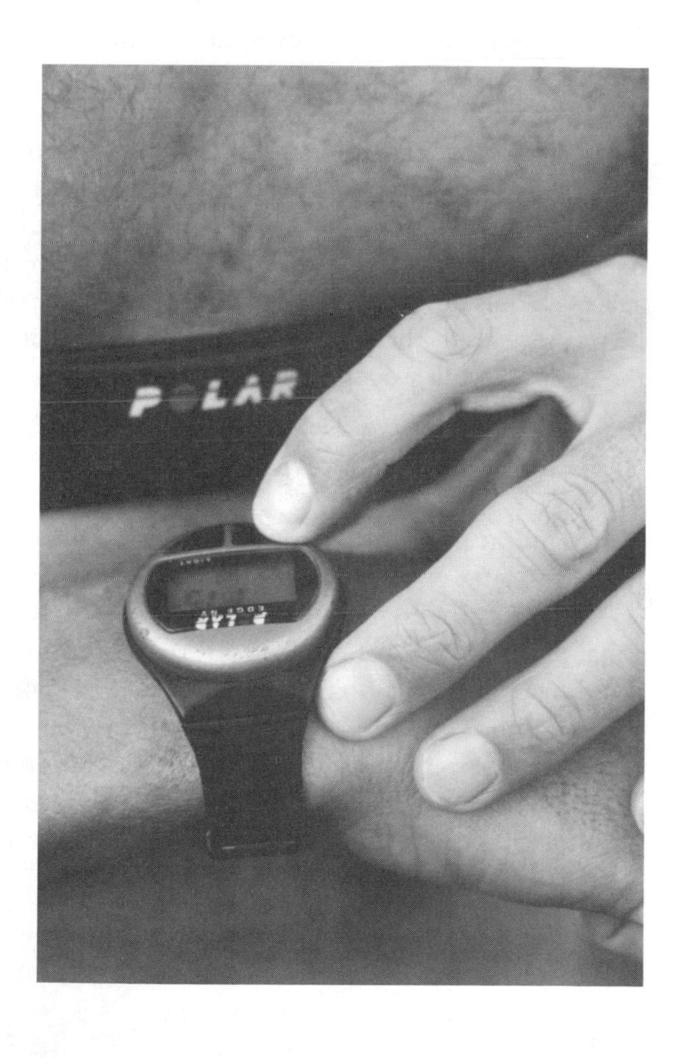

The question I am asked most frequently after "Why do you compete in triathlons?" is the how question, "How do you design a training program that fits?"

There are no secrets or mysteries to cross training. A successful training program has a few requirements, however, and these should be taken seriously. Essentially, answering the how question requires a dedicated commitment to regular and frequent exercise and the common sense to pay attention to your body's feedback, for good or ill. If you can find these two abilities inside yourself, not from the outside (whether from the cheerleading or nagging influences of a person or book), then you're bound for success. Tools (logs, heart rate monitors, other technology) can help you get to the how, but choosing to track your data will make them part of your own training strategy.

Keep a Log

The triathlon books I like to read the most are not any that are written for the public. No, the books I most appreciate are the ones that I write exclusively for myself every day—my own personal training logs. Your logbook is more important than any of the other triathlon books you might read. Having a journal is such an important part of triathlon training that I wrote the first triathlon log ever published and did so for everyone's use. (Although, most of all, I wrote it for me to use over my lifetime of training, since I plan on another 50 annual volumes.)

Think of your log as a training device—like a cyclometer for biking or a kickboard for swimming. It's a must if you want to get better. Think of your log as *your* first book: You write it, edit it, and eventually keep it on your bookshelf of important works. Think of your log as your confessor; tell it the way it really is, and if you don't want to show it to anyone, then don't. Your triathlon log is your personal journal, your way of letting it all out.

A triathlon training log enables you to record for all three sports data on distance, elapsed time, heart zones, weather, quality (or mood), comments, sleep, weight, weekly totals, stretching time, monthly distance averages, year-to-date totals, and much more. (See figure 9.1.) By keeping a log, you will change your behavior positively, and that alone can keep you on a training program.

Organization and planning can make or break the best of us. Completing your log page will become, with practice, as easy as brushing and flossing your teeth. No professional coach, trainer, or athlete can advise you properly without looking over a written log of your workload. Having your workout results to examine allows you to help yourself gauge the effect of sample training suggestions that you are keen to try, such as workouts you read in a magazine or book. Balancing training in three sports is hard enough; try not to do it in the dark. Keep a log.

Body Pieces

These days there are more options for recording your workout details. In addition to the tried-and-true pen-to-paper method, technology now provides some new and more graphical ways to record and display fitness data. Some recording methods may be too cumbersome for your style, but some may really turn your log into a dynamic report that can make your training lapses and successes very clear. If you're having trouble just putting pen to paper with your workouts, consider changing the tool you use to break the logjam and get those details spelled out.

With any digital electronic device, information is put into the chip that is used to calculate data. This information may not fit your circumstances. In the same way that actuary life expectancy charts

Figure 9.1

Sample Training Log Page

Date	Sport Activity	DST Distance	Time	Time In Zone					Key Workout Type
				Z1	Z2	Z3	Z4	Z5	
Weekly Summary									
Year-To-Date Summary									

Notes:

for insurance companies don't take into account the fact that you could very well live to 100 years of age, electronic devices can only make broad generalizations about what's really going on with your fitness. If you can think of your training as a symphony, be sure to use any tracking tool as only one instrument in the orchestra.

For this book, we tested two wearable devices that record some of the training data you might want to track. The names of the

Figure 9.1
(continued)

Averages	am Heart Rate	Body Weight/ Fat	Σ Altimeter	Weight Training Time	STRETCH Stretching Time	A,B, C,F Rating	Σ_{HZT} HZT Points

Notes:

products we tested are not as important as the idea of the products themselves. The benefit of these and similar devices is in the ease of tracking, not necessarily in the trustworthiness of the interpretations. Unlike a heart rate monitor that shows you what your heart is doing, wearable recorders of activities that don't relate to heart rate are not personalized enough and give only comparative data, sometimes based on dubious research.

Why, you might ask, are you even discussing these devices if they're suspect? Because they're cool, they're fun, and you can derive some logging and tracking help from them. Even though these devices are here to stay, one of the two devices that we tested is already going the way of the dodo bird, a victim of low sales or perhaps a bad business model. At any rate, even though it is hard to find a device that is tailored to record the level of detail that we suggest in our log example page, there is still a definite fun factor. If you are a lazy logger, try the body pieces available in sporting goods stores. But be sure you have a back-up system if your gadget suddenly ceases to work. The tried-and-true tracking tools described in more detail in the pages that follow are what will be around: heart rate monitors, body fat scales, and very likely some fitness-tracking Web sites.

Get a Heart Rate Monitor

Fifteen years ago, when I purchased my first heart rate monitor, they cost about $500. Today they cost as low as $60—about the price of a good pair of workout shoes. Monitors are readily available in athletic clubs, sporting goods stores, on Web sites, and through direct mail. At one time, heart rate monitors were only part of the professional athlete's world. Today heart rate monitors and heart rate training enable people of every fitness level to monitor their efforts and get the most out of their training time.

Heart Rate Monitor as a Training Tool

Training for a triathlon must fit you as an individual. We only have so much time to train, and that time must be spread between three separate sports—swimming, biking, and running. A heart rate monitor is the great equalizer in a multisport program. It gives you a precise way to determine how hard your swim, bike, and run workouts should be in any given week or month. Heart rate monitor training (known today as heart zone training; see chapter 5) gets the results you want over time. You won't spend too much time or intensity in one sport to the detriment of others. I'm convinced, and so are thousands of professional and amateur triathletes alike who train using this technological approach, that it will lead to the integration of your mind, your body, and your spirit into a triathlon training program that works for you over the long term. The plan in chapter 11, "Putting It All Together," can be most effectively used in partnership with your heart rate monitor feedback.

Body Fat Measurements

The measurement of percent body fat has become widely used as one of the indicators of fatness and fitness. Research has shown several interesting things about body composition, which is a way of assessing two types of tissue: fat tissue and fat-free tissue. The average inactive person loses muscle tissue and gains fat steadily beginning at about age 20. The research shows that even people of standard weight who maintain their weight as they grow older still gain fat and lose muscle tissue. For example, a person who at age 20 weighs 160 pounds may have 16 pounds of fat and 144 pounds of everything else (muscle, bone, organs, etc.), or about 10.4 percent body fat. That same person at age 55 may still weigh 160, but now has 40 pounds of fat and 120 pounds of everything else, or 25 percent body fat. Even though the person weighs the same at age 55 as at age 20, the body has "gone to fat," apparently due to inactivity. But studies also show that it's possible, even at age 55 and above, to build back muscle tissue and regain the correct balance between muscle and fat.

If you monitor your body fat or your fat-free mass regularly, you can take appropriate steps before serious changes take place. And you can also monitor the effect that a change in diet and training has on your muscle tissue. If you are too lean, particularly if you are a woman, you may refuse to believe that change has taken place without regularly monitoring and graphically representing body fat. For example, if you are taking in less nutrition than you need, you may be losing muscle and organ tissue, rather than fat. One proof of this would be through body fat measurements. Body fat measurement can help convince a too lean person that he or she needs a diet higher in nutrition and calories.

Much more common, however, is the person who is at the "correct" weight according to the height/weight proportion charts. He may look in the mirror and think he looks just fine. But his underdeveloped and seldom-used muscles may account for his light body weight. Body fat measurements, on the other hand, are likely to show that he still has too high a percentage in body fat and that he will need to get on a training and exercise program with correct food before he can change his body composition.

Body Fat Scales

Total body weight is meaningless to you as an athlete. Each of us has a genetically determined body shape that might be taller, shorter, or contain more muscle or fat than the person next to us. Vive la différence. It's the uniqueness of each of us that makes human life so rich.

A lean frame characterizes triathletes at the elite level, but the rest of us are statistically fighting the battle of the bulge. The problem is that your total body weight tells you nothing about how goes the battle. Changes in body shape will occur with training and proper nutrition, so all you have to do is tap into the right information.

A body fat scale is an important tool to measure your fitness successes. Rather like an ordinary bathroom scale, the body fat scale, once it has been calibrated with your height, gender, and activity level, can track your body fat as a percentage of your total weight. With a body fat scale, you can follow the percentage of body fat to decide when you need corrections in your diet and exercise plan.

Muscle carries more density and therefore more weight per square inch than fat. On a conventional scale, you might be weighing in at higher numbers that seem to suggest (because it looks like you're gaining weight) something isn't right in your training plan. Be careful. Athletes are known to be susceptible to all sorts of eating disorders. Keeping an eye on the body fat number through an electronic body fat scale can show you how your body responds in any given week in your exercise program. We're all watching the numbers, so be sure to track the change in body fat as opposed to overall weight as you train. It is easy to swap out that old bathroom scale for the newer body fat scale to be sure that this method of measuring body fat is the one most likely to stick.

Other Methods

Athletic performance depends in part on how quickly you can transport your body over the distance. A thin athlete is not necessarily a strong athlete. To keep tabs on your body composition (bone, muscle, fluid, fat), you may wish to benchmark it with a technique administered by a health care practitioner. Remember, even a body fat scale could be off by 3 or 4 percent. In a health care environment, however, you may be more likely to get a number that takes into account your genetics and individuality. Certainly you will get more numbers than the body fat scale can provide!

Rebecca Yao, who helped write this book, tested all the following methods.

BIOELECTRICAL IMPEDANCE ANALYSIS Rebecca paid a visit to her general practitioner doctor, who also specializes in sports. It was yearly physical time, so she had bioelectrical impedance analysis performed. Prior to the appointment, Rebecca had to follow a fairly strict protocol of no caffeine, no food, and certain other restrictions. At the doctor's office, she was hooked up to a machine with sticky electrodes placed on her ankle, by her heart, and on her wrist. A small current of electricity was generated through her body, and the machine decided the values shown in table 9.1, based on how slowly or quickly the machine received the current through Rebecca's body.

As you can see from the test data, if Rebecca had about 10 pounds of fat that she wanted to remove or transform into muscle, she would be well within a statistical safe zone. Her BMR (base metabolic rate) is calculated at 1,465 calories, and that's not calories from cookies. To get to an "optimal fat" range of 18–26

Table 9.1

BioAnalogics: ELG Quick-Comp		
YAO		
TEST DATA:		
	Date:	WED 07/26/00
	Age:	37
	Sex:	Female
	Height:	63 in
	Weight:	144 lbs
	Impedance:	549
RESULTS:		
	Body Fat:	31.1%
		44.8 lbs
	Lean Mass:	68.9%
		99.2 lbs
BMR:		1465 cals
Optimal Fat:		18%–26%
Goal Weight:		13+ lbs

percent, Rebecca would have to log the calories in a day to match 1,465 calories and train a certain time at a certain heart rate to burn calories by using her musculoskeletal systems. She would not eat fewer calories, because then her body would react as if she were in starvation mode (eating under her base metabolic rate of 1,465 calories) and would start dipping into the fat-free mass, saving the "fat" for the really lean times. It may seem ironic that she would have to eat to change her body fat composition. It's counterintuitive, but true.

Rebecca's doctor, Steven Hughes, M.D., a member of the American College of Sports Medicine, says there is also a happiness component to the data. He has a special interest in the problems of active people and is more than comfortable with Rebecca's level of activity versus her body composition. If Rebecca wanted to change her body composition, that would be fine, according to Dr. Hughes, as long as that change did not require extreme dieting or training to maintain a lower number. However, he didn't see any reason for

Rebecca to do anything differently. In short, Dr. Hughes interpreted her data and advised her appropriately. If you have this test done, be sure your results are interpreted by a knowledgeable expert who is aware of the limitations of the test data as they relate to you.

HYDROSTATIC (UNDERWATER) WEIGHING Hydrostatic weighing involves being weighed underwater after exhaling really hard. You can imagine how uncomfortable this method could be. Still, it is considered one of the more accurate methods, because the water displacement of your body density is easiest to measure with a high degree of accuracy. From there, body fat is estimated. It's still not error free. For example, it assumes that you are maintaining a constant bone density, which isn't appropriate for everyone. This test is offered at high-tech performance or cardiac testing centers.

AIR DISPLACEMENT (BOD POD) The Bod Pod is much the same as underwater weighing, but it measures air displacement rather than water. Rebecca tried this method at a sports medicine facility associated with a hospital. According to Rebecca, the displacement chamber looks so much like the Orgasmatron in Woody Allen's movie *Sleeper* that she had a fit of giggles throughout the test. Rebecca wore her tightest jog bra and shorts plus a beanie cap to enter the pod. (The beanie is to keep your hair flat on your head so the air doesn't get trapped in your hairdo and mess up the measurement.) This test was done several years ago, but the lean body weight was around the same as the bioelectrical impedance method (104.3 pounds Bod Pod versus the 99.2 pounds bioelectrical impedance method). Chances are that after running several half marathons a year as well as participating in triathlons, Rebecca's bone density is not decreasing from age 34 to age 37. So you can see how the numbers will vary, but they are close enough to give a good picture of body composition.

SKINFOLD CALIPERS Before using the body fat scale, Rebecca used a skinfold caliper to measure body fat. This method was offered at her health club and was the one her personal trainer used. Every couple of months, a caliper was used to pinch certain body parts to measure the subcutaneous fat. For this to be most effective, you have to get the same points every time, on the thigh, arm, hip, and back of the shoulder, among other spots. There are all kinds of skinfold calipers, some with a built-in computer with several different body fat percentage formulas, such as Durnin, Jackson-Pollock, or Slaughter-Lohman. Of great importance to the skinfold method is that the proper procedure be used each time. And you can't do it yourself because there are several sites that you cannot reach with the caliper in your own hand.

Web Sites

If you're already hooked into the Web, you're no doubt aware of a bunch of fitness-related Web sites where you can post your workouts to a personal calendar saved for you. Those of us who travel frequently and have Internet access at many of our destinations benefit greatly from this type of site. There's also a component of camaraderie when you receive daily e-mail reminders and other such site-generated mail. You can even sign up for a monthly diet service that logs food, suggests menus and shopping lists, and provides a chat room for support on your goals. Check it out through your favorite search engine by searching for the terms "fitness" or "sports training" or "diet."

What Does It All Mean?

What do all these tracking tools tell you? Well, they tell you that you're on the road to fitness. Whether it's a simple notebook where you jot down heart rate and a few other details or a downloadable heart rate monitor and a personal chat room, you're taking the time to follow your fitness commitment. Someone once said that what we can record, we can improve.

How do you interpret everything you're recording? No one person will be able to analyze all the data about your physical condition and come up with a cookie cutter program for you. If sports performance were more than just tinkering, we'd know from birth who could run the fastest and jump the highest. Fortunately, it's still a wonderful mystery and a thrill when we do better than we anticipated or when we witness an athletic feat that we might one day plan to train for and do. Over time and with diligent recording, the patterns of our training successes and slumps can be known. Tips and tricks to benefit us can be extrapolated from our data, even if the interpretation may be subject to interpretation.

How does it apply to or alter what you're doing? Tracking tools take the mystery out of the history, so to speak, but as is widely reported about financial markets, past performance is no indication of future success. Taking a good heart-to-heart look at our current state of fitness is always a plus. And when we alter our plans in fitness, we do take baby steps. Never swing so quickly to a new plan of action that you get dizzy just thinking about it. Other than the initial huge gains achieved from merely getting off the couch for the first time in years, the rewards of fitness are incremental and so should your course corrections be.

You'll change your program gradually as you collect your data and spread that information around to others for their opinions. You're still your own best judge of your readiness to move your fitness forward. So keep tracking, realize there is no quick fix, and try some baby steps of improvement as you go on.

chapter 10

the benefits of strength training

Being strong gives us energy. In the 1997 Eco Challenge, a multiday adventure race, I learned the lesson of strength by living with it daily. After 5 days of the 10-day race with little to no sleep and 20 hours a day of intense racing, I was without strength and tired. The race consisted of 40 miles of mountain biking, 25 miles of horseback riding, 120 miles of trekking, 50 miles of flat water canoeing, and 75 miles of class four white-water rafting. My team of four men and me faced one of the most dangerous and difficult mountain climbing routes ever created. The first of these was a dramatic and technically difficult 600-foot free rappel straight off the face of a ledge. A free rappel means that you hang from a rope and slowly lower yourself down while the winds swing you, while the rope heats as it passes through your jumar climbing device, while you focus on the moment with full concentration. The Eco Challenge is one of those high-risk races—the kind that I love.

Rope climbing is not my area of expertise. Before the race, I had only practiced three times with my equipment and harness. As I prepared to descend in the longest free rappel of my three climbing experiences, lowering myself down the height of the Empire State Building in New York, I was scared. Standing at the top of the ledge, my heart was racing. My heart rate monitor read 145 beats per minute without a muscle contracting. Adrenaline was pouring into my bloodstream, the adrenaline of fear. As I hooked onto the rope, the rigger who was assigned for safety reasons saw the fear. She said, "Sally, every other person has made it down this rope safely." In my mind, that was the challenge and the answer I needed. I thought to myself, "If they did it, I can do it."

It took both physical and emotional strength for me to dangle hundreds of feet in the air trusting my life and my safety to a single rope and a rigger whom I had never met before. And that strength came from years of training and in believing in my skills and myself as well as developing the physical strength that it takes to climb.

What continues to motivate me to do strength training is my desire to be physically and emotionally strong. For the Eco Challenge, I knew that survival was in large part dependent on strength. I needed to be as strong as I could so I could perform better, but even more, to help me overcome the obstacles that I knew I would face. Being emotionally and mentally strong is one of the principles that I live by.

Muscular strength and endurance are required as functions of our everyday lives. Our routine tasks around the home, such as lifting children, doing yardwork and housework, or moving furniture, require us to be strong. In the workplace, strength is also important for most people to perform their normal responsibilities proficiently. Weight training, also known as strength training, is a way for us to increase the size and strength of our muscles. Strength training is also important in almost all sports activities.

By gaining muscular strength, you become healthier. For those who suffer from back pain, specific strength-training activities can help reduce or eliminate the pain. By maintaining your muscle strength, you will also experience fewer injuries and maintain your muscle power as you age. For women, strength training is important to maintain bone mass and to help prevent osteoporosis. Strength training is like investing in a personal health insurance policy, because physical strength is something we use every day.

There are even more reasons to get stronger. For example, many people like to strength train because of the effect on their physical appearance, which can lead to changes in their self-esteem. Being buff is attractive, because it increases both the number of muscles visibly being used and the muscle mass. The benefits are displayed in one's more muscular appearance.

Strength Training and Athletic Performance

For many, weight training is an essential part of fitness training, because it leads to increased calorie-burning capacity (known as resting metabolic rate). By following a program of strength training, your body composition (or the ratio of fat to muscle) changes in favor of muscle. With increased muscle mass, there's an increase in the number of calories that are burned per minute when at rest. That is, those who train for strength burn more calories per minute just sitting than those who don't train for strength. By decreasing your body fat by 2 percent and increasing your muscle amount by 5 percent—a change in body composition that's easily seen by those who strength train—resting metabolism can increase by 10 to 15 percent.

Strength training also helps you avoid injury. When your muscles are stronger, you're less likely to suffer injury from poor mechanics (form). For example, as I noted in the running chapter, when your abs and back are strong, you won't suffer from strained stomach muscles. If your thigh muscles (quadriceps and hamstrings) are strong, you're less likely to pull your knee out of alignment when you run. Part of your strength training should include working on the muscles and fibers that support your joints.

Insider Tip

If strength training is new to you, take a class that teaches the techniques and different ways of training effectively and safely. It's all too easy to injure yourself if you don't have proper form.

There are two types of muscular strength. They are related but different:

1. Muscular strength: the ability of the body to exert maximum force
2. Muscular endurance: the ability of the body to exert repeated force

By definition, muscular strength is your ability to exert force. For example, if you can lift your child into your arms only one time, and doing so requires all the strength you have, then that is your maximum force. If you were able to lift your child again and again, that would be an example of muscular endurance. As another example, if you're riding a bike and your cadence, or revolutions per minute, is high, then you're exerting a low amount of force but with high revolutions and a small amount of weight. This requires muscle endurance.

There are different programs that lead to the development of muscular strength and muscular endurance, and they're primarily based on the types of exercises and the number of repetitions that you do when lifting a weight.

There are basically only three types of strength exercises:

1. Isokinetic strength training: slow-moving exercises through a full range of motion against a constant force or resistance
2. Isotonic strength training: moving weight against resistance, as in weight lifting.
3. Isometric strength training: applying force against an immovable object, such as a wall

Because of its close association with bodybuilding, strength training has amassed a large number of myths. Here are a few:

Myth: Strength training results in becoming muscle-bound and losing flexibility.

Fact: If weight-training exercises are performed over the full range of motion, flexibility improves.

Myth: Strength training, especially for women, just results in big muscles.

Fact: Gaining muscular strength and endurance by weight training increases both the number of muscle fibers *and* the size of each individual fiber.

Myth: Strength training increases cardiovascular ability.

Fact: There is little to no improvement in aerobic ability as a result of strength training alone.

Myth: Strength training takes a long time before results can be seen.

Fact: For those who are unfit, strength gains occur very quickly. This rapid improvement often results in motivation that leads to staying on the program.

Myth: Men gain strength faster than women do from strength training.

Fact: For the first twelve weeks, women gain strength just as quickly as men do. However, men generally increase their muscle size more than women do as a result of strength education.*

Myth: Strength training can hurt my sport-specific training, especially when I want to perform.

Fact: By adding strength training to your fitness program, your sport-specific workouts get better and your performances will improve.

Insider Tip

Call a friend who you enjoy being with and ask that person to be your strength-training partner for 4 weeks. Agree upon a meeting day and place. Design the training routine together.

Making It Fun

One of my favorite words is *fun*. If you make it fun, then your motivation and adherence to a training program are stronger. It's easy to include fun in most of the activities throughout your day. Find a training partner who will work out with you. Select a training partner who is as committed as you are. Select a training pal who has similar fitness levels as you, because it'll make exercising

*Scott Powers and Stephen Dodd, *Total Fitness: Exercise, Nutrition, and Wellness,* Allyn and Bacon, 1999, p. 125. Note: This muscle size increase in men occurs because men have twenty to thirty times more testosterone, which builds muscles, than women do.

Stretching Is Key

One key to maintaining a healthy body is to stretch regularly. This is particularly important when you're doing strength training. When you consistently practice your strength training, you build the muscle fibers you already have and you gain more. Unless you stretch these fibers, they'll be tight. This can lead to injury when it decreases your range of motion or pulls your joints ever so slightly out of alignment. Stretching also helps prevent that dreaded bulky look in women. Men, with their testosterone, won't worry so much about bulking up (although it can require a whole new wardrobe), but they still need to stretch to avoid stress on the joints and injury.

more enjoyable. Hire a personal trainer or buy a weight-training video so you can watch and learn the best techniques. Learn the different muscles involved in different strength-training exercises so you become more informed.

Good time management helps keep you on any exercise program, especially weight training. Find a convenient location or set up your own weight set in an environment that you enjoy. Set up an area in your house or living area for your exercise. Joining a good athletic club that provides a motivating surrounding and variety of equipment can also help you stay on your training program.

One of the keys to staying on any exercise program is desire. Do activities that increase your desire to do them again. Design a training routine that you enjoy. Make sure your routine includes variety, such as upper body training one day, lower body another day, and circuit training on the third day, which includes different stations with limited recovery time between them. You may have a tendency to train too hard at first and lift too much weight, which can lead to soreness and injury. Be gentle on yourself. Initially, lift less weight more times and gain muscular endurance. Later in the program, after strength training becomes more comfortable, lifting more weight fewer times can help you develop muscular strength.

Insider Tip

Set up an area in your home, office, or living space for strength-training activities. Make sure that the area is a comfortable environment with a pleasant ambience.

The Japanese principle of kaizen is one of the best practices for muscular strength and endurance. As we mentioned in chapter 4, kaizen means small, incremental improvements; it means constant change, such as a 1 percent improvement a hundred times that leads to a 100 percent change. By applying this philosophy daily, constant change happens and we get stronger. Getting 1 percent stronger every other day means being 100 percent stronger in less than a year.

Strength training should be challenging. Make a game of it by constantly challenging yourself to try different routines, different training systems, or different machines or equipment. Learn more about strength training and communicate with others who practice it. Create a new workout routine and challenge others to try it. Go to the Internet and learn more from Web sites that offer additional information.

Five Favorite Training Tips

1. More is not always better.
2. Work at your weaker sports but don't neglect your strengths.
3. Recovery is as important as the workout.
4. Be consistent.
5. Create a routine that is convenient for you so that you are more likely to stick to it.

—Dave McGillivray is the race director for the Boston Marathon and has worked on more than 500 events, including the 1998 Goodwill Games Triathlon. He has competed in eight Hawaii Ironman triathlons and thirty consecutive Boston Marathons.

Effect of Getting Older on Muscular Strength and Endurance

Peak muscular strength and muscular endurance occur in our late teens or early twenties. If you don't use your strength and endurance regularly after that time, you'll progressively get weaker. The same is true of your cardiovascular ability with age. After the age of 55, there is a second decline in muscular strength and endurance. This decline is more dramatic in men, probably because of decreased levels of testosterone. Even though at the same age women's levels of the reproductive hormones estrogen and progesterone also decline, those declines have little effect on muscular power.

Ultimately, if you want to feel healthier, improve your appearance, burn more calories, like yourself more, and just feel better overall, regular strength training works. That's a pretty tall promise, but when you do it, you'll feel the difference and the rewards.

The Law of Diminishing Returns

Strength training follows a very simple law of fitness training: Doing something is better than doing nothing, and doing something gets you a greater gain than doing too much. This is the law of diminishing returns, which states that with more exercise, you don't get a commensurate increase in exercise benefits. It's the initial training session that gives you the most effect. As a matter of fact, a little *can be* better than a lot. A lot of strength training may give you the maximum benefits but not the optimum benefits. In this case, optimum means the point at which you receive the most rewards for your effort as opposed to the ultimate or maximum level that you might achieve if you were to pursue the additional incremental changes past the optimum point for your physique. The greatest benefits come for those who are the least active and who are beginning a training program, because the improvements are the greatest.

Those people are going to realize a much greater health benefit than the already fit individual who trains even more hours. Sure, the extra few hours of training might result in some improvement, but not in the massive health improvements that you'll see when a sedentary person starts a training program.

The Differences in Muscular Strength Between Men and Women

You probably think that men are stronger than women. In fact, it depends on how you measure muscular strength. If you measure absolute strength, that is, the total amount that an average man compared with an average woman can lift, then it's true. In measuring upper body strength in absolutes, a woman is about 55 percent as strong as a man. In lower body absolute strength, a woman is 75 percent as strong as a man. This difference is usually attributed to the similar daily usage of the legs by men and women. We both walk and use our lower body muscles about the same amount in our daily tasks. This is not the case in our daily activities using upper body strength.

However, women and men are equally strong when relative strength is measured. Relative strength is the difference in muscular strength when taking into account the amount of muscle mass and the amount of fat mass. This measurement is expressed as "per fat free mass." Therefore, for men and women, the lower body strength, as a percentage of the amount of fat and muscle, is almost identical. Men and women have the same relative muscular strength.

Similarly, the ratio of strength between the upper body and the lower body of one individual is identical. For both men and women, upper body strength is about 70 percent of that of the lower body. Again, our legs and buttock muscles are stronger than our arms and chest muscles at the same ratio, regardless of gender.

Absolute strength is greater in men because testosterone increases after puberty. Prior to puberty, boys and girls have the same muscular strength and endurance. After puberty, women increase the production of estrogen and progesterone. Because the female hormones are not as anabolic (hormones that enhance muscle growth) as are male hormones, muscle mass in the female is not as greatly increased.

Research shows that both men and women achieve the same gains in muscular strength and endurance with strength training. Furthermore, all individuals lose muscle strength if they become sedentary, particularly after their peak muscle power periods that extend into their early twenties.

Let's Practice Strength Training

During the Day

Take a break during your day to do a little strength training. It's one of the easiest and best ways to reenergize yourself. Find a bench and use it as a piece of weight-lifting equipment by completing a few dips (see figure 10.1). Almost immediately, you'll feel the energy return and the dozy feeling disappear. It's one of the best midday stress busters that requires the least amount of time. Just a 3- to 5-minute break to walk around, strengthen some muscles (especially the neck and the shoulders), and stretch is better than drinking a picker-upper like coffee. Take several deep breaths of air afterward, go inside and calm yourself, and then hit the task that you took a break from and watch your productivity increase.

Muscular Strength and Endurance Training Program

There are different kinds of muscular strength and endurance training programs. Finding one that works for you is part of the joy of training. Experiment with different strength-training programs until you find a routine that works for you. To get you started, here is one of the basic weight-training plans that's widely accepted and enjoyed by many. It's based on performing a certain number of repetitions (known as reps) in a certain number of repeats (called sets), at either a percentage of your one-time maximum strength or by repetition maximums (RMs). "RMs" is

Figure 10.1
Dips

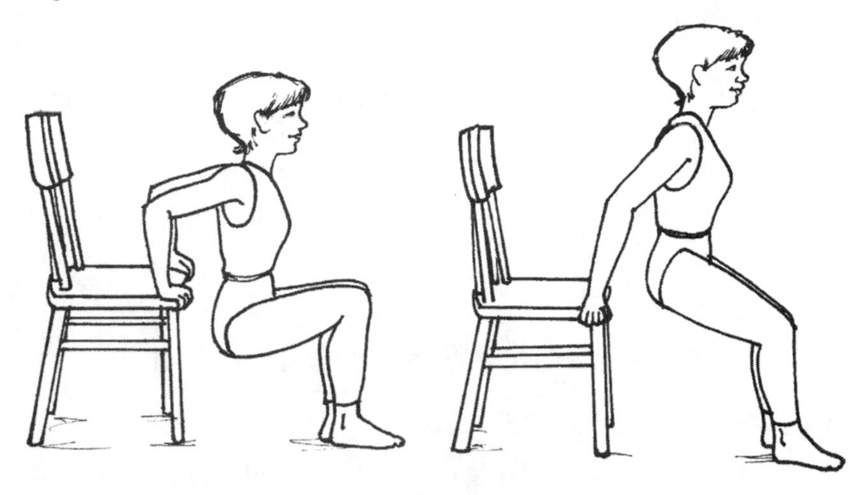

strength trainer lingo for the number of times you can lift a weight until you reach fatigue.

FOUR-PHASE STRENGTH TRAINING PROGRAM

Phase 1. Getting Started: 3 to 4 weeks

Frequency: 2–3 times per week

Duration: 2 sets

Intensity: 15 RMs

Description: This is a low-volume and low-intensity phase to initiate immediate strength gains.

Phase 2. Muscular Strength Phase: 2 to 8 weeks

Frequency: 2–3 times per week

Duration: 3–5 sets

Intensity: 6 RMs

Description: Also known as hypertrophy phase, it's a high volume of work with a low intensity of repetitions (15–30 repetitions of 3–5 sets).

Phase 3. Muscular Endurance Phase: 2 to 8 weeks

Frequency: 2–3 times per week

Duration: 3 sets

Intensity: 12–20 RMs

Description: During this phase, you are training your muscles to do higher intensity work over a longer period of time by increasing the number of RMs.

Phase 4. Support Phase: Lifetime

Frequency: 2–3 times per week

Intensity: Variable

Duration: 15–45 minutes

Description: This is an extended weight-training period during which your goal is to maintain your general strength conditioning level.

Here are a few simple reminders that will help you to continue enjoying your strength-training program, eliminate muscle soreness, and provide for measures of safety:

- A good warm-up should precede any resistance exercise, and a good cool-down should follow the completion of any exercise program. Always stretch after strength training.
- Proper technique and form are very important in both safety and injury prevention.
- Large muscles should be exercised before the small muscle groups.
- Breathing should be continuous while performing lifts. Holding your breath results in an increase in blood pressure and a reduction in the return of blood to the heart. *Always use a normal breathing pattern.*
- Following a training pattern that includes sections of time called periodization improves strength gains.
- Strength train in phases that gradually decrease in exercise volume and gradually increase in exercise intensity. This allows for progressive improvements.

- Plateaus in training occur and can be overcome by adding variability to your training with recovery periods, cross training, and changes in the routine.

Insider Tip

Set a goal to strength train and measure the before-and-after differences. Promise to complete at least the first phase of a periodization program that includes at least four phases.

Strength training may be the most misunderstood part of the entire fitness program because of the myths and propaganda that surround it, which probably came from its early heritage in bodybuilding. Strength training is one of the most important ways to increase your energy. And the joy of strength training is often felt after the workout because you increase your energy by using your muscles to get stronger. Rather than losing it because you don't use it (the weightlifter's mantra), rewrite it and obey the call of the strength trainer: You gain energy because you use energy.

Ask yourself the question, "What do I want?" If you want to be as strong as you can be in every corner of your heart, every cell in your mind, every muscle in its fiber, then strength training is the perfect energizing activity.

chapter 11

Putting It All Together

The Training Program

Training for triathlons is a blend of art and science. It's not easy to take three different activities and design them into an individualized and personal program that works for you. If you work out only in your favorite triathlon sports, you will most likely get a good workout, but you run the risk of ignoring your least preferred triathlon leg. If you work out only in your acknowledged "slow" triathlon sport, you may risk working out at too low a level to maintain your fitness.

Figuring out the balance can be daunting to the newcomer and frustrating to the experienced triathlete. Blending three sports together to benefit your overall conditioning to the point at which the race is an example of the best you can do is part of the art of triathlon. If you master this three-ring circus of sports skills and apply them in a scientific manner through analyzing your log, benchmarks, and testing, you will be on your way to the triathlon performance you desire. With some practice, you can learn both the art and the science of training.

When I first started to train for triathlons in 1979, I was a self-coached long-distance runner. I had finished races from a mile to a hundred miles. Approaching triathlon as an exercise scientist, I knew that I had to figure out how to balance all three sports and still include the key workouts from each discipline. It reminded me then, and today, of cooking, in which you blend a recipe of different ingredients and proportions based on the final meal.

For triple sports training, as with losing weight or getting rich, there are experts upon whom you can rely and relinquish your training program. Sports specialists, coaches, personal trainers, and ex-triathletes may try to sell you on their magical and mysterious secrets to training and racing success. In fact, however, there are no secrets or magic potions that, blended together, will guarantee that you'll cross the finish line first. Instead, I recommend that you put together your own program so you become a self-coached triathlete. Invest your resources into what these same experts should be selling you—consulting, encouragement, accountability, motivation, and psychological support. If you do choose to spend your time and cash following a training program that someone else creates for you, then make sure that you add to it your own self-coaching know-how.

There are two levels to the training program: a level for those who are new to triathlons and one for those with a background in sports training. Pick the category that fits you best, and train based on the guidelines and sample workouts that fit your background experience in fitness and sports training. If you're just starting to train for triathlons, begin with the *basic* tri-training program. If you're familiar with swimming, cycling, and running, then start with the *performance* tri-training program. If you have an extensive triathlon background, then you're probably interested in getting faster and getting your fittest, which is covered in chapter 13.

If you aren't sure where to start, try a fast-track basic tri-training, using the first level but only staying at that level for 4 weeks or less. After finishing that level, move onto the second level, performance tri-training. Both of these levels of training are contiguous and build upon each other, so it might work for you to move very quickly from level 1 to level 2.

Basic Tri-Training: Technique and Base Training Periods

To get started on your first triple fitness sports training program, dedicate a time frame (from 4 to 12 weeks) as your introductory period. The first half of this training, approximately 1 to 4 weeks, is spent on your *technique*. During the technique period, your goal

Five Favorite Training Tips

1. Rest is training.
2. Racing is the easy part.
3. Training is when you learn the keys that unlock the champion's mind within you: commitment, desire, playfulness, honesty, knowledge.
4. The heart rate monitor is a window into your body's response to training. It is one important tool for measuring your training load.
5. Most champions are viewed as eccentrics by their underachieving peers. Don't let false pride derail your progress.

–Sue Latshaw

is to build basic fitness conditioning and to develop techniques and skills in the three disciplines. The second half of basic tri-training is called the *base training period,* which lasts 2 to 6 weeks. During this phase, you sharpen and enhance those skills and build upon the base that you created in the technique period. The wider, or more thorough, the fitness base you create during the first half of base training, the higher the peak of performance you will attain in the second half.

The Technique Period: 1–4 Weeks

The technique period is the beginning part of the program. During this phase, you progress by developing your technical skills. This is your introduction phase, your first rite of passage to triathlon.

At this starting point, the emphasis in training is on developing your biomechanical efficiency, or your ability to move with the least amount of energy cost. In swimming, for example, biomechanical efficiency is achieved when you reduce your drag. During the technique phase, you progressively add more training time or training distance to your workouts.

For the first 1 to 2 weeks, you work out in all three sports in alternation, with a rest day between each. This means that during the first week, you swim one day, rest the next, bike the following, rest the next, run the following, and rest the next. Work out with a stopwatch and a heart rate monitor (or a heart rate monitor with a timer), using time and heart zones, not distance, as the determining factors of how long and how hard you should exert yourself. The duration of these initiation workouts is 15 to 35 minutes. The training zones are from zone 1 through zone 3, and you stay in each zone from 5 minutes to 15 minutes (see figure 11.1). Break your workouts into four parts: warm-up, preset/skill practice, main set, and cool-down.

WARM-UP The warm-up should be a slow, easy, relaxed period, at least 5 minutes long. It can include stretching as well as performing the actual sport at an easy pace. For example, when I run,

Figure 11.1

Basic Workout Profile

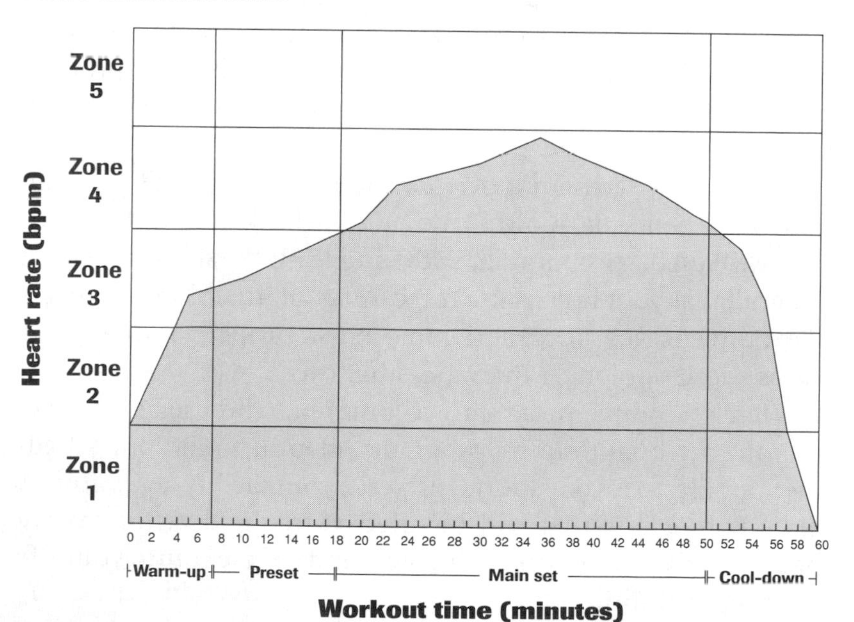

I start each run by walking slowly, increasing my pace to a slog (a slow jog), then jogging, and finally running.

PRESET/SKILLS Preset/skills is a training period during which you select a specific skill, do drills, and focus on improving that skill. In swimming, for example, you might choose to work on your flutter kick, so the preset drills might include a 2 × 50 using a kickboard.

MAIN SET The main set is the longest part of the training period and is the time when the most fitness benefit is achieved. You should be working hard during this set, using your monitor and staying in the appropriate zones (see chapter 5).

COOL-DOWN Like the warm-up, the cool-down is an easy period in which you slowly bring your heart rate down to its ambient level by reducing the intensity of the activity and recovering.

Memorize these four parts, and follow them each time you design or do a workout.

As you progress through the technique period, you'll add time, intensity, and distance to your workouts. The sum of these three factors is called training load, and you need to build it progressively and systematically. Training load is the basic way that you improve your fitness.

During the technique period, the new skills you'll need to develop depend upon old skills or your background. Work on your weakest or least familiar sport and learn the skills to make it as familiar as your best of the three. After all, triathlon training is like a three-legged stool, and you can't sit properly if one of the legs is shorter or longer than the other two.

Here's a sample program I recommend you use as a model for your personal training program. Adapt it to fit your schedule, your lifestyle, your sports interests, your facility accessibility, and anything else that will be affected by the decision you've made to incorporate something new and different into your life and responsibilities.

Sample Training Program Phase 1: Technique Period

Duration: 1–4 weeks

Number of Workouts: 3–4 per week

Total Duration: 15–35 minutes

Training Intensity: Heart zones 1–3

Training Frequency: Every other day, 3–4 single-sport sessions

Purpose: To learn the basic techniques and skills of tri training

	Swim	Bike	Run/Jog/Walk
Monday	15–35 minutes	0	0
Tuesday		Day Off	
Wednesday	0	15–35 minutes	0
Thursday		Day Off	
Friday	0	0	15–35 minutes
Saturday		Day Off	
Sunday	Sport that needs most improvement		

The Base Training Period: 2–6 Weeks

Once you've acquired the skills in the technique period, it's time to develop your aerobic power. Therefore, the final phase of the basic tri-training period, which lasts 2 to 6 weeks, is base training. This is the time when you train to build a foundation, or your endurance base, which is the fitness level you need in order to exercise for an extended duration without tiring. By developing your aerobic capacity, you improve your stamina, develop your sport-specific muscle strength, and reduce your risk of injuries.

Try to increase your base training level to the point at which you can work out for 20 to 45 minutes for 4 to 5 days per week in the middle three heart zones (zones 2–4). Keep in mind that you are only working out one sport per day. These workouts are called singles, and as you get fitter, you can add "brick" or bike-run or "doubles," which are any two sports in one day with a break in between workouts.

Sample Training Program Phase 2: Base Training

Duration: 2–6 weeks

Number of Workouts: 4–5 per week

Total Duration: 20–45 minutes

Training Intensity: Heart zones 1–4

Training Frequency: More often than every other day, up to 4 single-sport sessions in a row

Purpose: Work on developing your sport-specific techniques

	Swim	Bike	Run/Jog/Walk
Monday	20–45 minutes	0	0
Tuesday		Day Off	
Wednesday	0	20–45 minutes	0
Thursday		Day Off	
Friday	0	0	20–45 minutes
Saturday		20–45 minutes in sport that needs improvement	
Sunday		20–45 minutes, optional workout in your choice of sport	

When you feel you've learned the techniques and have developed your cardio base, it's time to take the next step in triathlon fitness training: the transition into the cross-training phase. You should make this transition when (1) you're comfortable swimming, cycling, and running at least 25 minutes continuously, (2) you're confident in the water, on the bike, and running, and (3) you feel the eagerness to move forward. You'll *know* when it's time to transition—it's one of those internal, bodily truths you'll be getting in touch with more and more.

The Cross-Training Phase: 4–8 weeks

The cross-training phase is a period of rapid improvement after you've completed basic tri-training. During this phase, your training progress is measured using a different metric than skills and endurance. Instead, you use a heart rate monitor with a watch function to obtain biofeedback during every second of your training. The training system is called Heart Zone Training, as was discussed in chapter 5, and uses four new components:

1. Time in zone to provide you with all the benefits of exercise
2. The training tree for training progressions
3. Heart zone training points to measure your training load
4. Key workouts

It's important to know your five heart zones, because training intensity is one of the keys to your success. So go back to chapter 5 and review the five training zones before proceeding.

You want to spend different amounts of time in different heart zones. Varying your training intensity is based on the principle of adaptation—in other words, the body responds best to stress and recovery by adapting to a higher fitness level. Training in zones gives you the data you need to apply exercise stress in the appropriate amount. It also tells you when you need to take the stress off to recover. As you get fitter, you can vary the amount of time you spend in different zones by shifting from the aerobic side to the anaerobic side of the training tree introduced in chapter 5 and reconfigured in figure 11.2.

One way of viewing training is to quantify the energy system or pathways that your muscles are using. *Aerobic* means "with oxygen," which means that there is always sufficient oxygen to meet the energy demands. *Anaerobic* means "without sufficient oxygen," and when your exercise speed or intensity gets too hard, there is just not enough oxygen for your energy system.

Figure 11.2

Heart Zone Training Time in Zone

	Aerobic Side			Anaerobic Side		Workouts
Race						
	Zone 1	Zone 2	Zone 3	Zone 4	Zone 5	
Peak/Power		10%	60%	20%	10%	2 speed 2 strength 2 endurance
Speed/Interval		20%	60%	10%	10%	1 speed 1 strength 2 endurance
Strength	10%	10%	70%	10%		2 strength 2 endurance
Endurance	10%	40%	50%			4–6 endurance
Base/Technique	30%	70%				3–5 base
Recovery						

The cross-training phase is a way of getting fitter by climbing near or all the way to the top of the tree. Doing so will make you as fit as possible and ready to perform at your best on race day. As you climb toward the top of the training tree, keep your focus on the trunk, or the goals that you've set for yourself. Note that there are five training branches on the tree, each branch representing a different stage in the cross-training phase. Your training program should be divided as a percentage of your total training time for each of the five different heart zones. Table 11.1 provides a handy worksheet to figure out how much time to spend in each zone every week, depending on which branch of the tree you're on.

Heart Zone Training points provide an easy way to measure training quantity—total training load per week or month. You can compare the difficulty of different workouts and, ultimately, track your training to achieve your goals. You earn one point per minute of your training in zone 1, two points per minute in zone 2, three points per minute in zone 3, and so forth. To determine your total points, simply multiply the number of minutes in each of the zones by the zone number. For example, for a 40-minute bike ride in zone 3, you would multiply 3 × 40 = 120 heart zone training points. Think of it as a scorecard.

The more heart zone training points you accumulate in one day, the more calories you burn and the more training you get. It's a practical, easy way to calculate training load, and it's blissfully simple to do.

Table 11.1

Time in Zone

Zone	Max HR	Zone	Base	Endurance	Strength	Speed	Peak
Z5	90–100%	Red Line	–	–	–	10%	10%
Z4	80–90%	Threshold	–	–	10%	10%	20%
Z3	70–80%	Aerobic	–	50%	70%	60%	60%
Z2	60–70%	Temperate Zone	70%	40%	10%	20%	10%
Z1	50–60%	Healthy Heart	30%	10%	10%	–	–
			100% min.	100% min.	100% min.	100% min.	100% min.

Finally, key workouts establish a specific purpose for the training session. There are basically three types of key workouts that you can use for each of the three sports:

1. **Strength:** Improving your power in the specific sport. Hill repeats are a good example of a strength workout; they lead to the development of your muscle power or your capacity for hard workouts.
2. **Intervals:** Also known as speed workouts, they are high-intensity repeats followed by recovery repeats to develop your anaerobic capacity.
3. **Endurance:** These workouts are of lower intensity and longer duration than the event for which you are training. They help develop your aerobic capacity.

For advanced triathlon training, the optimum number of key workouts is called the nine-key workout plan and consists of one strength, one interval, and one endurance workout each week in each of three disciplines, for a total of nine key workouts.

With your heart rate monitor, your understanding of training, and your tools and assessments, you can now begin to develop your own individualized and personalized triathlon training program for the cross-training phase. The program should be based on how much training time you have available to you. Each of us has a different time availability, so determine the amount of time you have and divide it into the zones based on the limb of the training tree on which you start your current level of fitness.

Next, write a training program and post it in a visible place. You'll eliminate junk workouts and save training time by having a plan and working the plan. It's an organized way of looking at your training. Test your training program by comparing the plan with the actual. To do this, compare your training plan with your training log or your benchmark. See how much difference there is between the two. When your log and your plan match, you have the highest possibility of being successful, of accomplishing your goal. (For more about keeping your triathlon log, see chapter 9.)

The sample training programs at the end of this chapter were designed for Paul Yao, a three-time sprint-distance triathlon finisher.

Because training is highly individualized, these sample programs won't fulfill all your needs for a training program, but they'll help you plan your own program. To better understand the logic of Paul's design for his cross-training phase, here is some background information about him:

> **Goal:** To finish faster than his last sprint triathlon in 8 weeks as well as change his body composition by dropping 3 percent body fat
>
> **Background:** Marathon runner, average cyclist, fair swimmer
>
> **Fitness scores** (see chapter 4): Swim scorecard—8, Bike scorecard—11, Running scorecard—13
>
> **Hours of training available:** 6–9 hours a week
>
> **Lifestyle:** Father, husband, business owner, no athletic background from school, responsible, smart
>
> **Current limb on the training tree:** Strength branch

The first workout shows the first training plan that Paul wrote. He quickly learned to write his plans in pencil, because after the first week, he discovered that he had overplanned and undertimed. At first, he didn't give himself enough flexibility and didn't have a back-up plan for missed workouts.

Insider Tip

If you do miss a workout, let it go into cyberspace. Don't try to make it up sometime during the week. Just let it go.

The appendix includes training tree branch charts for you to look up how many minutes you work out in each zone. If you have 60 minutes to work out, for example, and you are on the speed/interval branch, the chart will tell you how much time to spend in each zone so that you keep the quality of the workout session where you want it to be. Using these charts and the log page example from chapter 9 (or a blank piece of paper), put it all together for your own plan so you can begin to reach for the next branch on your training tree.

Weeks 1–3 of the 8-Week Triathlon Training Plan for Paul Yao

Limb on the Training Tree: Strength branch

Total Duration: 3 weeks

Training Time: 30–90 minutes per workout

Training Intensity: Heart zones 1–4

Training Frequency: 4–6 single-sport training sessions per week

Purpose: Work on getting stronger by using hills and swim drills

Date	Sport Activity	Time	Distance (approx.)	Time in Zones 1	2	3	4	5	Key Workout Type*
Mon.	Swim	30 min	800 m	3	3	21	3		I
Tues.	Weights	45 min							
Wed.	Bike	75 min	20–25 mi	10	10	55			SS
	Swim	30 min	800 m	3	3	21			I
Thurs.	Stretching	15 min							
Fri.	Run	60 min	4–5 mi	6	6	42	6		ST
Sat.	Bike	90 min	25–28 mi	9	9	63	9		I
	Weights	45 min							
Sun.	Rest Day	0							
				10%	10%	70%	10%		100%
Totals:			S: 1,600 m B: 45 mi R: 5 mi	29	29	200	29		287
			HZT Points:	29	58	600	29		803

*Key Workouts: I = Intervals, SS = Steady State, ST = Strength

Weeks 4–6 of the 8-Week Triathlon Training Plan for Paul Yao

Limb on the Training Tree: Speed/interval branch

Total Duration: 2 weeks

Training Time: 30–90 minutes per workout

Training Intensity: Heart zones 2–5

Training Frequency: 8 training sessions per week

Purpose: Train the systems to take the higher intensity load

Date	Sport Activity	Time	Distance (approx.)	Time in Zones 1	2	3	4	5	Key Workout Type*
Mon.	Swim	30 min	1000 m		6	18	3	3	I
Tues.	Weights	45 min							ST
Wed.	Bike	75 min	15–17 mi		15	45	8	7	SS
	Swim	30 min	1,000 m		6	18	3	3	I
Thur.	Stretching	15 min							
Fri.	Run	60 min	5–6 mi		12	36	6	6	ST
Sat.	Bike	90 min	28–32 mi		18	54	9	9	SS
	Weights	45 min							ST
Sun.	Rest								
					20%	60%	10%	10%	100%
Totals:			S: 2,000 m B: 43 mi R: 5–6 mi		57	171	29	28	285
			HZT Points:		114	513	116	140	883

*Key Workouts: I = Intervals, SS = Steady State, ST = Strength

Week 7 of the 8-Week Triathlon Training Plan for Paul Yao

Limb on the Training Tree: Peak Power branch

Total Duration: 1 week

Training Time: 30–90 minutes per workout

Training Intensity: Heart zones 2–5

Training Frequency: 8 training sessions per week

Purpose: Build distance by increasing speed

Date	Sport Activity	Time	Distance (approx.)	Time in Zones 1	2	3	4	5	Key Workout Type*
Mon.	Swim	30 min	1,200 m		3	18	6	3	I
Tues.	Weights	45 min							ST
Wed.	Bike	75 min	17–20 mi		8	45	15	7	SS
	Swim	30 min	1,200 m		3	18	6	3	I
Thurs.	Stretching	15 min							
Fri.	Run	60 min	6–7 mi		6	36	12	6	ST
Sat.	Bike	90 min	26–32 mi		9	54	18	9	SS
	Weights								ST
Sun.	Rest								
					10%	60%	20%	10%	100%
Totals:			S: 2,400 m B: 43 mi R: 6–7 mi		29	171	57	28	285
			HZT Points:		58	513	228	140	939

*Key Workouts: I = Intervals, SS = Steady State, ST = Strength

Week 8 of the 8-Week Triathlon Training Plan for Paul Yao

Limb on the Training Tree: Race branch

Total Duration: 1 week

Training Time: 25–45 minutes per workout

Training Intensity: Heart zones 2–5

Training Frequency: 3 training sessions per week

Purpose: Race benchmark, taper, and race well!

Date	Sport Activity	Time	Distance (approx.)	Time in Zones 1	2	3	4	5	Key Workout Type*
Mon.	Swim	25 min	800 m		3	18	6	3	SS
Tues.	Bike	45 min	12 mi		5	27	9	4	SS
Wed.	Run	30 min	3–4 mi		3	18	6	3	SS
Thurs.	Rest								
Fri.	Rest								
Sat.	Rest								
Sun.	Race Day	80 min	Sprint triathlon				80		
					6%	33%	55%	6%	100%
Totals:			S: 1,550 m B: 24 mi R: 6.2 mi		11	63	101	10	185
			HZT Points:		22	189	404	50	665

*Key Workouts: I = Intervals, SS = Steady State, ST = Strength

When You Are Ready for More: Resources

Books

Paula Newby-Fraser's Peak Fitness for Women by Paula Newby-Fraser and John Mora (contributor), Human Kinetics (1995).

Triathletes Training Bible by Joe Friehl, Velo Press (1998).

Triathlons for Women by Sally Edwards, Heart Zones Publishing, 2000.

chapter 12

eating to train and training to eat

First, the good news. Triathletes eat more than almost any other people. They eat more often, in greater amounts, more calories, more helpings, more of everything. If you love to eat, you've found your sport. Large helpings of healthful foods are yours for the consuming.

The other good news is that as a triathlete, you'll lose fat and gain muscle.

Now the bad news. The "flab to firm" transformation isn't immediate. If you look at the nonfiction best-sellers list, you'll always see a diet book listed that offers its followers quick weight loss in the dozens-of-pounds range. But between you and me, just say no to Name Your Fad Diet of the Media Month. In the long run, none of these quick weight-loss programs work, because they only temporarily shed pounds. Shedding bad habits, improving one's self-image and self-respect, and living a lifestyle that includes physical activity are the only programs that work for everyone and for a lifetime.

Record and Monitor

Your optimum diet is the particular combination of foods that stimulate your body to perform with maximum comfort and efficiency in a predictable way through a variety of situations. A well-balanced diet is a must for everyone, but it's particularly important for triathletes, who put themselves in unusually stressful situations. We can gauge the values of different food types to our individual metabolisms by recording and monitoring.

Write down and then look at the type, amount, and nutritional value of the foods you eat over a week. My simple answer for meeting the needs of my body is to assess this list by asking the question, "What will it give me and what will it cost me?" Food gives the body a source of fuel that it can burn for energy, plus certain other nutritional benefits, such as protein to repair muscle tissue. On the other hand, food can cost the body. It may provide empty (relatively nonnutritious) calories, such as a candy bar or soft drink. It makes sense that we put into our incredible triathlon machines only the food that gives us more than it costs. As you become more finely attuned to your fuel requirements, make a note of what works for you, how you feel, and how much energy you have.

Contrary to popular opinion, radically reducing calorie intake by dieting drastically does not promote the loss of body fat but instead causes the loss of muscle. The fact is, muscle weighs more than fat. Many first-time triathletes become disheartened when they increase their physical activity and their bathroom scale appears to mock their hard work by going in an upward direction. This is the point at which the intellect must rule the emotions. Body fat is vital to daily body functions; it cushions the joints and protects the organs, helps regulate body temperature, and stores vitamins. Everyone needs body fat to operate efficiently. As I discussed in chapter 9, an ordinary bathroom scale will not tell you what percentage of body fat or fat-free tissue you have. Confusing upward gains in body weight with becoming less fit and more fat is altogether too common. Then we start the "diet," and here we are on the weight issue merry-go-round once again.

As you pursue your triathlon training program, you'll be more encouraged by looking at the fluctuations of the body fat percentage instead of body weight. Monitoring your body fat percentage and noticing that you have more energy and are getting faster gives you a clearer picture of the benefits you're getting from your nutritional choices and training routine. Body fat benchmarking with your health care practitioners and home monitoring with a body fat scale, such as the Tanita Body Fat Monitor/Scale (retail around $79), helps you step off the mental merry-go-round.

Eating Rituals and What to Eat During an Event

The biggest rule is not to do anything in races that you don't do in training and are not completely comfortable with. I was never good at stomaching a lot of food before a race. I found that Power Bars worked well for me—I could eat one in the morning, and it sat well in my stomach for the race. But I also used Power Bars every morning before training (and yes, ended up being sponsored by them!). During the past couple of years of my career, I started having a Power Gel after warm-up and within 15 minutes of a race start, and sometimes another one toward the end of the bike. This helped my energy levels immensely (even though I never raced longer than Olympic Distance, i.e., 2 hours).

—Jackie Gallagher retired after 8 years as a Professional Triathlete at the end of 2000. She was appointed Head Coach of the Australian Institute of Sport Junior Elite Triathlon Program. She represented Australia in eight World Championships for three silver medals and one world title; Four Duathlon Worlds for two golds and a bronze. ■

Calories In = Calories Out

You can thank your incredible bodily machine for all that it does. As complicated as the body may seem, it's an unfailingly accurate calorie counter.

The truth is that for long-term weight control, one program works.

Diet experts agree.

Nutritionists agree.

Exercise physiologists agree.

They all agree that the only plan that works for a lifetime is built around the formula that I call the fitness equation:

Calories in - Calories out = Weight gain or weight loss

The formula follows the first law of thermodynamics, and it works.

Did you know that a 190-pound superactive male, such as a triathlete, burns 4,400 calories per day, whereas his sedentary counterpart burns only 2,250 calories? Did you know that a 140-pound, superactive woman burns 2,800 calories, but her couch-potato female friends of the same weight can only eat 1,400 calories before they gain weight? Would you like to eat that much—4,400 calories for men or 2,800 calories for women each day and still stay lean?

Look up your weight in table 12.1 and then ask yourself, "Would I prefer to eat twice as much and exercise *or* would I prefer to not exercise, eat half as much, and still be flabby?"

Eat More, Weigh Less

That's what triathletes do—they have to eat more if they want to keep from losing weight. They eat to gain or maintain weight, not to lose it. They're clued in to the way their bodies work—if you burn more calories in physical activities than you consume, then you'll lose fat and gain muscle. If you eat more calories than you burn off, then you gain fat and may lose muscle. Of course, diet and eating is a complex issue that can only be addressed in passing here.

What Americans are most prone to suffer from, however, is "creeping" fat. In *The California Diet and Exercise Program* by Stanford University's Dr. Peter Wood, a very clear explanation is offered: "The typical overweight American at age 50 has put on one to two pounds of fat each year since he [she*] was 20 years old. So, at 50, he [she*] is 30 to 60 pounds overweight—and it shows. But a gain of one to two pounds of fat each year means eating only 10 to 20 calories too much each day on average, or no more than a quarter of a small banana."

What Wood explains is that when you have a calorie imbalance on the positive, input side, you will inexorably become fatter.

---

*My addition. The same calorie imbalance occurs in women as well.

Table 12.1

Daily Calorie Allowance Table

Women						
Weight	**Super Active**	**Very Active**	**Active**	**Moderately Active**	**Low Active**	**Sedentary**
80	1600	1440	1280	1120	960	800
90	1800	1620	1440	1260	1080	900
100	2000	1800	1600	1400	1200	1000
110	2200	1980	1760	1540	1320	1100
120	2400	2160	1920	1680	1440	1200
130	2600	2340	2080	1820	1560	1300
140	2800	2520	2240	1960	1680	1400
150	3000	2700	2400	2100	1800	1500
160	3200	2880	2560	2240	1920	1600
170	3400	3060	2720	2380	2040	1700
180	3600	3240	2880	2520	2160	1800
Men						
Weight	**Super Active**	**Very Active**	**Active**	**Moderately Active**	**Low Active**	**Sedentary**
100	2600	2350	2100	1850	1600	1350
110	1800	2530	2260	1990	1720	1450
120	3000	2710	2420	2130	1840	1550
130	3200	2890	2580	2270	1960	1650
140	3400	3070	2740	2410	2080	1750
150	3600	3250	2900	2550	2200	1850
160	3800	3430	3060	2690	2320	1950
170	4000	3610	3220	2830	2440	2050
180	4200	2790	2280	2970	2560	2150
190	4400	3970	3540	3110	2680	2250
200	4600	4150	3700	3250	2800	2350

Meanwhile, lean, active people are successfully eating larger amounts of food than you but are remaining skinny. But it's not because of their "unnaturally high metabolisms." Really, genetics is usually not the difference between the overfat person and the lean one; it's the calorie in/out balance that's working in those active people's favor.

If you're training for triathlons for weight management as well as for fun, table 12.2 can be used to calculate the calories out (burned) in your fitness equation. You have to make your calculations from your own body weight, because calorie burning is dependent upon one's specific mass.

Table 12.2

Activities Calories per Minute

			Weight (pounds)			
Activity	**110**	**130**	**150**	**170**	**190**	**210**
Swimming (crawl)						
20 yd/min	3.9	4.5	5.1	6.3	6.9	
30 yd/min	5.5	3.6	7.1	7.9	9.7	10.5
35 yd/min	7.1	8.0	8.9	9.8	10.7	11.6
40 yd/min	7.8	8.9	10.0	11.1	12.2	13.2
45 yd/min	9.0	10.3	11.6	12.9	14.2	15.3
55 yd/min	11.0	12.5	14.0	15.5	17.0	18.5
Bicycling						
5.5 mi/hr	3.2	3.6	4.0	4.4	4.8	5.2
10 mi/hr	5.4	6.2	7.0	7.8	8.6	9.4
13 mi/hr	8.6	9.8	11.0	12.2	13.4	14.6
Running						
5.5 mi/hr	8.6	9.8	11.0	12.2	13.4	14.6
6.0 mi/hr	8.8	9.9	11.0	12.1	13.2	14.3
6.5 mi/hr	8.9	10.2	11.5	12.8	14.1	15.4
7.0 mi/hr	9.2	10.4	11.6	12.8	14.0	15.2
7.5 mi/hr	9.8	11.2	13.6	16.0	18.4	19.8
8.0 mi/hr	10.4	11.9	13.4	14.9	16.4	17.9
8.5 mi/hr	11.2	12.8	14.4	16.0	17.6	19.2
9.0 mi/hr	12.0	13.8	15.6	17.4	19.2	21.0
9.5 mi/hr	12.8	14.7	16.6	18.5	20.4	22.3
10.0 mi/hr	13.6	15.5	17.4	19.3	21.2	23.1
10.5 mi/hr	14.3	16.3	18.3	20.3	22.4	24.3
11.0 mi/hr	15.2	17.3	19.4	21.5	23.7	25.9
11.5 mi/hr	15.9	18.2	20.5	22.8	25.1	27.4
12.0 mi/hr	18.2	20.7	23.2	25.7	28.2	30.7
12.5 mi/hr	20.3	23.1	25.9	28.7	31.5	34.3

Eating Rituals and What to Eat During an Event

John Hellemans and his wife Ien (two of New Zealand's leading sports nutrition experts) both taught me a great deal about fueling the body. When I first went to New Zealand in early 1999, I was struggling badly with chronic fatigue and overtraining. Fixing my eating patterns along with my training intensities were the two things that allowed me to return to the sport and have some success.

I learned that it isn't just what you eat that makes a difference, it is also when you eat—before, after, and during training. On the morning of a race, about two to three hours before the start, I would have a large bowl of porridge. Not the most exciting of meals but very effective, and I never felt sick or hungry during a race. In the final couple of hours before a race, I would always have a sports drink with me, and I would drink about 700 milliliters to 1 liter in the final hour before the start.

The most important time for hydration, however, is in the days and even the week preceding the competition. The same goes for diet. One good morning of nutrition isn't going to save you from months of pies and beer. Trust me on that one.

If you want to know how many total daily calories you burn on the calories-out side of the equation, you must also add your basal metabolic rate, your calories burned on the job, and your calories burned in daily activities. Tables 12.3 and 12.4 provide some food for thought.

Foods In, Fuel Out

The truth is, you don't successfully race triathlons on your good looks and a secret diet. You do it by planning your food in, or

During an Olympic distance race, I wouldn't normally take anything to eat, because the race is so short.

The only time I would consider taking food for an Olympic distance was if I was worried about my fitness. And if I was that worried, I probably shouldn't have been racing. I would always have a large bottle of sports drink for the bike (two bottles if it was going to be hot). For longer races, I would take a gel type food and maybe some chocolate of some sort, because I love chocolate and if you can't eat chocolate in a race then what's the point?

—Ben Bright was born in Waiuku (meaning mud and water) in New Zealand's North Island in 1974. In 1990, Ben represented New Zealand at the Commonwealth Games and later the same year represented Australia at the World Champs, thanks to dual citizenship. Ben was the Australian Triathlete of the year at age 17. In 1993, he finished 5th overall at the Manchester World Champs. In 1994, he returned to junior racing to win the World Title. The 2000 New Zealand national champion and Olympic representative is currently taking an indefinite break from competition due to injury and is employed as a Triathlon Coach in Hong Kong. ■

Table 12.3

Job Calories per Minute

	Job Weight (pounds)					
	110	**130**	**150**	**170**	**190**	**210**
Driving (active)	3.0	3.4	3.8	4.2	4.6	5.0
Retail (light)	1.8	2.1	2.4	2.7	3.0	3.3
Waiting tables	3.0	3.4	3.8	4.2	4.6	5.0
Househusband/wife	3.3	3.7	4.1	4.5	4.9	5.4
Keyboarding	1.9	2.1	2.3	2.5	2.7	2.9
Ax chopping (fast)	14.9	17.5	20.2	22.9	25.5	28.2

Table 12.4
Daily Activities Calories per Minute

	Activity Weight (pounds)					
	110	**130**	**150**	**170**	**190**	**210**
Cooking	1.7	2.0	2.3	2.6	2.9	3.2
Eating	1.3	1.4	1.5	1.6	1.7	1.8
Sex (intercourse)	4.0	4.5	5.0	5.5	6.0	6.5
Showering/dressing	2.6	3.0	3.4	3.8	4.2	4.6
Sitting/talking	1.3	1.5	1.7	1.9	2.2	2.4
Sleeping	0.9	1.0	1.1	1.2	1.3	1.4

what you ingest, and balancing that with your fuel out, or how the food is used as energy.

That's the purpose of food: to be used as fuel and as nutrients for fitness. And as with your car, the higher the octane fuel that you use to fill up, the higher the performance of your motor.

Hippocrates got that message and wrote about it four centuries before the beginning of the Common Era. He noted, "Fat people who want to reduce should take their exercise on an empty stomach, and sit down to their food out of breath." He's talking about the same thing I am—eating more only if you exercise.

Hippocrates also added some additional sage words to his prescription. "Thin people who want to get fat should do exactly the opposite, and never take exercise on an empty stomach." He's right. The larger the carbohydrate stores that you carry before exercise, the better the performance. Note that I use the word "carbohydrates," not "proteins" or "fats." That's because in high-intensity exercise workouts, the principal sources of fuel are the carbohydrates.

If your food-in is high in carbohydrates, then your fuel-out will be high in energy. You should eat what you want your body to burn.

Note that fruits and vegetables are carbohydrates, so watch those rice, pastas, and grains servings. The nutritional value of a carbohydrate is important as well, and not all carbohydrates are created equal. Consider fruits and vegetables as your best choice when you're carbing up.

Remember, too, that you don't need to be embarrassed about eating healthy amounts of food and then have dessert when you're with your sedentary friends. As a triathlete, you're allowed to triathl*eat*!

When You Are Ready for More: Resources

Books

Jean Carper's Total Nutrition Guide by Jean Carper, Bantam (1989).

Nancy Clark's Sports Nutrition Guidebook by Nancy Clark, Human Kinetics (1997).

Nutrition in Sport by Georg Neumann, Meyer & Meyer Sport (2001).

chapter 13

How do I improve my performance and get faster?

You may be thinking, "Ah hah! The secrets are in this chapter! Finally, I'll be the quickest and best by following a few tricks." Well, yes and no. There's a difference between improving your performance and getting faster. Getting faster has to do with mechanical outcome, and improving performance involves changing your perception of what is possible for you, your life, and your future. The two go together and reflect each other as do sky and water. By improving first, you'll be in good shape to work on getting faster.

Improve Your Balance

In chapter 4, we covered some ways to assess your physical fitness and activity. Wouldn't it be great if you had a lifestyle scorecard that you could use to assess your life? For example, if you had 2.5 kids, a job that paid X amount of money, X number of cars, and a beach vacation every year, your life elements score would be equivalent to a "high" lifestyle. But as you subtracted some of those items, you'd place lower on your scorecard. It's tempting to measure life this way, not to mention the tendency to measure up to everyone else. If you've given that type of assessment method much validity in looking at life, you probably are missing out on the subtleties we must address if we want to improve our lives. There's more than meets the eye in a laundry list of life's assets and liabilities.

Stephen R. Covey, author of *The 7 Habits of Highly Effective People,* makes a good case for the need for balance in your life: "Success in one role can't justify failure in another. Business success can't justify failure in a marriage; success in the community can't justify failure as a parent. Success or failure in any role contributes to the quality of every other role and life as a whole." If our relationships, work, finances, spirituality, and community are out of whack, how will we find a way to improve our athletic performance? For most of us, it's likely that a single-minded pursuit of triathlon improvement won't do much more than create havoc in the rest of our lives. However, by examining how you might do better in your nonathletic roles, I believe you'll find more time, energy, and support to pursue the sport of triathlon.

I constantly hear how people have found more energy, more desire, and more excitement by training for triathlon. I talked to one person at a triathlon expo who said, "I can't believe how little time it takes to do the mundane chores of my life now that I eat better, weigh less, and have increased my physical activity. I can play with the kids without having to take a nap later, and I don't feel guilty that I should be doing something else." Others have told me that they know work will get done because their mind is sharper due to the benefits of a healthier life. Fitness provides increased energy so you can focus better on the priorities that the day brings. I've also heard people say, "I know how it feels to skip breakfast, stay up late watching TV, and try to work out, so I just don't spend my time that way anymore."

Be honest with yourself—where do you put your emphasis? Where are you really? Are you in balance, or are all your eggs in one basket? Ask others in your life to give you their gentle feedback on some rearrangements that might bring your life into balance.

Life is a bit like a three-ring circus. There's a lot going on all at once, and it's hard to take in all the action at one time. And sooner or later, the lions and tigers will appear. But life is not a high-wire act where one false step sends you plummeting down to the sawdust under the big top. You have room to maneuver before the clowns appear and the show is over. Be the ringmaster of your own circus, enlist the help of your troupe, and know that the show will go on, acrobats and all.

Improve Your Commitment: Hang in There

Take a moment to carefully examine your motivation for improvement. The heartfelt belief that you can do better for yourself is the one that will sustain you. Psychologists note that in every habit you wish to change, after you've made an initial improvement, there comes a time in the course of change when you realize how much further you have to go. This is when most people falter in their chosen course of lifestyle change. I like to think of this as the "phenomenon of pause." Even though we may have improved our behavior, perhaps the experience of some success draws too clear a picture of how much more work there is for us to do. Perhaps the power of truly achieving a lifestyle change is too scary, because inevitably that one change could lead to other changes. We humans can be a change-averse bunch. Watch for possible signs of discouragement in yourself that signal the pause, and guard against the voice in your head that says, "You won't get what you want. You didn't want it anyway, so why bother?" Actually, you will get where you are going if you recognize the phenomenon of pause but hang in there.

Performance gains are quite obvious when you begin a training regimen. There's air in those lungs, the blood is pumping, digestion is improved, and everything looks better, including your physique and energy. Even sex is better, due to increased blood flow to the capillaries. All is rosy. Incremental kaizen-style improvements may be harder to spot, so realize that you will see results when you renew your determination to make the change a permanent part of your lifestyle choice.

Performance gains past getting off the couch for the first time can come slowly. You may be looking at incremental improvements of 1 minute or even 30 seconds in your time, whereas your first set of improvements could have resulted in 10 or 15 minutes. It may seem discouraging to feel you're on a plateau rather than merely that you're climbing a steeper improvement slope.

Watch out for the "phenomenon of regression." Since you're on a steep slope, you could possibly take a misstep and slide back down. It's easy to think once attained, health and fitness are always possessed. Have you seen your friend, co-worker, or family member struggle with an issue, do really well, and then slide back to his or her former behavior? Afterward, everyone says, "And they were doing so well!"

Doing *well,* as we all know, is relative. The theory of exercise relativity says that no matter how fast you are, someone is always faster. And no matter how slow you are, someone is always slower. So guard yourself against slipping back to the way it was simply because you aren't improving as much as before. Sometimes you can improve just by not quitting. Dig deep into your original reasons for continuing or make up some new ones and keep on.

Improve Your Corner of Planet Work

Many companies have workout facilities, lockers, and showers so their employees can integrate their workouts comfortably into their workday. If you have such an employer, use these benefits as much as you can. Find other office pals who want to get into a routine and make a date to meet. It's unfortunate that such opportunities aren't universal, so if you have them, help yourself. Check with the human resources department of your company and find out if discounts are available at health clubs. While you're talking to HR, suggest that you'd like to see more recreation benefits offered. Who knows—you could start a mini revolution within your own workgroup. If you're an employer, what creative ways can you find to assist your employees in making their health work for you? In Japan, employee fitness is part of the workday, and the economic success of Japanese business is well documented.

Travel Training on Planet Work

Being proactive is Habit #1 in *The 7 Habits of Highly Effective People,* and it's the one I most remember when I'm traveling for business or pleasure. If I don't get a rental car, know where the hotel is located, or figure out where the decent non–fast food restaurants are, I'm one sad, stressed-out traveler by the end of my trip. Travel can be either an excuse to blow off your training plan for the week or a chance to get in some quality cross training. It's your choice.

Biking clubs often have fun rides on weeknights. But they can be hard to find if you are a visitor on a tight schedule. Local events usually have a bike shop as a sponsor, so call a local shop to find the name and number of the local bike club. Chances are they can rent you a bike, tip you off on the terrain, and even loan you a helmet. Local bike club rides are particularly good events to look for if you're arriving mid-week. You might consider packing your own tried-and-true bike helmet, but never mind traveling with pedals and shoes, unless you have a steamer trunk. For this one ride, you can use runners or your wing tips if you prefer.

Business Travel:
Your Fitness Ticket Off Planet Work

Running is a particularly good sport for which to find a race on a weekend in any given city. Check www.runnersworld.com for race locations and dates. Many events collect either all or some portion of the race fees for charity or community programs. Not only do you get a strong workout, but also a less fortunate person benefits from your workout. And remember, you don't have to run—you can walk.

Try to arrive a day or so before your business meeting and participate in the race first. Many races are run on Saturday or Sunday, so if your meeting is on Monday, arrange to fly on Friday evening or Saturday. With a Saturday overnight stay, most U.S. domestic airfares are much less expensive than what even an extra night in a hotel might cost. You'll no doubt find that if the costs can be more or less equal, your employer might like a well-rested employee, all bright eyed and glowing from an athletic event, representing the company at the Monday meeting. Besides that, you'll have a good feel for the local area after participating in a community fun run, and knowledge is positive power on Planet Work.

Advanced Exercisers

If you're part of the 10 percent who belong to an athletic club, check on reciprocal memberships. Your club might be part of a group that allows members of the group to use their facilities all over the world. You can even stay at some of the clubs, which tend to be centrally located and more moderately priced than a downtown hotel. If you haven't signed up for a club, check around to find one that has a reciprocal club program. You could even arrange for a sports massage. Sounds like a great way to make a travel workout appealing.

Swimming is almost impossible in a hotel pool unless the hotel has a 50-meter pool like the Peabody in Orlando, Florida. There are too many kids and not enough room in the usual kidney-shaped hotel pool. Before you book your reservation, ask the front desk if they have an arrangement with a nearby aquatics center. If you have some leeway in booking a hotel, pick one that has the fitness opportunities you want. Sometimes you'll have to drive a few miles, but what's that rental car for anyway? Swimming is the lightest travel sport to pack for—tangerine swimsuits don't take up much room. And you'd be surprised how often the hotel gift shop stocks swimming gear if you forget to bring yours. You may not be able to swim in their pool, but you can buy stuff at their shop.

Proactivity is already built into the basic travel mechanics, so I merely add one component, my fitness. I call the hotel to find out if they have a treadmill or weights. I also ask if there's a VCR in the room so I can bring my yoga tape if all else fails. I leave as little as I can to chance when it comes to a travel workout.

In some respects, leaving the ordinary routine behind can be helpful. Still, finding my choice of nutrition away from my refrigerator can be challenging. With time zone changes affecting my sensations of sleep and hunger, plus unfamiliar sleeping conditions that leave me more tired than usual, travel can be literally broadening in all the wrong ways. Many of us travel on business, usually the type of business that is rather important, so let's take care of ourselves while we take care of business. I think that everyone's global economy can improve by the simple act of remembering to bring workout clothes.

Ask Yourself:

- Is this trip a chance to drink with the Planet Work pals, or am I going to excuse myself after the business niceties, get some rest, and get in my 40-minute walk or run before tomorrow's meetings?
- Am I going to order dessert and high-fat foods that I don't make for myself at home as a convoluted reward for the stress of travel?
- Am I prepared to travel with a water bottle, pack my own healthy snacks for the airplane and car, plus get refills whenever necessary, so I can stay well hydrated and properly fueled?

Improve Your Attitude

Once I was in a small 10K fun run in a farming town. The day was beautiful, the run was flat, and as we ran along, all the cows in the pasture stampeded down their mile-long fence line next to the runners. I think the cows were at an 8-minute pace. It was an out and back course, so this happened on the way back to the finish line as well. It was a "mooooving" experience to see the cows running alongside us. We were treated not only to a good run but also to a few extra running companions. Most of the runners were chuckling and grinning at such a spectacle, and the mood was goofy and light.

Imagine my surprise when the first-place runner declined to accept the award trophy. He said, in front of the group of us waiting for age-group results and the random prize drawings, that they should give the first-place trophy to the next guy. It turns out that the first-place winner didn't want a first-place trophy with a time on it that was less than his personal best time for a 10K. Do you think he missed the point of the race performance that day? I'll say.

Ask Yourself:

- How much does this race mean to me?
- What does a good race look like?

Improve Your Motivation

Many athletes write to me about what motivates them. I love to read these letters, and I hear some of my own thoughts in their words. You may find yourself agreeing with the following sentiments from athletes, or you may have totally different reasons for continuing to train for triathlons. Your motivation can change over time and with your age, so compile your own motivational quotes to reread when you want a mental pick-me-up.

Years of Experience!

The beauty is that we never get to that point we are reaching for. There is always more tunnel to roam in trying to find the light. Mature athletes know this and have a sense of peace with this knowledge. It's about the journey. And in that journey we open previously dormant doors within our souls that would have never been opened without the seemingly unattainable push, the impossible task, the monumental physical undertaking. And we fail again and again. We learn in those failings that there are huge, wonderful lessons to be learned, and we appreciate those lessons handed to us. We find ourselves living as players, and not just in sport, but also in our work, in our relationships. As athletes, our growth is endless, and the treasured cup runneth over again and again.
—*Terri Schneider*

DAVE MCGILLIVRAY'S FIVE MOTIVATIONAL TIPS

1. You're fortunate to have your health. Take advantage of it and don't take it for granted.
2. Someone else in some other part of the world is training harder than you are.
3. The health benefits alone are worth the effort.
4. The worst injustice you can ever do to yourself is to underestimate your own ability.
5. We should live our dreams and know that people who say it cannot be done should not interrupt those who are doing it.

BARB LINQUIST'S FIVE MOTIVATIONAL TIPS

1. Be the organizer. Call friends to work out with. It's harder to bail if you know someone is depending on you.
2. Look through your logbook before a big race to see all the hard training you've done. If you don't keep a log book, you won't know how much you're improving.
3. When you are on a training run, visualize your competitors next to you. Play mental games like out-sprinting them to the tree.
4. Give yourself keywords to say to yourself while racing that have to do with technique, such as "long and strong" on the swim, "float da feet" on the bike, or "tall timbers" (running high in the hips and falling forward like a tree that's been cut down) on the run.
5. Remind yourself that triathlon is supposed to be fun, even when it's your job. If it's not fun, then add variety to make it so, change your attitude, or try another sport.

KEN GLAH'S FIVE MOTIVATIONAL TIPS

1. Enjoy training and racing.
2. Travel to new places.
3. Share the experience with others.

4. Don't let a bad race ruin a good postrace party.
5. Think about positive racing and training experiences and project them into your current racing situation.

FRANK COKAN'S FIVE MOTIVATIONAL TIPS

1. I was the class klutz kid; now finally, that's behind me. I tell myself this is no time to become a maturing klutz looking as old as, or older than, my chronological age.
2. I do not want to be disabled by diseases of self-neglect, stemming from mass effect of ignorance and thus accepted by the majority because "all the kids do it." Immobility and fat addiction are among the strongest contributors to the number one cause of death and disability—hardening of the arteries.
3. I like people with my view of life. There are plenty among triathletes who put their bodies ahead of their possessions. I enjoy training with them and socializing with them.
4. Everybody wants to be good at SOMETHING. Besides, even though being good in triathlon may not give one money, it does provide much of that which money can't buy: the best body one can have under the circumstances.
5. I am motivated by the progress, so I measure and record everything and save all the race results. Much better than collecting stamps.

Ask Yourself:

- What is the worst thing that can happen to me if I am fit?
- What would I really rather be doing than investing in my future health and energy?

Improve Your Support

Some of your friends are going to become strangers, and strangers will become your friends. By now, you've probably looked around

Planet Work and feel there might just be a little more. You're interested in going to a park for a short bike ride rather than sitting in the stands watching a professional ball game. Maybe you've made the invitation to your friends for a gentle hike on a Sunday, but they slept in. No one is interested in the new gear you just bought. You have joined a minority. It's like you're speaking a foreign language.

All of a sudden, no one understands where you're coming from. Most of the civilized world is overfat and inactive. You've just placed yourself in the 10 percent who plan some physical activity on a regular basis. Welcome to a taste of cultural bias.

The Ripple Effect

Triathlon is a metamorphic process. It results in personal and positive change. And by changing ourselves, we can change our society and make it a better place to be. When we change, all things change.

It's not pleasant to sometimes have to leave your pals behind while you increase your activity. But sometimes, to pursue your dreams, you must. In a perfect world, your current Planet Work pals, as well as your family and children, would hop on the path with you. They'd love you, they'd be intrigued by your newfound love of participating in physical activity, and they'd be along for the ride, whatever that means for them. That is support.

Still, some people you know will cease being part of your world. Probably the dichotomy between their inactivity and your proactivity is too great. It's too uncomfortable for them to see you changing your life in a positive way, and they don't want to be around you. It's a loss.

So have a small wake with flowers and music when you bury the past relationships, and be kind about what you think your friends and family should do about their own fitness. If you do take up the pulpit and look for converts, remember it's about health, theirs and yours. Explain yourself kindly but firmly. Do your loved ones a favor by not being judgmental and zealous about your lifestyle change, and do yourself a favor by not hurting yourself by making poor choices just to be with the ones you love. That's the most support and respect you can give to yourself and to others. Or as Dave McGillivray puts it, "We should live our dreams and know that people who say it cannot be done should not interrupt those who are doing it."

Ask Yourself:

- Have you met new friends who are also training for an event?
- Do you give and receive support from your housemates for their activities, physical or otherwise?
- Have you looked into a club, training program, or group that meets to discuss or work out?

Now Let's Get Faster

You've taken the steps to improve by bringing balance to your life and by examining your attitude, motivation, and support. You've made a stronger commitment to your health and level of physical activity by figuring out how to incorporate training into your travel and turning up the volume of your positive mental messages. Through lifestyle improvement, you gain the wiggle room to spend the energy and time you've saved on training techniques that can get you faster finishing times.

Specificity of Training Your Triathlon Skills

It's time to drop the basketball, tennis, golf, and other recreational pursuits. These activities are certainly enjoyable, and during off season or recovery weeks, they have their place. But this chapter is discussing performance, and performance is sport specific. To a triathlete, that means swim, bike, run, lift weights, and stretch. If you're spending your sport activity time pursuing other activities, that's good for you as a recreational athlete. Recreation can lead to personal satisfaction. But as a triathlete, if you're frustrated when you look around at your local age-group competition and know that you have the possibility to do better but aren't, now might be the time for greater concentration on triathlon-specific training. Recreation does not train you in the specific skills that you need as a triathlete.

How to Train Less but Get More

One goal you can attain is to decrease your training and increase your performance. There is an inclination to think that the opposite of this is true. You may read that to get fitter or get faster, you need to train more. This simply is not the way that the human body responds to exercise experience.

Increasing training time may seem like a good idea, but it's not always the most prudent. You can increase your time or intensity in training, but not both. Whichever one you choose to increase, try to increase it by only 10 percent per week at the high end. At some point, you won't make any additional gains from piling on more training. You will have reached a training plateau. That's when you need to hold your training plans static or back off before challenging yourself further. You could redistribute your heart zone training points so you aren't necessarily gaining points (even using the 10 percent rule) but instead are mixing your types of training while you're spending time on a plateau.

When I was first starting to train to run marathons professionally in the late 1970s, the standard rule of thumb was that to run long distances fast, one had to train to match the race. This is called the specificity rule among exercise scientists. It means that to perform well, you have to match the specific requirements of the event with specific training. My training volume progressively increased as I approached a peak race, often exceeding 100 miles, and I would proudly record how well I had trained. It wasn't until many of us started to add cross training to our workout regimen that we ran faster with less training volume.

Here are some tips on how to train less and get more:

1. PLAN YOUR TRAINING To do this the best way, write a training plan. Spend some time making sure that you include the key workouts—endurance, speed, and strength—as you climb the training tree. We've provided you with an example of a plan in chapter 11 to get you started.

2. KEEP A TRAINING LOG If you log your workouts and focus on them, you'll discover that some days you have junk workouts, or a workout without purpose. Eliminate them.

3. WORK YOUR PLAN Precision training is like a mirror. When your written plan mirrors your training log, you've achieved precision training. The saying "Plan your work, work your plan" is central here.

4. SPEND TIME IN ZONE Training intensity is key in the training load formula:

Frequency × Intensity × Time = Training load for that activity

The best way to keep track of training intensity is to monitor and measure it with a heart rate monitor.

5. STAY ON THE PLAN I often see individuals who can set goals, fill out the entry form for an event, plan their workouts, tell each other what they're doing, but then derail from the whole process. They never make it to the starting line, which, as I've said before, is more important to me than the finish line. To stay on the plan, don't forget to add the support, motivation, and inspiration sides of your training. Without this emotional part of training, the physical side suffers.

6. SHIFT YOUR PARADIGM It may be counterintuitive for you at first to train less to get fitter, but it works. Imagine a training graph with all the fitness benefits on the *x*-axis and with time on the *y*-axis. At the top of the graph is 100 percent fitness in all three disciplines (see figure 13.1).

Look at the two points on the graph. They're both at the same fitness level, but the one on the left shows the effects of overtraining and its negative response. Overtraining results in staleness,

Figure 13.1

The Paradigm Shift

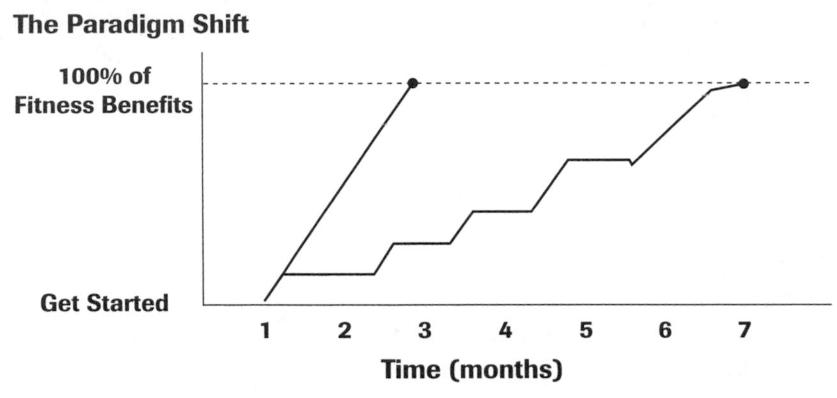

potential injury, stress, and other hazards. The point on the right, climbing toward peak fitness, is positive, with continued improvement each week. Stay on the right-hand side of the training graph.

7. VARIABILITY Variability training is new to most people in the pursuit of fitness. The body loves variety and typically responds by improved fitness. It's the spice of life message and works in performance training as much as in other parts of our lives. By getting rid of monotony through variety in your workouts, you'll improve. Try new types of workouts, such as riding a mountain bike in place of a road bike session. You're still training specifically for triathlon, but you just spiced it up a bit. By adding variability, you'll see that through the stress of the new stimulus your body will respond in positive ways.

8. TRAIN SYSTEMATICALLY The greatest influence on results for top-level competitors comes from using a training system that standardizes your training in order to optimize it. For example, I once worked with a young Ironman competitor, and in both of his races he performed poorly because he arrived injured at the starting line. After long conversations about his training, he admitted that he had trained for a full year for the race, averaging 25 to 30 hours per week, or 1,000 to 1,500 hours per year. He was overtrained because he didn't allow time for recovery. I suggested a new training program: undertraining. On his third Ironman, he finished two hours faster than in either of his previous races. He now is applying the principle that measuring and monitoring an appropriate training load and allowing for recovery or regeneration will improve his performance.

9. ADD MORE REGENERATION OR LOAD AND UNLOAD YOUR TRAINING Some folks call it recovery and others restoration, but a more complete look at periods of renewal in training is regeneration. This is a phase of training both within a training plan and between plans. Add regeneration if it's not part of your training program. For a good description of regeneration, read *Successful Endurance Training* by Georg Neumann. He writes, "In the regeneration phase, the state of equilibrium (homeostasis) of the bodily functions disturbed by load and demand regulation is restored." If you allow enough time for recovery in the training load, by unloading some of the workouts, your body will have the time to adapt and usually improvement will occur.

10. DISCOVERY Use yourself as an exercise lab that you want to test. Training is a blend of art and science. Concoct some training recipes that match your physiology. You're the master chef.

Annualize Your Training Plan

It's physically impossible and also undesirable to remain in peak performance mode every single day of the year. The challenge that athletes face is to make that peak performance moment happen on race day or at least race week. The other weeks we're just winding in and around the performance zone, trying to combine rest and good nutrition and to taper our training to hit our personal targets on race day. Setting a one-year training plan, or annualizing your training plan, helps both set goals and provide you with the direction you need to take over the 12 months of training.

Perils of Overtraining

The worst mistake I ever made was undoubtedly in my preparation for the Olympic Trials in 2000. I simply pushed too hard. Leading up to the selection trials for the Sydney 2000 Olympic triathlon team, a few things went wrong for me. I fell and broke two ribs while running 11 weeks out. After that, I made the normal but fatal mistake of trying to make up for lost time. This led to my fighting off illness in the last couple of weeks and getting more and more tired and run down. Because the Olympic trials were so important to me, I still ignored the signs, and by the time of the trials, I had pushed my body right over the edge and ended up with a debilitating, chronic, overtraining fatigue syndrome.

I failed to make the team, but at least I killed myself trying!
—*Jackie Gallagher* ■

To peak in the week of your big event, you need to plan your training. Most professional triathletes annualize their training, choosing to peak at their most important race of the year. You'll have cycles of stress, adaptation, and recovery throughout the season, but it's a good idea to pick one race as your focus and plan your training for that race. Of course, you may also want to participate in other races throughout the season, which will cause you to have smaller peak race weeks over the course of the year.

To improve, you need to change your training load and system. When you do, your body will adapt to the increased workload. This is exercise adaptation. This is why you need to vary your training. You don't need to increase the time and distance of your training forever, but once you've found a good balance, it's time to vary your intensity and your amount of time in each heart zone. You also need to include rest days in your training plan, to give your body time to recover from the increased workload. If you don't take a day off once in a while, you risk injury or burnout. You'll eventually find the way that works best for you. It can be a monthly cycle, a 10-week cycle, or a quarterly cycle, all within your annual training cycle. Here are a number of different types of workouts that will lead to faster finish times.

STRENGTH WORKOUTS Running or biking up hills is, as we all know, harder than going on the flats. Hill training will make you stronger and is especially important if your race course has hills. Here are two ways you can incorporate hills into your training.

Hill Repeats Warm up for 10 minutes or so. Run or bike up a hill, working as hard as you can. Walk or ride slowly back down the hill for recovery time and then go up the hill again. Try three to five repeats at first and then work your way up. This is a high-intensity workout, so don't try this more than once a week. It's also good to schedule your speed training on days that you have adequately recovered from your hill repeats and vice versa.

Training on Hills Run or bike a route that includes hills. You can try to keep your heart rate down or your speed consistent or just aim to get up the hill more efficiently over the course of your training. Repeat the same course occasionally, so you can judge your improvement.

SPEED WORKOUTS To get faster, you must train faster. Once you've gotten comfortable with the amount of training you're doing and your ability to go the distance, you'll want to incorporate various training techniques to get faster. Here are some of the techniques, with examples of how to do them.

Intervals Intervals are used in training for all three tri sports. Training in intervals means doing the same distance at a fairly high intensity repeatedly, with short recovery breaks between repeats. Interval training is a way of teaching your body to handle a higher intensity and get it used to sustaining that level of effort over a longer period of time.

Swim Intervals Swim 4 × 50 yards at 80 percent of your max HR, with 10 seconds of rest between each of the four 50s. If you're not using a heart rate monitor, this will be harder to do, but you can judge your perceived exertion. Aim for about 8 on a scale of 10. You can increase the number of repeats you do as your swim skill increases. You could also start at 25 yards instead of 50 if you can't swim that far at first, or move up to 75 or 100 yards if you'd like to work longer intervals. It's a good idea to mix it up and not do the same workout every time so your body continues to work to adapt.

Fartlek As we discussed in chapter 8, *fartlek* is a Swedish word meaning "speed play" that is now in common English usage. You can practice fartlek in all three of the triathlon sports. When running or riding your bike, pick a landmark coming up (such as a tree or building) and sprint to that landmark. When you get there, reduce your speed and go at a more relaxed pace. Then pick another landmark to sprint to. This is harder to do in the water, but you can speed up and slow down as you swim. The whole idea is to have fun and get in some speed work.

Checking in with Your Progress

As I've said throughout this book, there is no global theory on the best way to train. There isn't a coach or exercise scientist who would honestly admit to having all the complexities of the physiology of sports and training adaptations nailed down. Rather, there are many schools, hypotheses, frameworks, and a bit of quackery from those who take on the responsibility of helping others improve their performance. There is no one school of champions; there are many.

The following list is an attempt to provide you with a way of looking at how you can change your training to elicit the positive response of improved performance. Take these points into consideration, learn more about them, experiment with them, or otherwise add them to your own individualized and personalized approach to improving your performance.

1. Would you improve your performance if you were self-coached or coached by another?
2. Are you following the training plan accurately?

Insider Tip

Training plans that are designed by coaches for athletes are sometimes not followed. A research study led by Carl Foster, Ph.D., found there was a significant difference between the training plan provided by the coach and the one executed by athletes. Foster concluded that this discrepancy may be the culprit in the high incidence of poor adaptations to training.

---

3. Have you measured the changes in your fitness level during your training progressions?
4. Do you quantify the amount of exercise that you experience?
5. Are you focusing more on your training load than on your training volume?
6. Have you gone over the fine line between improved performance and deterioration?
7. Do you eat a balanced and nutrient-dense diet with possible supplementation?
8. Are you regularly experiencing flow (see chapter 18) during your training?
9. Are you practicing variability training by including variety in your workouts?
10. Have you set goals that are higher than what you can now attain?
11. Are you developing the more advanced skills required to improve your performance?

12. Do you allow a period in your training for regeneration?
13. Do you include competitions in your training to measure progress and to gain experience?
14. Are you working toward improving your biomechanical abilities?
15. Are you working toward learning more about training methodology, physiology, sports nutrition, sport psychology, and so forth?
16. Have you learned the primary sources of your personal motivation?
17. Have you participated in sports camps, clubs, online training programs, or other support systems?
18. Have you discovered that group training is more enjoyable and stimulates your commitments?
19. Are you noticing and responding appropriately to negative stressors in your life?
20. Are you aware of performance enhancers, such as altitude training, heat acclimatization, and ergogenic substances?
21. Are you encouraging your friends and loved ones to support you in your efforts to train and attain your goals?
22. Are you drinking an optimum amount of fluids during and between your workouts?
23. Have you invested in the quality of training and racing equipment that you need to achieve your results?
24. Have you decided who is really your true competitor?

One of the best ways to determine if your physical performance is improving is to measure it with one of the following standard measuring tools, which are either performed in the lab or in the field.

Laboratory Performance Tests

- Spiroergometry: a test that increases load; at allocated testing points, measurements of oxygen, heart rate, and lactate are taken

- Measurements of velocity during sport-specific performances

Field Performance Tests

- Competition as a diagnostic measure
- Time trials to measure speed, heart rate, and biomechanics, such as stroke count, turnover rate, or cadence

The purpose of these measurements is to determine if your aerobic and anaerobic performance capacities are enhanced. Because the results of these tests are sport specific, each of the three disciplines within triathlon needs to be measured individually. For laboratory purposes, special equipment, described below, has been developed to assess the relationship among training load, training effect, and the direction of training adaptation:

- Swimmers: current channel, rope-pulling ergometer
- Cyclists: high-performance cycling ergometer
- Runners/Walkers: treadmill

Field tests are more practical and easier to administer, yet they're subject to error because of the problem of standardization, or the ability to create constant conditions. The equipment to measure lactate and oxygen consumption remains pricey today for most who are training at highly competitive levels. One of the basic axioms of training is that we can best manage what we can monitor and measure. For improved physical performance, use the results of the previous questions to help you manage your training program better.

Planning, logging, doing the workouts, testing, and benchmarking your progress are just some of the secrets we've already revealed in previous chapters. These basics help improve your performance either in a workout or a race. Your good patterns and practices will in the end also improve your performance. So now that you've taken a look at where you are in your triathlon lifestyle and tried some different workouts, retest your benchmarks from a performance standpoint. How do you score on the distances you benchmarked in chapter 4?

Check your log—you'll no doubt see some improvements on the scorecard.

When You're Ready for More: Resources

Books

George Sheehan on Running to Win by George Sheehan, Rodale Press (1994).

The 7 Habits of Highly Effective People by Stephen R. Covey, Simon and Schuster (1989).

Videos

The Cutting Edge (MGM)

For the Love of the Game (Universal Pictures)

The Karate Kid (Columbia Pictures)

Rocky (United Artists)

Strictly Ballroom (Miramax Films)

Vision Quest (Warner Bros.)

chapter 14

open water swimming

Swimming in a lake, ocean, or river is one of life's great pleasures. The sand, the wind, the sparkling water make everyday cares float away on the fresh breeze. A sunny beach vacation is the most popular way to spend our leisure time. There's something for everyone at the beach—kids, grandparents, teenagers—and now there's something for you, the athlete.

Summary of Open Water Swim Training Goals

- ✔ Locate the best open water swimming spots near you.
- ✔ Swim in open water at least once prior to the race each season.
- ✔ Be comfortable in your wet suit, goggles, and cap.
- ✔ Know the basics of open water swim safety.

Open Water Gear (Swim Equipment)

Should I Get a Wet Suit?

Yes. A wet suit is a key piece of triathlon gear today. You need to practice swimming in a wet suit before your race, and you also need to practice removing it in transitions. Here's what you'll want to consider.

WET SUITS: WHAT THEY DO AND WHICH KINDS ARE OUT THERE There are many types of wet suits—scuba, water skiing, and open water swimming, to name a few. Swimming wet suits are form-fitting and made out of a type of rubber that is supple and that easily cuts through the water. If you can't find one at your local triathlon retailer, you can find one online. Wet suits cost between $200 and $400, but they save you 1 to 5 minutes in a race.

SELECTING A WET SUIT You'll want to try on different kinds of wet suits and simulate swimming movements in them to see which ones fit and move best for you. Just like clothes, wet suits from different manufacturers fit differently. And there are different models (long johns, short johns, and two-piece wet suits) to choose from. If it fits your body type, buy it.

GETTING YOUR WET SUIT ON I recommend using a body lube on your arms, legs, and neck, both to keep the wet suit from chafing and to make it easy to remove. Commercial products are available for this purpose, or you can use oil-based cooking spray. If you notice that the wet suit is still difficult to get on and off, consider cutting off the legs at the ankles a bit. You can whack off a hunk with regular scissors and thereby expand the circumference of the suit at each ankle. Wet suit manufacturer Piel has come up with an ingenious double-zipper wet suit, which makes it a breeze to get off.

TESTING OUT YOUR WET SUIT Particularly important in wet suit testing on dry land is to do a bunch of strokes and turn your head as if you're breathing in the water. Wet suits can sometimes chafe at the neck, which can be anticipated and fixed with a little gel or lotion. If it's hard to move your arms, you might need a bigger size or a different wet suit altogether.

WHAT IS THE WATER TEMPERATURE? If the water is too warm, you can overheat in a wet suit, as American Tim DeBoom found out when he was pulled, apparently from heat exhaustion, from the swim in the April 2001 Ironman Australia. The water temperature was 73 degrees Fahrenheit. Conversely, if the water is too cold, without a wet suit you risk the effects of overexposure to the cold or hypothermia. This condition is equally serious and can result in poor performance. There are very few races where wet suits are required. One of them is Escape from Alcatraz, which includes a mile swim in the San Francisco Bay. Find out from the race organizers ahead of time whether or not you need a wet suit.

Swimming in the Cold

I have many fond memories of an amazing triathlon relay between London and Paris in which I was fortunate enough to take part in 1984. This was a crazy idea of the first person to bring mass triathlon to Great Britain—Mike Ellis—and was in pre-wet suit times. The swim section naturally included crossing the English Channel (with the exception of the 5 miles roughly forming the French shipping lanes). To prepare, I would train in our local 100-yard pool (yikes!) in Cambridge when it opened at Easter. Of course, I was the only nutter, since the temperature was 48 degrees Fahrenheit and I tried to swim one more length each time I went in. I was always hypothermic on emergence and could hardly get dressed, but a "nice cup of tea" kindly supplied by the pool attendant soon sorted out the body temperature.

The race itself took place at the beginning of June, and the official sea temperature was 53 degrees Fahrenheit. My team had been hurriedly assembled (since previous candidates magically withdrew in the last two months) and included British long-distance swimmer Juliet Smith and two mainly runners, Fran Ashmole and Brenda Yule.

Race rules were that each team member had to survive a minimum of 15 minutes × 2 in the water, total (so that someone couldn't escape their marine duty). And, if it wasn't possible to finish the swim, then a huge time penalty would be awarded, and the team would be permitted to continue on the bike section in France. The rest of the team was on an

DO YOU HAVE TIME TO PRACTICE SWIMMING IN A WET SUIT? Like any other piece of gear, you need to practice using your wet suit prior to the race. Be sure to allow yourself enough time to play around with your wet suit before the race, because you'll want to minimize any race day surprises from your gear. You need to get used to how your wet suit feels and the way it affects your swimming.

accompanying fishing trawler–in open air, no cover–but it did provide a useful, if short, rest while we traversed the French shipping lanes. Suffice to say that the female body fat helped us just a bit, and out of 11 teams, we finished the swim (and hence also the final classification) ahead of the British Royal Navy and the Royal Air Force, all of whom collected the large time penalties. The British Men's team, containing, among other luminaries, Steve Trew, as well as the U.S. Navy Seals, were the two teams who found the sea too cold or the seasickness too much to cope with and had to abort pretty early on.

What will always remain in my memory, though, was the teamwork. Those who were stronger in a particular section mucked in to help the rest, and our support team was just amazing. Those familiar with Wimbledon Football Club will know they have a reputation of being "hard" footballers, but their physician of the time joined us for the weekend to sort out our aches and pains. When she declared that "her" footballers were wimps in comparison with us very amateur endurance athletes, it caused a wry smile or two!

It was a wonderful experience–although I am now quite happy that we can use wet suits when the water is that cold!!

–Professor Sarah Springman was fundamental in setting British triathlon along the road to its equity policies, and they remain a central tenet of the International Triathlon Union's work and decisions. Sarah has an amazing career as athlete, administrator, and mentor. ■

This is because a neoprene wet suit is like wearing a buoyancy device—you'll float with it very easily. Because of the buoyancy, your swim technique is altered. Your legs are on top of the water rather than in it, your arms are somewhat restricted, and your alignment in the water changes. This is why you need to practice with the wet suit before the race.

ARE YOU A GOOD SWIMMER? Wet suits can help people with less than stellar swim skills be faster swimmers because they help you float and maintain body position. But if you're already a good swimmer, a wet suit can help you swim even better. The extra flotation provided by a wet suit changes your body position and stroke and gives you an advantage over swimmers without them, so I recommend them to even the best swimmers.

Goggles

Rather than using goggles that closely encircle your eye socket, which is a pool goggle, some triathletes are turning to a new type of goggle, an open water goggle. These resemble a miniature version of a face mask from scuba gear, except your nose isn't inside. These new goggles allow the watertight rubber seal to go on your forehead, over the top of your eyebrows, close to your temples on the side, and about mid-nose on the bottom. Because this style of goggles is more comfortable and provides for much improved peripheral vision, it's very popular. I prefer open water goggles, such as the Aqua Sphere brand, because they rarely leak, they don't leave ring marks around your eyes, and they're hydrodynamic and flexible.

Goggles come with different lenses. Use the clear goggles, especially when the swim is in murky water, fog, or overcast weather. It's the same as on a bike: use green or amber-colored lenses in bright sunlight and clear water.

Safety Checklist

- ✔ Never swim in open water alone or at a pool where there's no lifeguard.
- ✔ If you ever need assistance in the water, the universal signal is to raise your hand and wave for help.
- ✔ Wear a brightly colored cap so you're visible in the water.
- ✔ Always be aware of others in the water with you, both for your safety and for theirs.
- ✔ In open water, you must have someone with you in a boat or on a paddleboard or with a flotation device.

- ✔ Know you can cover the distance before you swim in open water.
- ✔ Remember to keep an eye out for hazards and obstacles in open water, such as broken bottles on the bottom, submerged tree limbs, or power boats and jet skis.
- ✔ If you're swimming in the ocean, be aware of special hazards such as jellyfish, barnacles on docks or steps, and undertows.

Let's Practice Open Water Swimming

Open water swimming can be scary. There are no walls, no lane lines, no pool bottom, no markers to keep you on course, not to mention from 50 to 1,500 other swimmers out there with you. In the pool, you didn't have to deal with waterweeds, or even fish and fowl. Get out there and experience the open water. Learn how to swim a straight course. When you learn open water swim skills, finishing the swim portion of a triathlon is energy saving for the rest of the race.

Learn in the Pool

Since the majority of triathlons are held in open water, wouldn't you think of open water swimming as a basic skill? Shouldn't people do the majority of their swim practices in open water? No! I must emphasize strongly that your swim skills can be best learned in a pool under the watchful gaze of a swim coach, trainer, or lifeguard. Open water practice just isn't that accessible to most of us, especially on a regular basis. Most swimmers know that the best way to get stronger in swimming is by repetitive laps in the pool. When you do find the extra resources required for open water swimming (a partner, a boat with life vests, a swimmable lake), you'll already be sufficient in your swim skills to approach open water issues. Please learn to swim in the pool, not the lake, river, or ocean.

Practice, Practice, Practice in the Pool

You can simulate open water swimming in the pool by closing your eyes when you swim so you don't see the line on the pool bottom. With your eyes closed, try to swim as straight as you can, and when you open your eyes, check your progress. Try this exercise a few times at various speeds to get a sense of how your body might pull you off course when you can't see clearly.

In the pool, swimming in a circle, rather than touching the wall or doing kick turns, is good open water practice. See how long you can swim around without touching the edge of the pool. You can tread water or use the breaststroke instead of freestyle, but make a point of not touching the sides or the bottom. Sometimes in a swim workout, I won't touch the sides at all. It throws off the split times in the written workout, but it's a good mental reminder that I'll be swimming hard without the momentary pause every 25 yards.

Also, swimming in the deep end and swimming in the pool when the swim team practices are good pool simulations of deep water. Deep water feels different and is harder to displace. Not only will you feel that sensation, but you will also get a better workout in deep-end lap swimming. When the swim team works out, besides seeing how effortlessly they swim, you'll also get to swim through lots of chop, which will resemble the waves in open water.

Insider Tip

Get some friends to swim in a pool lane with you. Start off at the same time, sprinting as fast as you can. Crowd each other in the lane, bumping and jostling. This will be a good approximation of the frenzy of a swim start. Practice this until you feel comfortable with bodies all around you in the water.

Find Your Swimmable Open Water

Pool practice is fine. However, anyone who plans to do a triathlon must practice open water swimming at least once in an actual open body of water prior to the race. Swimming at your favorite beach, whether it's by a lake, river, or ocean, is a great way to experience the open water. There's usually a roped-off, monitored stretch for swimming, and you can do your laps away from the beach activities. But always take a buddy—swimming in open water by yourself is not worth the risk.

Practicing open water swimming is especially important for those who are new to the sport of swimming, but even someone with years of competitive swimming experience needs to get out in the open water before the race. There are many differences you'll want to experience so you can eliminate as many race day surprises as possible. To simulate a swim start, try the drill in the Insider Tip (page 212) in a lake or ocean within the roped-off and lifeguarded area.

Sighting

Before you get out there in open water, you need to learn some new tricks. The first is sighting. This involves raising your head out of the water and looking ahead to make sure you're still on course. You'll want to learn to swim with your face in the water, or else your neck might get sore from hyperextension, and you'll certainly be using extra effort to move through the water. You'll want to look up and sight every eight to fifteen strokes. Practice this in the pool until you're comfortable with it. This will help prevent you from swimming off course and adding minutes and yards to your swim.

Insider Tip

Count your strokes. After every eighth stroke, sight. This counting keeps negative thoughts out of your mind. The eighth stroke is a "Tarzan" stroke, in which you take a big swoop of water and arch your back to bring your head up out of the water to sight on a buoy.

Bilateral Breathing

Open water has a number of unique challenges. Waves, current, wind, and sun are nature's additions to the other swimmers and watercraft obstacles that may already be in the equation. Bilateral breathing can solve many of the challenges of open water. When the wind is blowing or waves are coming in, if you only breathe on one side, you could get a mouthful of wave. Breathing to the shore side will keep you sucking air, not water. Bilateral breathing also allows you to look both ways in the swim to help with sighting and possible water hazards.

Drafting

Advanced swimmers know that swimming is an arms-dominated sport, and you can get plenty fatigued in the first leg of a triathlon by just using your arms. If you can tap into other swimmers' energy by drafting behind them, you'll save yourself 8 to 15 percent of effort to use on the bike and run.

To draft, look for the bubbles that mark another swimmer's wake. Slide into that swimmer's slipstream so their body is pushing through the water like the prow of a ship and you're following behind like the stern. Be sure to sight so you don't follow a faster swimmer off course. If those bubbles aren't going where you want, stroke to the side and swim until you can hook onto another stream of fast bubbles.

What to Expect in an Open Water Race

Water Conditions

Ocean swims also have currents and undertows, so watch out for those conditions when swimming in the ocean. You shouldn't have any problem with large marine creatures, since the splashing about of all those triathletes will very likely keep them away. Though rare in triathlon, jellyfish and, in tropical waters, Portuguese man-of-wars have made their appearance. These have stingers that can be very painful or even incapacitating. And stepping on a sea urchin can sideline you for a month.

When a triathlon swim is held in fresh water, the vegetation in the water is another hazard. It won't hurt you, but water plants can get annoying when you touch them or just brush along your limbs and frighten you. Sometimes, before a race, the vegetation is trimmed back so you don't have to swim through it. But it's still there below you, and I know people who get unnerved by the thought of it.

I recommend you practice open water swimming as many times as it takes for you to be comfortable. Open water swimming can be challenging and sometimes scary because it feels like it's just you out there in deep water. You need to be confident of your skills and ability before you take off on a half-mile or more swim. Swim parallel to the shoreline and keep on the lookout for hazards, such as branches and other submerged objects. When you're near the shore, watch for broken bottles, cans, and other debris. Like sea urchins, stepping on debris can sideline you.

Swim Start Conditions

Be prepared for some challenges at the start of the swim portion of the triathlon. Whether a wave start (groups of 35 to 100 starting together in each wave) or a mass start, there may be some contact during the swim start. Usually during the first 200 to 400 yards, everyone is gung-ho before they settle into their swim pace.

Seed yourself, or position yourself according to your swim speed, in your wave. If you're a fast swimmer, position yourself at the front of the wave. If you're slow, stay to the back or the outside of the wave. It's okay to wait until everyone else is gone before you start. Those who wish to avoid any contact and are unsure where in the wave they should be should stay in the back behind the other swimmers. This helps everyone, especially if the start area is small.

Wherever the swim is held, there will be swim safety volunteers on the swim course to make sure everyone is safe. There's no penalty if you need help during the swim. Again, the signal that you're in trouble is to raise your arm. The swim safety supporters will get to you and let you hang onto the craft they're in (canoe, kayak, surfboard, etc.).

It's not a good idea, however, to swim from lifeguard to lifeguard to complete your swim. The lifeguards and water safety personnel are there for emergencies, so respect that.

Figure 14.1

Open water swim course examples

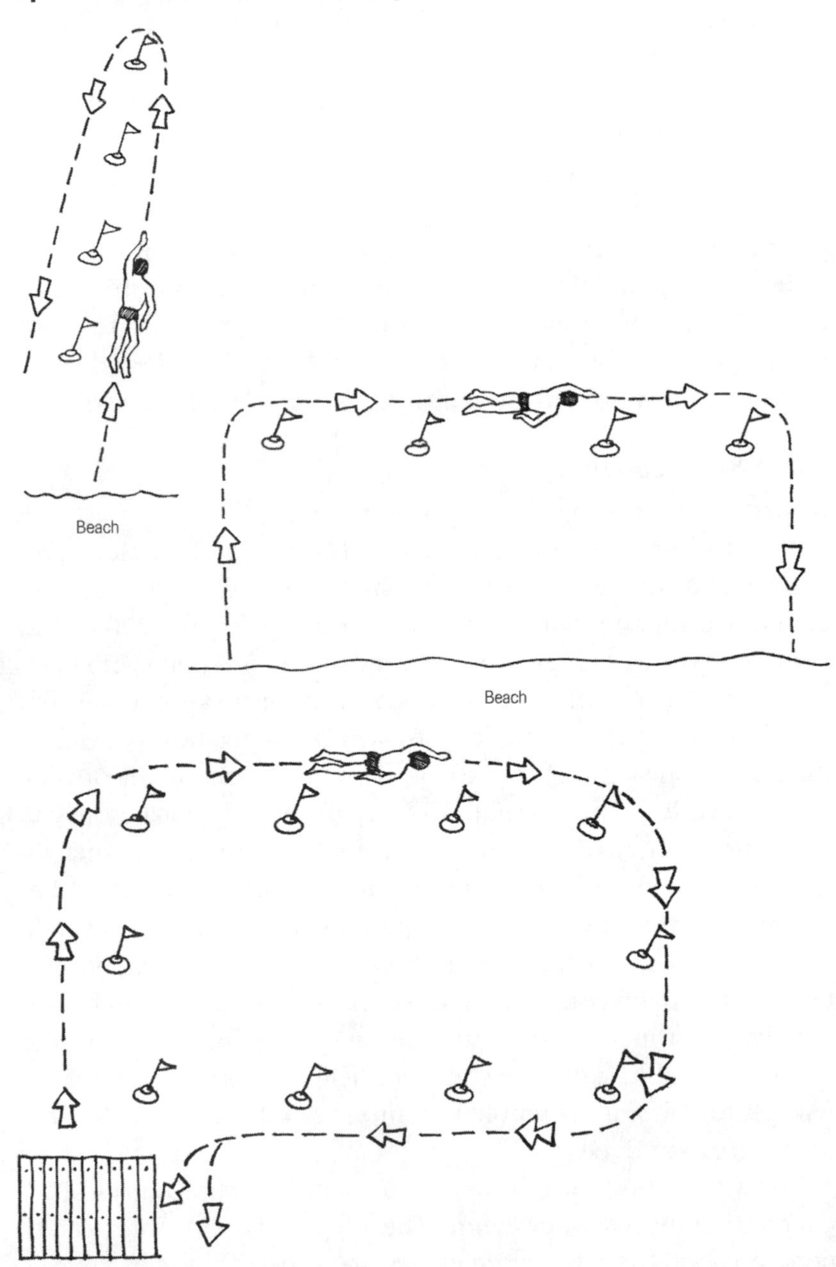

Open Water Swim Skills Checklist

- ✔ Know how to sight.
- ✔ Know how to breathe bilaterally.
- ✔ Know how to swim in a straight line.
- ✔ Conquer the fear factor by practicing open water swim starts with your buddies.
- ✔ Know how to put on and feel comfortable in your wet suit.
- ✔ Know how to keep your goggles on and fog-free.

When You're Ready for More: Resources

Books

Open Water Swimming by Penny Lee Dean, Human Kinetics (1998).

Local Scene

Your city, county, and state parks and recreation departments can tell you about water quality, when beaches are open, open water swim practices, and open water swim events.

Know Before You Go

My first ocean triathlon was on the occasion of Sally's induction into the Triathlon Hall of Fame. My husband, Paul, and I were looking forward to a nice banquet, quietly hobnobbing with triathlon's finest, but of course there was an event connected to the gala affair, and we found ourselves signed up for the sprint triathlon portion.

That morning, Paul and I showed up a little late for the race start, banking on that VIP parking pass and paying a little too much credence to Sally when she said, "If I had my way, I'd show up 5 minutes before the gun went off." What we didn't hear was the part where she said, "But I always get there 30 minutes before so I can hear about the course conditions."

On this day, Oceanside, California, was experiencing the largest surf for the day in 10 years. We should have known, because there were many surfer dudes out there having a blast. We also should have known, because the lady at the bed and breakfast two blocks off the beach said she was surprised to be able to hear the ocean. Or we should have known if we had shown up in time for the course conditions talk.

But we didn't know, and after I threw on the only wet suit in the group, we ran into the waves and started. Well, the other 200 people ran up the beach 150 feet and ran into the water there. Turns out there was a huge current flowing north and we almost exhausted ourselves trying to swim south to the buoy. If we'd listened to the course talk, we would have been cruising out and north to the buoy rather than trying to swim a triangle from the beach.

The next buoy to the north came very quickly, and I was puffing myself up at the thought that I was one strong swimmer, until I rounded the buoy to try to swim south back toward the shore. And north of me, the Oceanside pier, largest and longest pier on the Pacific Coast, kept looking bigger and bigger as I swam my hardest in place, in the ocean.

Finally, I managed to catch up with a group of triathletes who weren't swimming at all but sort of bobbing around. Heck, I swam right past them, when all of a sudden, a huge wave hit me and I pinwheeled under the water, seeing a lot of sand mixed with water. I am relatively fearless in the water and actually was having a bit of a chuckle on myself because I figured out why those other triathletes had stopped and were looking over their shoulders. They were looking at the timing of the waves and preparing to dive beneath them. With my wet suit on, I popped out of the water like a cork and proceeded to swim in, this time looking over my shoulder every five strokes. Mike Plant, the race director, greeted us with a big smile and said, "Now you'll have something to talk about." Right, Mike.

Paul didn't fare so well. A less-accomplished swimmer, he was swept into the pier and got a barnacle abrasion on his shin. We have a great picture of Paul on the bike with blood dripping down his leg. Many triathletes were swept through the pier and had to run up the beach a half-mile back to their bikes. Sally was so busy helping swimmers get to lifeboards that both Paul and I beat her out of the water.

This is also the race in which Rudy Garcia-Tolson, a 10-year-old with artificial legs, blew by me on the run, but that's another story.

—Rebecca Yao, from Bellevue, Washington, has completed fifteen sprint triathlons so far and volunteers to coordinate the largest peer athlete mentoring program in the United States as part of the Danskin Women's Triathlon Series. ■

chapter 15

staying in the game

Or wins a battle but loses the war? Both health and performance are tied together. Since you're working out for your health and the demonstrations of health that a good athletic performance represent, let's see how to keep at it as long as possible. Potential roadblocks of a physical nature can slow you down or stop you altogether on your fitness journey. Here are a few signposts to recognize so you'll know you're on the right road.

Maintaining a Proper Training Load

As an athlete, you want to be fully aware of your overall health and well-being. You want as many days as possible where you feel energetic, lively, and alert. When you're training and eating appropriately, your mind is sharper, the world is beautiful, and everyone is in love. When you're overtraining, you could be down on everything, not interested in any sort of physical activity, and fairly sleepy. Plus your friends suddenly avoid you.

Overtraining is not the same as simple mental burnout from too many early swim workouts; it's an imbalance between time in training and time in recovery. One of the great things about triathlon is that because you're training in three different sports, you have less risk of overtraining in any one of them. But even with training different muscles, you can still get fatigued or find you're experiencing more colds than usual. That can be partly due to overtraining.

It can be hard to spot overtraining, because a certain amount of stress is part of the "training effect." Here's where you can rely on your trusty friend, your log. Check your log to see if you've increased your workouts over the 10 percent rule. Is there too much volume or intensity? Or perhaps too little recovery? Be a detective and check for inappropriate bumps in your fitness journey. One of my favorite clues to spotting overtraining is the Delta heart rate test, as was discussed in chapter 4.

Keep Properly Hydrated

When training during hot weather, it's best to train either early in the morning or in the evening when it's cool. It's nice that most races are held early in the day. By the time the sun comes up, you're sitting in the shade, admiring your race medal or ribbon. Our bodies are not particularly good at telling us when we're thirsty. By the time we get the signal, we're already dehydrated. So if you have a choice of training times or routes, pick the shade and the coolest part of the day.

You'll also want to experiment with how much fluid and how often you need to drink to meet your body's fluid needs during your training. Most athletes prefer small, frequent sips of sports drinks both to keep them hydrated and to avoid stomach cramps that come with drinking too much fluid at one time. You'll want to discover what your body needs before race day.

Five Favorite Training Tips

1. Enjoy it
2. Be consistent
3. Slightly undertrained is much better than slightly overtrained
4. Eat well and eat soon after training
5. Never wipe your butt with a leaf from an unknown plant

—Ken Glah

Remember, when you get thirsty, you're already dehydrated. When you're in a race, take advantage of every water stop, even if you feel great and are going strong. It generally isn't recommended to take in the water you're swimming in during a triathlon, so you should drink before the swim. You should also have water bottles on your bike and drink everything in them before you start the run. Drink even more (use bigger water bottles) when it's hot. Dehydration, when ignored, can lead to heat stroke or a stint in the medical tent at the end of the race.

Heat illness can lead to brain damage or even death. It is therefore vital to take in enough fluids and to stop exercising immediately if you develop the symptoms, which include a weak rapid pulse, headache, dizziness, weakness, vomiting, and low blood pressure. Low blood pressure can eventually lead to heat stroke, causing mental confusion, convulsions, and increased body temperature. If you experience any of these symptoms, get to a cool place immediately and start drinking chilled fluids. Lie down or take a cold bath. If symptoms are severe enough, you must get to a doctor.

Water Intoxication (Sodium Deficiency)

The flip side to dehydration is having too much water. This is called hyponatremia (low blood salt, otherwise known as water intoxication). It usually occurs when training or racing for long periods in hot weather and is one of the big problems athletes have had to overcome at the Ironman in Hawaii. When you're going hard, you sweat, and as you sweat, you lose salt. If you drink lots of fluids but don't replace some of that salt, you could be in danger of hyponatremia. Taking salt tablets and drinking sports drinks can help you avoid it.

Symptoms of hyponatremia include weight loss (during training, from water sweated out), headaches, dizziness, and swelling in your hands and feet. The catch here is that if you don't consume much sodium on a regular basis, your body will adapt and you won't need as much. If you do eat a high-sodium diet, make sure you replenish the sodium lost in your sweat when training in the heat.

Cold Exposure (Hypothermia)

Most of the exposure to the cold can be addressed by dressing properly. If you have appropriate sports apparel in fabrics that wick away the moisture from your body, and common sense, you're unlikely to experience this extreme condition.

Hypothermia can be a problem in the wintertime, when outdoor temperatures plummet. It can also happen if you train when it's wet and windy. The best precaution against hypothermia is dressing properly for the weather. Wear waterproof but breathable fabrics when it's raining, and don't wear cotton (which holds water either from the elements or from sweat and does nothing to keep you warm). Taken to its extreme, hypothermia can lead to frostbite. Wear layers so you can remove one or more articles of clothing as you warm up from your exertion. Your body temperature goes up when you're training, so you don't need to dress as if you're going to be standing outside in the snow. But do be careful to wear a hat, gloves, and warm socks when training in severe cold, because cold causes your blood vessels to constrict, reducing blood flow to your extremities and therefore making them colder.

If you do get overchilled training in the winter, warm up gradually. Remove damp, sweaty exercise clothes and wrap up in something warm and dry. You might want to take a hot bath or shower and drink something hot like tea or spiced apple juice. If there's a howling blizzard outside, don't go out. You can go to a gym or buy equipment for home if you live in an area with severe weather. In bad weather, you not only risk overexposure to the elements, but you also risk being struck by a falling tree limb, slipping on ice, or getting lost in conditions of low visibility.

Muscle Cramps, Low Blood Sugar, Blisters

No one is really sure what causes muscle cramps, but they can happen to anyone. If you hydrate properly and eat a diet rich in potassium, calcium, and magnesium, cramps shouldn't cause you too much trouble. If you do get a cramp, stretch and massage the area. You may be able to continue training.

Low blood sugar is caused by not eating regularly. Your body needs fuel in order to perform. It isn't recommended that you eat right before exertion, but two or three hours before should be fine. Don't exercise on a completely empty stomach or you could become disoriented or faint. If you train first thing in the morning, experiment to find out what foods don't make you nauseated. Sometimes a banana or a piece of toast will keep you from having low blood sugar.

For training sessions that are longer than an hour, you may want to take food with you to keep your blood sugar level up. Finding the one that works for you should be done during training. There is a large market of energy bars and gels, which should be consumed with water to aid in digestion. If you find these products distasteful, experiment with regular food, such as bananas or bagels. The key is to find a food that doesn't upset your stomach and will give you energy during long training sessions.

Blisters are caused by friction, usually on the feet. Make sure your shoes fit properly. When you buy new shoes, especially for running, you may want to trade off between your new shoes and your old ones. But don't wear your old running shoes until they're completely worn out, because that can cause injury from foot rolling or lack of padding. If you prefer to train without socks, you might want to use lubrication on your feet. Drugstore petroleum jelly and commercially marketed sports lubricants work for this.

Common Sport-Specific Injuries and Ways to Avoid Them

In swimming, the biggest risk of injury is to your shoulders. Competitive swimmers train close to 5,000 yards per day, which adds up to 200 lengths of the pool at 15 to 25 strokes per length. Most shoulders were just not designed to put up with that much repetitive motion. To avoid stress on your shoulders, ease into swimming gradually. Take your time at the beginning of your training and work up to swimming a huge amount of laps. You might also want to get some stroke coaching to make sure your arms are moving properly. Freestyle doesn't put too much stress on your body if you do it correctly. In addition to stroke coaching, look for a video or book that shows proper form.

Pain from biking, aside from saddle soreness, is generally in the wrists, knees, neck, and lower back. Most of this type of soreness can be avoided by buying a bike that fits you in the first place. Buy your bicycle at a reputable bike shop and ask them to use a fit kit to make sure the bike is the proper size for you. Go back to your bike shop and look at adjusting the height of the seat or handlebars or both if you regularly experience pain when biking. Women and men are built differently, and so are their bikes. Men usually have longer torsos, so they need more room between the saddle and the handlebars. Women generally have proportionately longer legs, so they need to make sure the saddle is the correct distance from the pedals. A bike that fits should not be uncomfortable.

For best results, align your body on the bike in the best position you can. As you sit on the saddle, lean forward from the hips, keeping your chest up and checking to see that your back remains flat. Your neck and shoulders will be relaxed as you gently place your hands on the handlebars, because you're using your abdominal muscles to keep you in position rather than allowing the full weight of your torso to fall on your wrists. This position will take some practice to hold as you ride.

Probably the biggest danger in biking comes from falling off your bike for any one of a number of reasons. The best way to keep from crashing is to practice good handling and train yourself to automatically use hand signals for turns and stopping. Always wear a helmet and learn the rules of the road. Ride with an experienced biker or a group to practice your handling skills in tight situations. A grassy field is a good option if you wish to try riding elbow to elbow with a few friends. You'll be surprised at how much jostling you can take without falling on top of each other. With this practice, your confidence will grow.

The Worst Thing That Happened During Training or Racing

The worst accident I ever had was training on Australia's Gold Coast in the early 1990s. I was out riding with friends. We were coming down a notoriously steep hill, and I didn't take one of the corners. I hit the gravel on the side of the road, flipped the bike at about 70 km/h, landed on my head (luckily I was wearing a helmet), and slid down the road on my back. I was fortunate that I only needed a few stitches in my back. On the whole, I have been pretty lucky with crashes. The worst injury I ever had was a couple of years ago when I lifted something the wrong way and hurt my back. I did some nerve damage that doesn't want to be fixed and unfortunately has brought my racing to an end.

—Ben Bright ■

Because triathlons are held outside on roads, you need to practice in the same conditions, if not on the same roads you will bike. Learn road courtesy, such as always letting people know you're passing and pointing out debris on the road. It may sound strange, but in a race situation, triathletes still point out road hazards to their fellow racers. If you want to look cool and experienced, you'll do a quick finger flick to point out a bit of glass or bump as well.

When you run, your greatest risk of injury is obviously to your legs. Joints are particularly vulnerable. If you try to do too much too soon, you could strain the muscles or joints. Taking the time to warm up, stretch, and cool down can go a long way in keeping you injury free.

Spend the money on the shoes at the specialty sports stores to get the right shoes. Pay attention to any kind of pain in running, and if it doesn't go away with stretching or time, see a sports doctor. Taking an anti-inflammatory, such as ibuprofen or aspirin, can help, as does icing immediately after you train. Another potential problem when running is developing shin splints. This is a sharp pain down the front of your shins, and if left untreated, they can lead to stress fractures. Ice the area. Take time off from running or run in the deep end of the pool using a flotation device if necessary to keep from impacting the joints. This lets the shins heal.

Strategies to Help Stay in the Game

We all like to have good reasons to get out of unpleasant situations. It must be the "dog ate my homework" syndrome. When you've first started on or recently returned to the fitness road, your newly active lifestyle can became uncomfortable up to the point where you're looking for ways to get out of it. You want to just slink back to your old routines, take it easy, and have a big piece of cake. I'm not suggesting that you might hurt yourself on purpose to get out of your training plan, but if you get an injury, that's a signal to change your training, not to take a big detour on your fitness road. If you hurt your shoulder, you can still use your legs. If you have a sore ankle, that won't keep you from your abdominal crunches.

The Worst Thing That Happened During Training or Racing

I battled Achilles tendonitis throughout my career. In fact, the worst bout of it was through 1996—my most successful year. I believe everyone has a weakness and a (physical) breaking point. My Achilles was mine. It was something I had to learn to deal with and manage. Because my motivation for success was so high, I often put up with a lot of pain, but I also learned to minimize the impact of my weakness on my performances. I still tape my ankle for stability and manage my lower leg problems with lots of massage (often self-massage), ice and stretching.
—*Jackie Gallagher*

All athletes experience injury at some point in their careers, and you will too. Physical therapy, a change in training, rest, and recovery time will get you back in the full swing of things. In the meantime, you'll just have to get a bit creative with your training, won't you?

Strength training, stretching, massage, and proper fit with proper equipment are some of the elements of an injury-free training program that you can incorporate into your week so you can save some of the creativity for other interesting pursuits.

Strength Training

Strength training increases your ability because it increases the amount of muscle you have. As you get stronger, you'll find you can do more. Strength training does not, however, do anything for your cardiovascular fitness. It is possible to be very strong and well muscled and still get winded going up stairs. A good training program includes strength training along with aerobic training.

When your muscles get stronger, they're better able to handle an increased workload. Stronger muscles also help hold your joints in proper alignment when you run, bike, and swim. If you've never lifted weights before, I recommend you find a trainer to show you how and to make sure your form is correct. Improper form (as with anything else) can cause injury.

Stretching

Stretching is vital in avoiding injuries to your joints and your muscles. When you exercise regularly, your muscles get tight from contracting and building, and you need to stretch to maintain flexibility and release the pressure of your muscles pulling on your joints. In extreme cases, tight muscles can pull your joints out of alignment and cause injury. Yoga is helpful, but it is sometimes thought that yoga can relax your muscles too much for peak performance. Do make sure you stretch properly, avoiding stress on your joints. Stretching should not cause pain. If you don't know how to stretch for all three of triathlon's sports, find a fitness professional or fellow triathlete and ask.

Massage

Massage can alleviate tightness in the muscles and help ensure that your joints are aligned properly. Massage also increases the effectiveness of blood circulation. One scientific study showed that 10 minutes of deep stroking and kneading of a lower leg almost doubled the blood flow to that area for more than 40 minutes. Ten minutes of exercise, on the other hand, increases (not doubles) the blood flow for only 10 minutes.

Of course, physical activity pumps considerable blood and oxygen to the muscles, exchanging oxygen-filled blood for carbon dioxide-filled blood. But it also increases the amount of waste that needs to be removed. All of this is a vicious cycle that can lead to muscle soreness. The purpose of massage is to break that cycle. Massage flushes the tissues with blood without creating the by-products that accompany exercise. Too bad you can't massage your way through a triathlon.

There are many different kinds of massage, so make sure you go to a certified massage therapist who works with athletes. You can also try rolfing (dry tissue manipulation) or shiatsu (Japanese pressure-point massage), but generally the best kind of massage to get for athletic performance is deep tissue massage (otherwise known as Swedish massage, but generally known as sports massage).

Whatever sport you play, sports massage could give you 15 to 20 percent extra performance, extra protection, extra time per game, per season, per race, per career. This means a lot to you, whether you're a professional athlete who depends on bodily skill and power for your livelihood, a serious amateur, or even an athlete who plays a sport strictly for recreation. With sports massage, you can do what you do better, longer, and more easily. You will raise your performance level at the same time that you lower the stress levels on your body. You can go for massage as needed when you feel your muscles are tight, or you can set up a regular schedule. Massage can be a preventative strategy, not to mention it feels good.

Proper Equipment (Running Shoes, Helmet, Bike Fit, Clothing)

One of the most important things you can do to stay in the game is wear the proper equipment. An ANSI- or Snell-approved bike helmet is not optional; it's required. Well-fitting running shoes can make the difference between a great season and a season spent on the couch nursing your knees. Buy your equipment at stores that hire people who are involved in the sport, so they know what's involved and can help find the best equipment for you. Ask the bike store personnel to use a fit kit to find a bike that fits your body. Take running shoes for a short spin before you buy them, preferably on a hill so you can see if your feet slide. Wear comfortable clothing that doesn't pinch, chafe, or bind and is made out of breathable, wicking fabric and gives enough support. When training, wear clothing appropriate to the sport. I know I've said all this before, but it can make the difference between getting the most out of your life and making physical activity a miserable experience.

When You Are Ready for More: Resources

Books

Athletic Massage by Rich Phaigh and Paul Perry, First Fireside Edition (1986).

Bicycling Medicine by Arnie Baker, Simon & Schuster (1998).

Lore of Running (3rd ed.) by Timothy Noakes, Human Kinetics (1991).

Nutrition in Sport by Georg Neumann, Meyer & Meyer Sport (2001).

chapter 16

Race Day

D-Day

Everyone is feeling it, and there's not a good name for the sensation. Let's call it prerace jitters. The symptoms are nervous stomach, monkey mind, and last-minute buying frenzy. You've taken all the steps, read this book, followed it like a training bible, improved your diet, cleaned and checked your equipment and gear, and now it's D-day—deployment time. What can you expect to experience over the entire event weekend? Read this chapter and visualize your race before the event takes place. It could save you from listening to that monkey of self-doubt, and maybe keep you from buying the entire store at the expo!

It's a Weekend, Not Just a Day

The triathlon begins long before the sounding of the starter's signal. You might receive a confirmation in the mail or on the Web, you might be receiving announcements from other events now that you're on the list because the race directors or timing company has provided marketers with ways to contact you. For most races, you'll be asked or required to attend a race packet pickup the day or days before the race.

Particularly larger triathlons insist that you attend a prerace expo the day before the race. This is where and when you pick up swag (free items passed out by the vendors to get you to try their stuff), sign away that you're responsible for your own self—a liability waiver—and so forth. Many of the race bags include your race numbers (for the bike and on your shirt or race belt for the run), so sign the waiver and get your body marked for the swim. There are usually also tables for the race sponsors, course talks, bike repair or inspection, and vendors of triathlon-related items.

You can handle expo attendance in different ways. If you have a specific attendance time assigned based on name, age, or other factors, then go when you're supposed to. If not, coming early usually means longer lines and more swag. Coming late means short or no lines but also the possibility that you might miss out on a free water bottle or the latest sports gel. If there are freebies to be had, try them. You never know when something you haven't seen before will be perfect for you. Triathlon pigs binge on swag;

Top Five Things Not to Do in a Race

1. I never change my breakfast or my race nutrition just before the race.
2. I never clean the drive train just before the race. When old dirt is scraped off the cogs, the shifting changes. When solvents get in around the bolts, these may let loose. I once rode the whole Ironman with a jockey wheel hanging at an angle ready to fall out.
3. I never change goggle settings since the strap slipped out and I swam without them in Kona. That is painful and my eyelids swelled enough to push my biking goggles away. The swelling got sweated away in two hours, but still . . .
4. I never listen to competitors talk about how hard they trained, and I no longer make predictions about how many will beat me. I concentrate 100 percent and only on my own performance.
5. I never quit since I have learned how quickly one feels better in a sag wagon. A few minutes of restful drinking and eating works wonders, especially when you hear of your competitor having as bad or worse time.

–Frank Cokan, M.D.

we recommend that you don't grab all you can carry, though—leave some for the other racers.

Be prepared for lines during the packet pickup. Be patient and don't get cranky with the race volunteers manning the tables. They're giving up their free time to help you. Thank each and every volunteer, because it couldn't be done without them. If you have a problem with something anytime during the weekend, write a note to the race organizer after the event is over. If there's a danger, however, try to find someone in charge right away and explain what's going on.

Likewise, if you enjoyed the race, write the race organizers a note about your experience. Race directors are human, too, and poorly paid at that. Who doesn't like to know that they've done something right for a change?

Check Out the Race Course

Most of the time taken up by the expo and one of the most important parts of the expo is the course review talk. Be sure to attend. This is given by the race director or a race representative and is likely to have the most up-to-date course information. Any questions you may have regarding set-up time for your transition gear and when you can take your bike out of the transition area after the race will be addressed during this talk. The race director usually has course maps and can explain any last-minute details. Sometimes, the course is altered due to construction or permit requirements. They'll give you the final decision on whether wet suits are permitted and in some cases required. You're responsible for knowing the racecourse, so be sure to attend the racecourse review as many times as you need to in order to get the details.

Also, if possible, check out the actual racecourse in person before the race. If it's in your hometown, take the opportunity to train on the racecourse. Drive or ride the bike and run routes if you can, to see where you'll be going and know the challenges that it offers. Take a look at where you'll be swimming. Sometimes

> **Top 5 Things Not to Do in a Race**
>
> 1. Try new food, equipment, or routine
> 2. Cheat
> 3. Curse at volunteers
> 4. Be inflexible in your race plan
> 5. Set unreachable goals and then quit when you fail to meet them
>
> *–Sue Latshaw*

it's at a public beach, so you can get in for 10 minutes or so to paddle around. This isn't a workout, just a chance to test the waters.

Get Your Gear Together and Get Prepared

As you start to pack your gear for the race, separate it into four parts: swim, bike, run, and postrace. Double-check against the gear checklist to be sure you have everything (see chapter 17). Compare the gear checklist with your own list and check off all items. Spread out everything that you think and know you need. Make sure you have everything. Take out anything that you haven't used before, be it a pair of shorts or a specialty sports drink. If you haven't tested it, it doesn't belong in your race bag. By the time you get to race day, you'll want to have tested everything thoroughly and know what works for you. If you want to wear socks for the bike and the run, then bring them along. It might add a few seconds to your transition time to put them on, but if you're more comfortable or they prevent blisters on your feet, then it's worth it.

Do what prep you can the day or night before your race. Put the frame number on your bike, pin your run number on your shirt or attach it to your race belt. Fill your water bottles and have them ready. Make sure everything fits in your travel bag and put it all in there.

Top 5 Things Not to Do in or Before a Race

1. Doing something different on race day. Here are some of the most common:

   Trying a new food or drink on race day.

   Racing a bike that you have not had time to properly train on first.

   Using a new model of racing flat.

2. Using a full wetsuit because it is faster, even though the water is too warm for it. You then start the bike feeling like you just had a liter of margaritas in a hot tub.
3. Flying in to a race the day before. Even if you leave early on the day before, you still won't get enough sleep two nights before the race (a crucial night for sleep). If you leave late in the day before the race, then you run the risk of delayed flights, disappearing luggage (most likely your bike), and a heart rate for most of the day that is higher than what you will be racing at the next day.
4. Not bringing earplugs. If you don't have earplugs, there will no doubt be a party in the hotel room next to you.
5. Telling your friends the time you will finish at an Ironman. Just like washing your car will cause rain, announcing your projected finishing time will cause one or more of the following:

   Huge surf and strong currents for the swim.

   Headwinds the entire bike ride.

   Torrential rain at the end of the bike that gives way to a sun so strong that you are afraid to walk through aid stations because you think your shoes will get stuck to the road.

—Ken Glah

Eating and Sleeping

Eat a hearty meal the night before the race. This is not the time to try that exotic cuisine. You'll know from your training and testing foods what works best for you. Traveling for a race can limit your food choices, but plan ahead, especially making arrangements for food the morning of the race. Many times hotels do not offer food as early as you'll need to eat. I've been caught several times with no breakfast provided at 4:30 A.M., so contact the hotel to find out if you might need to go grocery shopping.

If you can't sleep the night before the race, rest comfortably with the thought that this is normal and common. The really important night for sleeping well is two nights before the race, because for most, it takes two days for the effects to catch up with you. Traveling to a race might involve some additional sleep strategies, such as choice of hotel location (a nonconstruction zone works best), room selection (not by the elevator or ice machine), and other personal preferences. Rest knowing that the chances are that your fellow racers aren't sleeping either. You'll no doubt have a restful sleep the next night after the race.

The Worst Mistake in Training and/or Racing

The worst and most public mistake I ever made while racing was during the 1992 Nice Triathlon, where I neglected to take any food with me for the bike leg and completely blew to pieces at about 90 km. I proceeded to lose 12 minutes in the last 30 km of the bike. I made it about 14 km into the run before I fell over and basically went to sleep on the road. I woke up in an ambulance on the way to the hospital. I was under the false impression that there would be food available during the bike ride.
—Ben Bright

Race Day

Get to the race site at least an hour before the start of the race. This provides time for parking, unloading your equipment and gear, getting body marking, waiting in lines for portable toilets, setting up your transition area (details are in chapter 17), getting your logistics arranged within the transition area, talking to friends, drinking fluids, and most of all, taking pictures.

The race day is the best day. It's the time when your investment in your training and preparation are rewarded. Savor it. Remember, your fellow athletes, especially in your age division, are your best friends. They'll help you throughout the race as companions or as a target to race harder.

There are many, many tips for D-day. Read them, and as you gain experience after completing your first or fiftieth triathlon, add to them and share with others.

Focus on Where Your Bike Is Racked

One of the most confusing moments may well be the one spent finding your bike after the swim. At the USTS National Championships in Las Vegas, my bike was racked next to the portable toilet, which therefore served as a marker for more than one activity for me. As we left the transition area, I said to my compatriot and fellow master triathlete, "Look hard, our bikes are both next to the outhouses."

She didn't acknowledge my statement, so I put my hand on her shoulder and repeated the sentence. After the race, she thanked me for stopping her—she had found her bike with ease, because we both took the time to do a double-take on where we had racked them. The real point that I learned is that by helping others, I usually find I help myself more. I suspect you've already discovered this fact of life.

—Sally Edwards

Swimming Tips for Race Day

- Splash a little water on your shoulders and back while you wait for the swim start. You'll avoid the shock of the water temperature by sampling it first.
- It's nice to take a small practice swim to warm up the muscles, check the water temperature, and test out your goggles yet again before the start.
- Remember to swim a straight line by raising your head to sight every eight strokes.
- If you are nervous, focus on your swim stroke, keep your face in the water, and use the best freestyle stroke you know. You *will* get through it.
- You won't save energy going slowly and using breast-stroke. You'll only get cold, and it will take longer to transition to the bike leg.
- Do not swim from boat to boat. The lifeguards need to be able to move their flotation devices around in case someone is in trouble.

Biking Tips for Race Day

- Check your tires for debris after you walk your bike to the transition area. Many times there are needles, burrs, or thorns in the grass that you might not notice, because you're usually riding on the pavement.
- Clip your helmet on your head before you unrack your bike.
- Walk your bike out of the transition area.
- Follow the transition rules set by race management with regard to walking, riding, or running in the transition area.
- Set your bike in the appropriate gear prior to the race. If you're starting the bike leg on an uphill, use a lower gear than you would if the course were flat at the start.
- Stay to the right as you ride. When it's time to pass another rider, then move to the left to pass.

- Talk to the other riders whenever there's a safety issue. Let other bikers know that you're passing or attempting to pass.
- Drink on the bike. The amount of fluids depends on the factors of the day.

Running Tips for Race Day

- Drink fluids at the aid or fluid stations. However, it may not be to your advantage to drink the electrolyte or energy drinks offered if you haven't tried them in your training.
- Stay to the right as you run. Yell "trail" to ask another runner to yield the path.
- You're feeling the effects of cumulative fatigue during the run. Be more careful overall, because the effect of fatigue is loss of coordination and often the ability to think clearly.
- Make sure your race number is visible when you're in sight of the finish line. You'll help the finish line announcer and the photographer figure out who gets the picture proof. Many races today use an electronic timing chip to measure runners' elapsed times. Regardless, you still must wear your race number in front of you during the run.
- If there's a finish chute, walk through it in an orderly manner so the finish line volunteers can record your finish place and time.

The Insider's Report

Doing the race from within as a triathlete is one perspective. Seeing the race from outside as a spectator is another. But the perspective that is not often recounted or seen by the triathlete or the spectator is the one of the insider who sees what is happening behind the scenes.

In triathlons, there's an inner maze required to organize and produce the event. When Jim Curl and I wrote the first book on race management, *How to Organize a Triathlon: A Race Director's Guide* in 1983, we wanted to stimulate the rapid acceleration of triathlon events in order for the sport to grow and be seen as well organized and managed.

When Greg Rorke, the president of Danskin, first called me on the phone in 1989 and asked if Danskin could hire me to be their national spokesperson, I flatly and firmly said no. I said this in large part because I only wanted to be associated with a quality event with a company that would commit to the sport long term. Mr. Rorke was a good salesperson. He promised me that the Danskin Women's Triathlon Series would be the best, and he's proven himself right. He asked Maggie Sullivan to be the vice president of sports marketing, and the company subsequently enthusiastically embraced the sport and their national women's series, so that today, a dozen years later, Danskin deserves the credit for being the longest and best sprint triathlon series on the planet.

The Heart of Triathlons: What It Takes to Make Them Happen

The following is from Maggie Sullivan, who is the Vice President of Sports Marketing for Danskin. She is also the co-author of *Caterpillars to Butterflies: If You Can Dream It, Why Not Tri It?* Since 1992, she has directed the Danskin Triathlon Series to its premier position as triathlon's largest women's property and the sport's longest-running series in the history of the sport. She has summited glacial mountains, led 70,000 women to their first triathlon finish, and resided with pride for 26 years in New York City. Maggie produced the largest triathlon in the history of the sport, with 4,000 participants, at the Seattle Danskin Women's Triathlon on August 19, 2001.

"Perhaps I was destined to be in the event production business—a business that tests my tenacity repeatedly, requires me on numerous occasions to dig deep for an extra dose of any number of character attributes (not to mention energy), a business that requires more than an average injection of self into one's work, and ultimately a business that requires interacting with people—a lot of people.

"My upbringing (one of nine children), work ethic (genetic), and my choice of cities to call home (New York City), when combined, provided me with a pretty sturdy foundation for such a career. When one couples that with my sheer enjoyment of being a part of developing properties, either on an entertainment level or a participant level, there can be no question as to why I've stayed in the business for 32 years.

"Unlike many, I can't say, 'I always knew I'd be in the sports business.' I can't even say I've always liked sports. My thoughts early on went more the way of being a Rockette on stage in New York City, and then while in school, a psychologist. Here's how it went for me, and I wouldn't trade it for anything.

"I cut my teeth in the sports production business by way of 19 incredible years in men's professional tennis—which was and remains, in many respects, the entertainment business. The lessons learned on multiple fronts in those years have served me incredibly well in the 13 years I've worked in the sport of Triathlon, though the two are worlds apart in many ways. The most important difference for me has been in the approach.

"My first career focused on building 'entertainment properties' that people could *watch*—no small task mind you, if done professionally—but far and away different from a *participant-driven* undertaking, which in the end is all about building properties for people to *experience.* Many of the nuts and bolts remain consistent, but what is required from the top on down in a series' management team and the local race director teams in each city, particularly on race weekend, certainly does change.

"The undertaking of developing and building a triathlon series that is nationwide in breadth can be viewed on two levels: the series level and the race level—both are critical to the results. First the series work, since it provides the framework into which the individual races will be housed and establishes the standard by which the race will be executed.

"The focus of a series director for a nationwide series needs to be, naturally, nationwide. The concerns of a series director (this is from the vantage point of the Danskin Women's Triathlon Series director) include but are not limited to:

- Race city identification
- Race director identification
- Sponsor identification, sales, and management
- Public relations and publicity
- Collateral materials (entry brochures, program, advertisements) development, printing, and distribution
- Budgeting
- Insurance
- Database management
- Web site development and maintenance
- Affiliation of charity
- Site signage
- Site materials
- Participant materials (souvenir tanks, finisher medals, swim caps, race numbers)
- Waivers
- Incident reports
- Expo development and execution
- Consistent site presentation
- Timing company
- Media on race day
- Announcer
- Spokesperson
- Collateral programs development
- Series staffing
- Travel

- Determination to have prize money or not
- Preseries training seminars
- Prerace program materials, travel, talent, etc.
- Shipping

"The work on a series level is virtually year-round, with the effort on the following year's series starting before the current one is even underway. This is due in part to the nature of corporations and their budgeting timelines, length of time necessary to develop certain programs that may be a part of the series' mix, and so on.

"Depending on how the work is handled, in-house or outsourced, the depth of hands-on involvement and time investment by a series director varies.

"On a local race director level, the concentration is focused on the specific city within which the race takes place. The concerns are varied and include but are not limited to:

- Identification and securing of race venue
- Layout of race site
- Design/identification of race courses (swim, bike, run)
- Permitting
- Interfacing with local municipality (parks and recreation; police; fire; medical; department of transportation; etc.)
- Securing safety personnel for race
- Developing volunteer base
- Budgeting
- Marketing event regionally
- Securing of local hotel
- Sourcing and securing of structural materials for site
- Identification of and layout for registration expo facility
- Receipt of, recording of, and transportation of inbound freight
- Identification and training of key coordinators

- Managing race management team
- Build out and breakdown of race site (fencing, scaffold towers, transition areas, tents, parking)
- Participant food and beverage
- Local race sponsors

"Here the work starts off more gently (depending on the number of years utilizing the same site), with days or in many cases weeks of work devoted to putting all the pieces municipality-wise and venue-wise in order and then roars toward closure on race weekend with less frenetic movement in the weeks that follow.

"Sound easy? It's anything but. A solid and successful race is, at the end of the day, the results of a true collaborative effort. A good fit between series' management and local race director personnel is essential. The word 'relationship' comes to mind. That is what needs to be developed in order for a seamless race presentation to occur and for there to be a beneficial return to the series' business partners—a solid relationship between a series management team and a local race director team. And like any other relationship, these take time.

"The challenge, on a simplistic level (which in actuality isn't very simple at all), is keeping many, many balls—more than a few of them of real consequence—in the air simultaneously. The business is rife with detail, personality management, needs assessment, and management and is one that repeatedly tests the best in a variety of ways. It's a balancing act, which when integrated properly and in a professional and timely manner, gives you a good shot at a successful series/event production. However, the true proof of our work in the sport of triathlon comes via the participant and her experience. It is she who will be the ultimate determining factor of our efforts.

"The rewards forthcoming from work in this sector of the sports world are innumerable. Knowing that what you do makes it possible for tens of thousands of women to know who they are and what they are capable of is invaluable."

chapter 17

transitions

The Fourth Event

Triathlon is a sport of threes: a triple fitness sport, a tri-training event, and a swim-bike-run format. But there's also a fourth leg spliced in between each part of the race, a place known as transitions. Transition 1 (T1) is the swim-to-bike transition; transition 2 (T2) is the bike-to-run transition.

Getting through the transition is part organization, part luck, and part being able to move under the stress of time ticking away and your competitors making ground on you every second you spend there. You can't get to the finish line fast if you're futzing in the transition area.

In a recent Danskin event, I was the sweep triathlete, or the person who makes sure everyone is off the course before it is closed. I slowly left the transition area to accompany the "final finisher" on the bike leg. I took my time transitioning, because when you volunteer to be last in the race, there's no point in hurrying. As I caught up with the final woman, a motorcyclist drove next to me to say that I had erred, because there was a woman riding her bike behind me. I did a quick U-turn and rode back to find her. The cop was right. Since I knew I was going to be out there with her for at least an hour finishing the bike leg, I asked her, "What do you do for a living, and what happened in your transition?" Incredulously, she said, "I'm an officer in the Air Force. I lost my helmet in transition and spent 40 minutes trying to find it and get another one out of a friend's car. Then one of the women who had started in an earlier wave and finished offered me her helmet." Certainly, that's one way to get through a triathlon, but with a little preparation you can do better.

A Complete Gear List for Triathlon

The first part of making transitions easy, fast, and smooth is to get organized. Being organized consists of having the right gear and having it arranged sequentially in your transition area. There are two different equipment rules for you to follow:

Rule 1: The less you need, the faster you are.

Rule 2: It's more important to have what you need than to be fast.

Select which of these rules applies to your racing style. In the clothing area, for example, the less you wear, the faster your finish. However, the corollary to this rule is: It's better to look good than to go fast.

Following are lists of essential and some nonessential gear.

Prerace tri gear

- ✔ Travel bag
- ✔ Bike rack for your car
- ✔ Warm clothes and rain gear
- ✔ Towel for the ground

Swim

- ✔ Suit
- ✔ Goggles
- ✔ Cap
- ✔ Goggle defogger
- ✔ Towel

Bike

- ✔ Helmet
- ✔ Clothing
- ✔ Bike

- ✔ Tools
- ✔ Seat bag
- ✔ Socks
- ✔ Bike shoes
- ✔ Bike frame number
- ✔ Eye protectors, sunglasses
- ✔ Bike frame number
- ✔ Full water bottle(s)
- ✔ Frame pump or CO_2 system

Run

- ✔ Race belt
- ✔ Shoes
- ✔ Sunglasses
- ✔ Race number
- ✔ Run clothing
- ✔ Hat
- ✔ Lace locks

Other items

- ✔ Heart rate monitor
- ✔ Bike gloves
- ✔ Bike computer
- ✔ Floor bike pump
- ✔ Camera
- ✔ Personal items: reading glasses, comb
- ✔ Sunscreen
- ✔ Extra water bottle
- ✔ Food
- ✔ Clothing for before and after the race
- ✔ Plastic bags for rain protection
- ✔ First aid kit

After the race gear

- ✔ Change of clothes
- ✔ Food and beverage of your choice
- ✔ Towel for after the race

Setting Up Your Transition Area

Get to the race site early. Wear your swimsuit under your sweats, because there may not be anywhere to change. Try to pack all of your race gear in one bag, because you'll be carrying it as you push your bike from the car to the transition area.

When you find the rack you've been assigned (bike racks are usually set up by race number), rack your bike. Spread your towel to the right of your back wheel, and place your gear bag to the right of the front wheel. Next, set out your gear sequentially in the order in which you're going to use it. Lay out your bike shoes, put the clothes you plan to wear for the bike (if any) on the shoes, lay your helmet on your aerobars with the straps out, ready to don. If you don't have aerobars, you can put the helmet on top of your bag.

Put your running shoes (if different from your bike shoes) either next to or just behind your bike shoes, with your race belt on top. You might have to wear your race number while you're on the bike, either on a shirt or using the race belt. Be careful, since the race numbers made of Tyvek squares tend to flap in the wind, which is annoying. Also take time to affix your bike number (if one is provided) on the top tube so it doesn't crawl backward and chafe your inner thighs. Make sure you have water or your tested sports drink in your water bottles, which should already be in your bike cages. Lay out any food or other supplies you might need.

Take a minute to think it through. Hopefully, you've already practiced transitions in training, so you know what to expect. Once you're set up, walk from your bike rack down to the entrance to T1. Then walk back to your bike and count the number of bike racks to where you racked your bike. Do the same from the entrance back into T2, so you can again find your spot at the end of the bike leg. If you can't remember these two numbers, find some other way to find your particular bike out of the hundreds or thousands that will be racked in the transition area. Look around to see if there are any landmarks or structures that will help you find your bike more easily.

Remember that once the race starts, that spiffy purple bike you're planning to use as a landmark to find your own bike may not be there if its rider finishes the swim before you do. Some people use balloons (when allowed by race organizers) or a special towel laid across the saddle to find their bikes.

The Eight Parts of a Triathlon

Yes, there are three legs to a triathlon. But each event has its own start and its own finish line. Yes, there is one transition area, but spliced between each of the legs of a triathlon is a transition, which means that there are really two transitions, not one. What you need to be prepared for is eight parts of a triathlon, not three or four.

The Eight Parts of a Triathlon

3 starting lines + 3 finish lines + 2 transitions

- Start of the swim
- End of the swim
- Swim-to-bike transition: T1
- Start of the bike
- End of the bike
- Bike-to-run transition: T2
- Start of the run
- End of the run

Part 1: Swim Start

The announcer will call you to the starting line. In smaller-scale triathlons, everyone begins together. But in many larger or more sophisticated events, the race begins in waves, or groups of individuals who are in the same age division. There are usually 2- to 5-minute delays between the start of each wave. Stand with the individuals who are in your start wave. As you wait for your wave, review your swim plan: How far apart are the buoys, what color and size are they, is there a current or wind, are there waves, what can you sight on, and where is the sun rising?

At this very moment, you may be tempted to change your prerace strategy, particularly because you're standing, scantily dressed, waiting for the swim to begin. This is an anxious time, when self-doubt may rear its ugly head, but don't let the excitement of the prerace activities alter your determination or focus. Stick to your plan.

As the starting signal sounds for your wave, enter the water with measured caution—you don't need to charge in with flailing arms and wild screams. It's common for first timers to experience hyperventilation at the start of the race. If this happens to you, just roll over on your back in the swim or wait until you regain control of your respiratory pattern. If it's your first triathlon, use it as a learning experience as much as anything.

After you pass that first buoy and clear it, take the time to get your bearings. Breaststroke for a few yards if you need to (remember to keep an eye out for those around you), and follow the most important rule of swimming: breathe.

As you round the last buoy and head toward the swim finish line, relish the moments—the swim is almost over. Do a mental body check: Survey your body and scan your energy level. Use the information to focus your attention on performing as you planned in the next part of the race. Swim until your hand touches the bottom and then stand. While you are walking, running, or trotting through the shallow water toward the finish chute, you might feel a loss of your equilibrium. All levels of athletes could experience this brief sensation. It often happens when you quickly change from the prone to the vertical position.

Part 2: Swim Finish

Take off your goggles and swim cap and look up at the clock or your wristwatch to make a mental record of your swim split. This information should give you some data to think about with regard to the first leg of the triathlon.

In most events, you'll encounter timing volunteers at the swim finish who will take your time splits. These volunteers will direct you toward T1, the first of two transitions.

Part 3: Swim-to-Bike Transition, T1

Your bike and gear are waiting for you in T1. Because you took a good look and know exactly where your bike is racked, you can easily run up to it without confusion. But don't sacrifice comfort for speed in transition. Take enough time to get properly organized. Make sure your bike shoes (if you wear them) are securely fastened and that you've put your gear on comfortably: sunglasses, helmet, and any personal items.

The transition area is like a pit stop. Think, "What do I need to get while I'm in the pit stop to keep this body machine on the bike?" The answer may include fluids, fuel, medical help, petroleum jelly, and sunscreen. In the Ironman, as with pit stops in car races, people are in the transition area to help you. If that's the case in your race, now is the best time to use them, because they won't be able to help you while you're out on the course.

Ride or walk your bike out of T1. Every race has its own rules about exiting with your bike. Some allow you to walk and others to run out of the area with your bike—ask in advance. Start your heart rate monitor, if it wasn't started before the swim, and your bike monitor, which starts your bike timer as well as records distance and speed, because the bike leg has begun.

Part 4: Bike Start

I love the start of the bicycle leg. I'm fresh, happy that the swim is over, and excited. What I need to do at that point is relax and ride according to my prerace strategy—either in miles per hour or, as I prefer, beats per minute *and* miles per hour.

I remind myself to be careful to avoid the draft position, which is sitting in another rider's slipstream. This is a violation of the rules in many triathlons. You must constantly maneuver to stay out of a position violation situation, and in races with mass starts, this isn't easy to do. There are some draft legal races, so be sure to know the current definition of this position violation according to USA Triathlon (USAT).

Be wary of the riding skills of the other riders. Always give yourself the benefit of the doubt—you may be a better rider than they are. Talk to riders as you approach and shout out that you're passing. Always pass to the left, and don't cross the centerline of the road.

As you ride, you may notice a few body signals of your own that you'll need to heed. Start drinking almost immediately from your water bottle. If the bike portion is more than 25 miles, you may need to eat during the ride as well. Don't depend on the race organizers to provide either water bottles or food along the course. You may also notice that your legs are tighter than usual. To help with any tightness, stand and stretch or backspin on the downhills.

Part 5: Bike Finish

As you ride toward T2, the second transition, start to prepare mentally for the change. I sometimes forget to push the stop button on my bike computer or monitor. But there are more important things to remember, like slowing through the chicanes (the traffic cones that are set up to slow you down as you ride into or out of a transition area) and riding or walking your bike with extra care in the transition area. Remember, runners will be exiting down the corridors between the bike racks.

As you enter T2, look for the finish clock and make a mental note of the time. Quickly find your position on your designated bike rack. Rack your bike. That leg is over.

Part 6: Bike-to-Run Transition, T2

Do not unsnap your helmet until you're off your bike—it's a rule. Slip off your bike shoes, slide on your racing flats, tighten your lace locks, grab your hat or visor, put on your race belt or number, and *go*.

For many, there's a tendency to hang out in the transition area, eating, drinking, and getting organized. You can if you want, but you're eating up time that you may value later. However, keep in mind that the transition area is a checkpoint. If you need help, now is the time to seek it. It's better to get it now than to be sorry later.

As you take those first few running steps away from your bike, you may feel what I call the "bike-to-run grip." It feels like your quadriceps have rigor mortis; they can be so tight that it's hard to take a normal stride length. This is normal, however, so expect it—it happens to everyone.

How do you alleviate the decimating feeling of the "grip"? There's no one best answer, but a couple of tricks sometimes help. Try backspinning on the bike as you coast to the T2 transition area before the dismount. Or before you start the run, try to stretch out your legs. In training, practice getting off your bike and immediately running (what is known as a brick training session), and train the discomfort away.

Part 7: The Run Start

Start your timer (if it hasn't been running since the swim start) as you exit the transition area and try to set an even pace. You probably will have to run a mile before you can feel truly comfortable at your chosen speed; it seems to take that long for the musculature to adapt to the transition. You may need to reach down inside yourself for some strength and perseverance.

Other runners will pass you, just as swimmers and cyclists have done. But you'll pass other runners as well. The jockeying for position among those with the same single-sport specialty makes triathlon fun. Those with a strong cycling background passed the swimmers and the runners in their leg, whereas those with a strong running background now get to pass those who were stronger in the swim and bike. Obviously, those with strong backgrounds in all three have the best chance of holding their position. That's the solution to winning in this sport—balance.

Part 8: The Run Finish, The Race Finish

As you approach the final finish line, look up—there will be a finish clock with the time. You're guaranteed that it's going to display the time of the first starters, those in the first wave, and you're probably in one of the later ones. Remember the time, though; you can subtract out your wave handicap when you're thinking more clearly. Or, better still, look at your watch or monitor—it's best to rely on your own timing anyway.

Then throw your shoulders back, hold your head up, and run across the finish line, arms held high and spread as wide as the smile on your face.

You're a triathlete.

After the Race

Live it up. Food and drinks and some type of a party are usually waiting for you at the finish line. But most of all, meet people. Triathletes, as a rule, are a friendly group. Introduce yourself, make new friends, share one another's experiences, and learn from each other. It'll surprise you how many others want to do the same with you.

I like to have some small reward planned for races that count—a gift to myself. After all, I've earned it, and you, too, should treat yourself to a reward for a great accomplishment. It can be something small, like a new training device, or something big, like dinner for the support crew that joined you on this magnificent day.

The Days After

How great you feel the day after may surprise you. It's one of the bonuses that is rarely discussed after triathlons—how little they really seem to take out of you.

I set the master's world record at the 1990 Ironman Japan, and Erin Baker won the pro division. Two weeks later, we saw each other again at the finish line of an international distance triathlon. It was as if we were psychically linked as we simultaneously said to one another, "Did you notice any effects on today's race from the Ironman?" We both acknowledged that we didn't feel anything that could have hurt our performance—no lingering fatigue, injury, or lack of enthusiasm. We both won again.

Give yourself several days or possibly weeks for regeneration time. This was your first triathlon of many more to come. Write a new training schedule, build a new base, and reach a new peak. No matter what, take it easy. You may have to nurture a blister or a black toe back to health, and you'll undoubtedly need to devote attention to both the mental and the physical regeneration to some degree.

You may be different from Erin and me. You may feel some negative side effects of your first triathlon. If so, take it even easier. Sleep. Rest. Relax. Take a day off work. If you sit at a desk during part of your day, raise your feet slightly higher. Get a massage. If you choose to train, do so in low heart zones, slowly, briefly. Remember to drink lots of fluids and eat complex carbohydrates and nutrient-dense foods.

The Fever

If you feel like I did after my first triathlon, shivering on the banks of Stonegate Lake and being recorded as a DNF ("did not finish"), participating in your first triathlon is like a raging, hot fever. I was hit hard, floored. Then when I finished my first Ironman, my fever was ignited to new levels of fervency. Upon my return to California from Hawaii, all I did was talk about triathlons. I started new triathlon races (and wrote a pamphlet on how to do it); I helped found USA Triathlon; I wrote the sport's first book; I opened triathlon retail stores; I spoke at clinics, at races, to tri clubs, to anyone who would invite me.

Later I discovered that this fever was love, and I hope you feel the same for the sport after your first triathlon.

chapter 18

training the mental muscle

Sports psychologists suggest that conditioning the mind is as important as training the physical body. For example, long before you do your first physical triathlon, you can complete your first mental triathlon using visualization, which I call our mental videocassette system. Picture yourself at the starting line, ready to begin the swim. A phantom starter begins the 5-second countdown for your wave, and you're off—a videotape replay of a race that hasn't yet happened. Visualization is one of the ten mental positive training techniques, described in this chapter, that I use to prepare for the epic event.

The mind thrives on positive training, just like the pectoral muscle does, and, interestingly, training the intellect is not unlike training skeletal muscle. The mind flourishes because of mental challenges that include positive stress and adequate recovery. It deteriorates or deconditions from an absence of stimulation or stress, just like muscle tissue does. Training the mind is best accomplished by following the same process used in physical training: setting goals, planning, executing, measuring, and evaluating. When challenged by this training, the mind responds by the process of adaptation, and when there is adequate recovery, the result is a stronger mind. You can use mind-training techniques as part of your triathlon training regimen. Just like you train using techniques such as endurance, speed, and strength, conditioning the mental muscle involves the following ten techniques.

Visualization

When Brigitte McMahon broke the tape to win the first Olympic gold medal for triathlon in the Sydney 2000 Olympics, it was not only exciting because she raced the final 1K against Michellie Jones, the prerace favorite, but it was also anticlimactic. She had mentally replayed the race so often and was so familiar with the scene at the finish—breaking the tape—that it might have lacked a sense of drama for her. The terms "visualization," "imagining," and "mental rehearsal" can be used interchangeably. They all refer to the process of imagining the upcoming challenge, so you become more familiar and comfortable with it. Since your subconscious doesn't distinguish between real experience and imagined experience, you can write your own script with whatever outcome you desire. Your internal television screen can then play back your successful effort, removing doubt and replacing it with positive expectations.

Feedback

Feedback is necessary for monitoring and measuring your triathlon performance. Triathletes who use feedback stay connected with what they're doing and remain in control of where they're going.

There are two sources of feedback—internal and external. Internal feedback, also known as biofeedback, comes from within the body as kinesthetic awareness, or the awareness you gain from the sensory experiences of your muscles, joints, and tendons. External feedback comes from other participants, coaches, spectators, the environment, and the equipment you're using.

Using feedback to make adjustments to your skills or to your goals can result in an improvement in your triathlon experience. For example, at the starting line of the Gulf Coast Triathlon, a half Ironman distance, I watched each of the age-group waves start the swim as I waited my turn. Standing motionless, fully clothed in my wet suit, and waiting calmly, I looked at my heart rate monitor and the number on it was 145 bpm. This high heart rate is called an anticipatory heart rate and is the result of my emotional heart being excited and ready for the start. When my starting line heart rate number is 76, I usually perform poorly, because my emotional commitment to doing my best is absent.

Mind-body biofeedback is one of the most useful techniques for both training and racing. A good analogy of this technique is the thermostat of a furnace. You must pay attention to and monitor the emotional and physical stress you're experiencing and regulate your own thermostat. Ideally, you want to keep the mental and physical stress balanced, and you have the ability to enhance your performance at only a little extra psychic and physical energy cost. I call this pace-sensing ability your "perceptostat."

How do you know how high, hot, or hard to set your perceptostat in order to maximize your performance? The answer is that you need a large dose of experience to regulate your perceptostat. Training your mind and body together is a blend of art and science, and as you get to know your body and its responses, and as you gain athletic maturity, the easier it is to make informed decisions. If your feedback mechanisms are honed and you're training in harmony with your mental and physical self, then you should feel like your training is going like clockwork; it feels like it clicks, or is in synch. When this happens, living the life of a triathlete is at its best.

Focus

Sometimes even when you're monitoring your body and pacing yourself according to your plan, you can unexpectedly experience fatigue. If it happens during a race, then you have to find your inner grit, reach inside your mind, and find that pathway to your determination, no matter how narrow it may have become. This is extreme focus, or what I like to refer to as blind focus, when all your energy is fixed like a laser beam on the target.

I used blind focus at the end of one of my 100-mile endurance runs. It was the Western States 100 Miler, and for 20 hours and 7 minutes, I concentrated all my attention on the race. I felt like I was in a trance and that I was united with all existence through my mantra, the steady beat of my footsteps. I was in a state of total focus, an awareness of all conditions, people, feelings, and experiences. It was only by committing total focus to my ultra marathon performance that it was possible for me to achieve my goal to finish and do my best, and, in this case, also win the race setting a new course record.

Studies of top performers have measured the ability to concentrate during training and racing. These studies have discovered that winners *associate* (or totally stay in the present moment) during a race, whereas those who *disassociate* (or mentally go on autopilot) don't do as well. Those who strap on music as they train and drift off mentally during training and racing don't reach the same physical and mental conditioning levels. Winners are aware of nearly every move they make, every feeling and thought they have, especially when they're racing. Focusing on performance gets results.

Monkey Mind

The voices of doubt, defeat, and negativity lurk along your triathlon training and racing route. You have to be ready to deal with them, to provide answers as they play their mind games, because what might begin as a whisper in your ear may become a thunderous question, "Why are you doing this to yourself?" You might hear your inner voice support these negative thoughts and try to persuade you to slow down, quit, cancel, or simply not show up. How can you anticipate and counter such psychological deterioration?

First, focus on your goals; try to remember what first attracted you to triathlon. Second, when you draw up your training or racing plan, have incremental goals, so that as you achieve them, you feel the effects of kaizen—small, constant improvement. If you take the entire training period or a long race like the Ironman as one relentless continuum without multiple starting lines and finish lines, it can be an even tougher mental challenge. Having a series of shorter races that build up to your main race planned in your training schedule breaks your training into incremental goals.

In a race itself, for example, when I start, I focus just on the swim leg rather than on the entire race. My goal at the starting line is to get to the finish line of the swim, and as I approach that marker, I then begin to focus on T1, the swim-to-bike transition. I set these smaller goals throughout the race, which then becomes a succession of starts and finishes and transitions, none of them so distant that the voice of doubt can nibble at my resolve.

Anxiety

Stress from worrying results in a shift in our biochemistry. Our metabolism slows down and begins to hoard fat calories and preferentially burn glucose. But worry steals more than calories from our bodies—it also scrambles our brain. The physiological response of anxiety is tightening of the muscles, undue fatigue, and racing heart rates. Together, worry and anxiety are counterproductive. When I arrived in Hawaii for one of the many Ironmans that I've finished there, I saw one of my training partners, who had arrived early to acclimate before the race. He was a mess. He looked worn out and unkempt, with sunken eyes and a frazzled appearance. Knowing what a powerful triathlete he was, I wondered what effect the pre-event anxiety would have on his performance. He fizzled. The anxiety he felt while he hung around waiting for the day of the race had sapped his enthusiasm. Since he had nothing else to think about but the race, he worried it to pieces.

Relaxing during stressful times is a talent that comes from an ability within yourself to keep the fires roaring while simultaneously keeping your mind at ease. You must have confidence in yourself and your capabilities and be able to listen to your body and respond to its changes. When anxiety strikes, the body often goes into survival mode with numbness and disassociation. But if you use the technique of body scanning and staying focused on the moment, you'll have real-time biofeedback information to make changes and adjustments as you train and race. Practice this technique by scanning yourself—your physical as well as your emotional components—as you go from your feet to the top of your head. Do this to check up on what kind of effects the race has on your muscles, digestion, hydration, mental attitude, and so forth. You'll be amazed at the extra energy that's freed up for your performance when you replace the worry by relaxing into the performance.

Pain

There are different kinds of pain: There is mental pain, and there is physical discomfort. Your ability to tolerate and deal with pain is a large part of the metamorphosis of becoming an athlete. Some pain can be ignored, and some should be heeded. Some pain should even be welcomed. When you're training or racing at the highest training loads, you're guaranteed to experience some pain. Be sure that the fear of injury and its companion, pain, do not become elements that self-doubt uses to chisel away at your resolve.

There are ways of reducing pain, especially the low-grade physical discomfort. One way is to focus on the location of the pain, directing your mind to that point and working on some biofeedback ways of sending relief to that area. Another method is to apply hand pressure and hold the pressure for several minutes. Changing your biomechanics can reduce pain. For example, changing the angle of your swimming stroke or the gait of your running stride or shifting your weight on your bike seat can alleviate some pain.

Self-Awareness

It's easy to be confused about the difference between self-awareness and self-consciousness. They are actually two different states of mind—one is good for a triathlete and one is bad. When you're self-aware, you're not thinking about how you may look to others; you're simply processing information about how you are doing in the events that you're experiencing. Because triathletes continually monitor their body's responses, they have heightened self-awareness. Monitoring the body's response provides information about your current race state. From this information, the triathlete may process and make management decisions about adjustments to his or her racing plan to accommodate the condition and improve performance.

Self-consciousness, on the other hand, means you're looking at yourself from the outside as you perceive others may see you. You then judge yourself on what you think others may see, and it interferes with your performance. Whether you think others see you positively or negatively, it's still an outside focus and can flaw your performance.

To develop self-awareness, learn to listen to your body and feel what good training and racing days are. Visualization is an important mental skill for developing the ability to create your desired outcomes. Triathletes who have developed their self-awareness have an advantage over those who haven't. For example, you can decrease the tendency toward accidents or injuries by tuning in to your body and what it's experiencing. Some triathletes push themselves beyond normal pain and keep going when their bodies are screaming out for them to slow down or stop. To achieve your goal, staying within the comfort zone is essential, because within it, smart triathletes listen to and respond to their bodies.

Flow

Flow is one of the richest and most memorable experiences of sports performances. It's a state of consciousness in which the mind and body are in total synchronization and everything is effortless. In the early 1970s, Mihaly Csikszentmihalyi first explained the phenomenon and later, with Susan Jackson, wrote *Flow in Sports*. Flow is when you're performing perfectly, having a peak experience. Flow is variously described by those who have experienced it as "in the zone," "natural high," "in control," "floating," "on a roll," "switched on," "in the groove," "on auto," "everything clicks," and "flowing." It's the ideal performance state.

To achieve flow, you need to create a balance between the challenges that you face and the skills that you have to overcome the challenges. Anyone, from a fitness-oriented participant to an elite performer, can experience and enjoy flow and the mental rewards that come from this optimal experience.

Flow is achieved most often when you know what it is you're trying to achieve or what the goal is. By entering a triathlon or racing in one, you have to set your goal—whether to finish, do your best, or beat the clock—and your psychic energy is then harnessed to achieve that goal. That's one of the reasons triathlons are so much fun—they provide an opportunity for flow to occur.

Goal Mind-Set

When there is purpose in training, motivation naturally appears. By setting goals, all actions are directed and more focused in both the short and the long term. When you understand and know your intentions, you can best direct actions to achieve them and avoid the distractions that draw you away from them. A goal mind-set is one that uses motivation driven by desire rather than by defeat—the two greatest motivators in an athlete's life. Goals draw our actions toward them. Goals provide the positive push.

This goal mind-set is best created by knowing exactly what it is that you're trying to accomplish. Visualizing your outcome, or what first attracted you to triathlon, helps to create a goal mind-set. A goal is a blueprint, a finish banner with the words on it that you yourself write about what you want to achieve.

To be successful, set goals that require a reach and are higher than what you're currently doing. To achieve them, you need to draw out the blueprint, hone the required skills, and use all your resources to achieve them—especially the development of your physical and mental muscles. The best way to achieve a goal mind-set is to know where you're going. Without goals, or when goals are not realistic or valued, there is little motivation for training. In the absence of motivation, there is little energy or challenge. And if motivation is low, emotions often turn toward anxiety or worry, and training is usually compromised. Quite simply, setting your mind to achieve your goals is the building block of motivation.

Emotional Mind

Connecting the two hearts—the emotional heart and the physical heart—is vital to success in most aspects of our lives. The emotional heart is responsible for the positive feelings of passion, joy, love, confidence, hope, and happiness. It is also in control of the negative feelings of fear, anger, depression, anxiety, panic, and unhappiness. The physical heart is the cardiac pump. It distributes oxygen-rich blood to all corners of the body every minute of our lives.

When the mental and the physical muscles are simultaneously fit, then you can achieve maximum productivity, health, and happiness. Table 18.1 shows a working model using five different

Table 18.1

Emotional Heart Zones

Zone Number	Emotional Zones	Zone Description	Energy or Stress	Zone Benefit
Zone 5	Red Zone	Out of control, frantic, total panic, disconnected, emergency, stat	Extremely stressful	Toxic
Zone 4	Distress Zone	Worried, anxious, angry, scattered, fearful, reactive	Stressful	Cautious alert
Zone 3	Performance Zone	Focused, in the flow, positive stress, fulfillment, completion	Energy giving	Achievement
Zone 2	Productive Zone	High concentration, effective, energetic, prolific	Energy giving	Results
Zone 1	Safe Zone	Meditative, relaxed, affirming, regenerative, comfortable, compassionate, peaceful	Energy giving	Energizing

heart zones to achieve a positive emotional and physical balance in sports and life.

Zone 1 is the Safe Zone. The safe zone gives us energy. It is where we go to recharge our batteries, to calm ourselves, to get peaceful, to refocus our energy. The safe zone is very personal, and it is important for you to design your own safe place.

Zone 2 is the Productive Zone. The productive zone is a range of feelings in which you may spend much of your time at home, work, or play. In this zone, you are getting things done and feeling pretty good. You are relatively peaceful and focused, going about your day-to-day responsibilities. In zone 2, you have access to both your emotions and your thoughts.

Zone 3 is the Performance Zone. The performance zone has all the features of zone 2 except that it's characterized by greater focus, concentration, positive intensity, and accomplishment. You are probably in zone 3 when you do something you really love, whether it's work, play, or relationships. You reach flow best when you're working in zone 3.

Zone 4 is the Distress Zone. Zone 4 drains us of energy. The distress zone is a state where the bad stuff starts to happen. It is characterized by feelings of fear, worry, anger, anxiety, depression, guilt, and helplessness. This is where the stress response is triggered and physiological changes begin to affect heart rate, blood chemistry, and activity in all the cells and organs within the body. The ability to think clearly declines, and the emotions begin to take over. In zone 4, we become much less productive in our work and much more destructive in our relationships.

Zone 5 is the Red Zone. The red zone is a place you never want to go. This is out-of-control behavior, raw emotion with no rational thought. It is characterized by aggression, violence, and hysteria. This is where abusive and destructive behavior happens. It is highly toxic to the person in zone 5, as well as to anyone else nearby.

These five zones represent a different emotional and physical moment, time, and experience. To fully use the emotional heart zones systems requires an individual to develop four abilities: emotional flexibility, emotional strength, emotional responsiveness, and emotional resiliency. When this is accomplished, the mental and physical muscles are at a state of peak performance.

Once you start to use the ten keys regularly to train the mental muscle, the opportunity to achieve your fitness and sports goals appears. The combination of these ten keys leads to living the life of a triathlete. For many, this is a transformational process that takes them from a low-energy, stressful, chaotic pattern into a high-energy, satisfying, and joyful way of living.

Before I sold a company that I cofounded, Fleet Feet Sports, I met with several leaders in the Japanese sports business community who traveled to our offices in California to buy the rights to our retail athletic footwear franchises for Japan. During that meeting, I asked why they wanted to import our footwear stores to Japan. The president of the company answered that it was a cultural imperative within Japan to transform the country through a process called "watch, do, be."

I was confused. This expression was unfamiliar to me, and I asked for an explanation. He said that, historically, the Japanese people *watched* sports—they didn't participate. Over the years, with the growth of recreational and fitness sports activities, Japanese society slowly developed into more of a participatory sports culture. Ultimately, what Japanese society wanted and what they wanted to buy from Fleet Feet was a state of being. In this state, all people would have a lifestyle in which fitness and health would be part of their everyday life, and therefore they would have evolved to the highest level of being. All people would experience flow.

chapter 19

your first triathlon race

Some of you may never enter a triathlon—you may be cross training for fitness, not for the finish clock. Or maybe you're reading this book because your family member or friend is training for a triathlon. If so, you can skip forward to the next chapter, if you'd like. But possibly, if you read this chapter, it might change your outlook on the subject—it might make you think, "Well, I suppose, maybe it just might be worth it to train for and enter a race."

I hope you do.

Racing for me is like the topping on the dessert of fitness—it's the sweetest part.

Choose a Triathlon

Just because you enter a race doesn't mean that you have to *race* it. Racers can give it all in order to achieve peak performances. Or you can, if you choose, use racing as a learning experience. Even now, I occasionally train through races, entering them for the fun, for training, and for camaraderie, but not to compete.

Today there are hundreds of triathlons in the United States to choose from. Look for them in the calendar sections of *Triathlete* magazine, *Inside Triathlon,* the USA Triathlon Web site or newsletter, your local newspapers, or on the bulletin boards of your local triathlon club or tri or sports shops. After you've completed a few triathlons, the races will find you—entry blanks will appear in your mailbox.

Sprint Distance

You may want to start with a sprint distance event. The race could be sanctioned by USA Triathlon, which means that you'll have

Table 19.1

Triathlon Distances Table

	Swimming		Biking		Running	
	km	**mi**	**km**	**mi**	**km**	**mi**
Junior Youth (7–10 years old)						
	0.1	0.06	5	3.10	1	0.62
Senior Youth (11–14 years old)						
	0.2	0.12	12	7.45	3	1.86
Short/Sprint Distance						
	0.3–1	0.24–0.62	8–25	5–15.5	1.5–5	1–3
International Distance						
	1–2	0.62–1.24	25–50	15.5–31	5–10	3.1–6.2
Olympic Distance						
	1.5	0.93	40	24.86	10	6.21
Long Distance						
	4	2.48	50–100	31–62	10–30	6.2–19
Ultra Distance						
	3.2+	2+	100+	62+	30+	19+
Ironman						
	3.8	2.4	180.2	112	42.195	26.2
Hyperman *						
	11.4	7.2	540.6	336	126.585	78.6
Decatriathlon **						
	38	24	1802	1120	421.95	262

km = kilometers / mi = miles

* Not an official distance, it is three times the Ironman distance in three days

** Not an official distance, it is ten times the Ironman distance to be completed in maximum eighteen days.

From www.Runtheplanet.com; Copyright © by Run The Planet Inc. Seattle (United States of America).

to become a member (it's a good idea to do so anyway). The sanction means that the race organizers have completed the necessary paperwork required by the national governing body, and while it's not necessarily a guarantee of quality, it's an effort in that direction.

Or the race could be a Tri for Fun event. These are low-key, low-competition events designed for low-stress enjoyment. Tri for

Funs may have no prizes, no fancy timing systems, no finish line food or hoopla. But there's also no pressure on you to have high-tech gear or to excel. Tri for Fun races are short, local events, so the hotshots probably won't appear. These races can be any variety of distances, depending on the terrain at hand.

One of the women who works with me decided to initiate herself into the sport at a Tri for Fun. At the second transition, she was putting on her running shoes and a fellow worker and more experienced triathlete came up to her and said, "Julie, how can you be through already? I only just finished myself." Julie laughed, saying in return, "I'm in the transition. I haven't started the run yet—that's how much you beat me by." Undaunted, Julie finished the event at her own pace and had a lot of fun.

TRAINING FOR THE SPRINT DISTANCE If you're selecting THE race for you this season and it's a sprint, that's cool. And rather than go into every training principle on the laundry list for a sprint triathlon, focus on the principle that gets top five billing: training specificity. In my book *The Heart Rate Monitor Book for Outdoor and Indoor Cyclists,* the Training Triad—specificity, overload adaptation, and threshold training—are thoroughly explained. The principle of specificity for triathletes is defined as "working in only the specific activity or event in which you plan to perform." That is to say, specifically train for the specifics of the event.

Sprint distance triathlons are what their name implies—short. Training for short distances is different from training for ultra distances, primarily because they depend on your training the anaerobic and the aerobic energy pathways to utilize a blend of fuels to power you to your finish. In addition, training to finish is different if your goal is to train for peak performance.

Take the Danskin Triathlon event (½-mile swim/12-mile bike/3.1-mile run) as an example. When cross-training for the Danskin to finish, your training volume can be relatively low, as little as 3 hours per week of low intensity, or zone 1 to zone 3 intensity. If you cross-train to win your age division at the Danskin Triathlon, you need to increase the volume (frequency and distance), as well as train at higher intensities to achieve that goal. Competitive triathletes at the sprint distance train for more than 3 hours a week and include zone 4 and zone 5.

Olympic/International Distance

A longer-distance triathlon that's becoming quite popular is the Olympic or International Distance triathlon. Here's what Joanna Zeiger, a Ph.D. in genetic epidemiology and a new professional triathlete, has to say:

> The Olympic triathlon distance, 1.5 kilometer swim, 40 kilometer bike, and 10 kilometer run, requires a combination of speed and endurance. You cannot spend too much time going all out, because most races last just over two hours. But there are many points in the race where your heart feels like it is going to pound out of your chest. In the Olympic format, the cycle portion is draft-legal, meaning competitors can ride in packs. The rider leading the pack exerts more energy than the riders in the back. The ideal situation is for all of the riders in the pack to rotate to the front so that there is not a single person doing most of the work. Many times this does not occur, and a few people get stuck dragging around the rest of the riders (this can be extremely frustrating). The draft-legal format is advantageous to weaker riders who are strong runners; they can rest during the cycle portion and then run very fast.
>
> While I prefer the non-drafting races as a true show of strength and ability, I have come to appreciate some of the benefits of the draft-legal format. For one thing, the draft-legal format is certainly exciting for the spectators. Also, since the ability of so many of the racers is comparable on the swim, often 20 or 30 people come out of the water at the same time, making it difficult to

> monitor a non-drafting course. Finally, the draft-legal format adds in the elements of skill and tactics, giving a new and different twist to racing. I would also argue that one should not totally neglect the bike portion in training. The stronger you are on the bike, the less the 40K will take out of you, and consequently the faster you can run.

TRAINING FOR OLYMPIC/INTERNATIONAL DISTANCE TRIATHLONS

Training principles provide a framework in which to wrap your training values to create your main beliefs about your individual training plan. Threshold training is one of the three principles of the training triad and is an important component to training smart for Olympic/international distance triathlons. The training triad model is represented in figure 19.1.

Training for the international distance range of distances (see figure 19.1) is more arduous because the distances are the power of two over the sprint distances. That is, the training distances, like the race distance, are twice as long as the sprint distances. For performance training, using the power of the distance training is a good way to set your weekly mileage and yardage. Set your weekly volume as a multiplier of the race distances and increase your distances until you reach the time constraints that you have in your weekly training time. As your training load increases using the power of the distance, multiply the swim, bike, and run race distances by a power of three. After several weeks, use the power of four as your weekly volume.

Figure 19.1

Training Triad Model

Threshold training, another corner in the Training Triad, is a powerful training principle, because it calls for training at the heart rate point that divides aerobic from anaerobic metabolism. It's a principle of training "at, about, and around" your anaerobic threshold. This is your crossover exercise intensity—when you pass over the point where there is sufficient oxygen, aerobic energy, to maintain the stress level of the workout.

Adding threshold training to your workouts results in huge increases in endurance and speed by raising your anaerobic threshold. It also results in the expansion of your fat-burning range so you become a better and more efficient fat-burning individual.

Even Longer-Distance Triathlons

It's a choice to do longer triathlons. Doing well at a shorter distance doesn't mean that one day you'll be looking at the starting line of an Ironman, a Vineman, a Tinman, or an Ultraman. Triathlon has changed from its early beginnings in the 1970s and 1980s such that you can be a top athlete specializing in a given distance. It's foolish to think that the athlete doing sprint distances is less capable than the athlete participating in endurance distance events. Sometimes the distance is a matter of choice, having to do with lifestyle. But do keep an open mind—all sorts of people and athletes finish a long course triathlon, from the physically challenged to the Clydesdale/Athena class participant. For more information about these categories, check out www.challengedathletes.org and www.teamclydesdale.com.

Of course, if your only success has been in entering the same race or distance year after year so you can spank all the local age-group talent, maybe it's time to get another perspective. Enter a longer-distance triathlon, even as a fun event. Who knows, you might just expand your horizon a bit. And with 40 percent of the Ironman participants toeing the line for their first Ironman, the probability is that you, too, will do an Ironman.

Training for Endurance or Ultra Distance Triathlons

The extra long races, the really, really big distance races like the Ultraman and the Ironman, require a special commitment, focus, and lifestyle commitment. Training for them is not for everyone. Training for them is only for those who have the aerobic capacity, the biomechanics, and the ability to juggle enormous time management stresses. The average finisher, not age-group competitor, trains for 15 to 20 hours per week just to finish the Ironman still standing.

Designing an endurance triathlon training program that fits into your life requires the overload adaptation principle of the Training Triad. If you overload a muscle group, it responds first by getting tired or fatigued. When allowed to rest and regenerate, the muscle responds by adapting to this new load. Through this adaptation process, muscle groups improve their strength and endurance capacities. You get fitter and can perform at this new training level more efficiently. The key to the overload adaptation mechanism is that there is adequate time in the positive stress recovery cycle for regeneration. That is, time needs to be built into the training program for low-intensity, low-load training days.

I love the long races—whether it's the Race Across America, the 100-mile Iditashoe snowshoe race, the Eco Challenge, or the Ironman triathlons. But I can absolutely say they're not for everyone. And if you're the type who loves the challenge, I have one word of advice for you: Build up to them; don't jump into them. Starting with an Ironman triathlon as your first is foolish. Instead, develop a long-range training strategy so that you arrive at the starting line with years of training, experience, and savvy.

Famous Races You Can Do

I think you'll be hooked on the sport of triathlon after your first event, and you might want to try one of the more famous ones. Here are the details.

Danskin Women's Triathlon Series

Since 1990, the Danskin Women's Triathlon Series, the largest and longest running series in multisport history, has created the opportunity for more than 70,000 women to cross the finish line of a sprint triathlon. More than half the Danskin triathlon finishers are doing their first triathlon or even first athletic event ever. More important, each Danskin triathlon hosts Team Survivor, a fitness opportunity for women in all stages of treatment, recovery, and survivorship of cancer to train for and participate in their first triathlon in a supportive environment.

Many professional triathletes, including Jennifer Gutierrez and Michellie Jones, raced in the Danskin Women's Triathlon Series as a rite of passage. The Danskin Women's Triathlon Series is one of the driving forces in the involvement of women in the sport of triathlon. If you're female, don't miss this event. The Danskin is the most inspiring, fulfilling experience you can have in your triathlete life.

Wildflower (200 Miles South of San Francisco)

You have to camp. It's a co-ed event held at San Antonio Lake in Monterey County, California, in May. But it sells out in January. The scenery is beautiful. With bands and festivals and camping, it's all that an outdoor multisport event should be.

Although Wildflower is in its nineteenth year, the 4-hour mark has yet to be crossed in the long course, which is a measure of the

My Favorite Race and Why: Wildflower

It has a festival atmosphere, a challenging race course, beautiful scenery, and awesome race organization. It is such a treat to race on Saturday, and then have an early morning church service, overlooking the lake and worshiping with fellow triathletes on Sunday. Of course, when you win a race, it makes it a favorite, but the icing on the cake was the Sunday morning church service.

—Barb Linquist

course's difficulty. The 1.2-mile swim, 56-mile bike, and 13.1-mile run are some of the most challenging course segments around. There's a 1-mile hill on the bike right at the start, and then comes Nasty Grade, a 5-mile, 1,000-foot hill. With 60 percent of the run on backcountry trails, the Wildflower tests the skills of the professional, elite, age-group triathlete, and first-time long-course competitor alike. It's a very difficult Half Ironman.

A unique feature of the Wildflower is the Triathlon Club Team Competition, in which age-group triathletes from club teams compete for club team points and a team title. Triathlon club team members receive points for completing the course, for finishing in the top ten overall, and for finishing in the top ten in their age group.

In addition, the Wildflower has an Olympic Distance Triathlon, with an amateur age group and a relay team event. This world-class course includes a 1.5K open water swim, a 40K extremely hilly bike course, and a brutal 10K run course. This race

The Toughest Half Ironman

After my first Ironman Triathlon in Kona, Hawaii, circa 1980, I received a phone call from Dave Lewis, the Fleet Feet retail storeowner from Salinas, California. Terry Davis, the current owner of the Wildflower Triathlon and then an employee of the park services, had asked Dave to create an event that would bring in revenue for the park. Terry asked Dave, who asked Sally, "Would athletes from all over come to do a triathlon in Lake San Antonio?"

I drove down to Salinas and designed the course with the comment to both of them, "The triathletes will only come to the middle of nowhere–Lake San Antonio?–if you make this course hard enough."

It's a hard course. Thousands now race there, and after twenty-odd years, the course is still hard enough.

–Sally Edwards

has been selected to host the USA Triathlon National Collegiate Championships several times. This USA Triathlon national event features more than thirty of the top college triathlon teams from all over the country.

If you like more wilderness in your racing, the Mountain Bike Triathlon portion of the Wildflower is a sprint distance event with a 0.25-mile swim, a 10-mile bicycle course (mountain bikes only), and a short 2-mile run. Age groups begin at 8 and under and continue to 70+.

Mrs. T's

Held in August, Mrs. T's Chicago Triathlon is billed as the world's largest triathlon. They plan three days of racing, with individual and relay team competition at the junior, supersprint, sprint, and international (Olympic) distances. They usually have around 6,500 adults and 700 kids participate.

Mrs. T's defines the distances for 2001 as follows:

> Sprint distance triathlon (for age group): 0.75K swim, 22K bike, 5K run
>
> International distance triathlon (for age group, pro and relay team) 1.5K swim, 40K bike, 10K run

There's $40,000 in prize money and a kid's triathlon for the 7–14 age groupers. An interesting distinction is made for mountain bikes. Mountain bike competition is included in the sprint division of the Mrs. T's. Tires must be at least 1.625 inches wide, but you're eligible for a special category, and prizes go to the top three men and the top three women overall. Let's hope you get to ride slicks.

Ironman (Various Locations Around the World)

In 1998, the Ironman Hawaii celebrated its twenty-year anniversary. Today, the Ironman has grown to a large franchise of races, each with qualifying spots for the Ironman Hawaii, the "world championship," as it's now billed. Actually, some of the other race courses are tougher for a variety of reasons, and at least one, Ironman Florida, is scheduled after the championship. But reality is not what the Ironman is all about. Anyone who hears the

The Original Mrs. T's, aka USTS Chicago—1983

The first thing you must realize is that the race was dead.

The United States Triathlon Series went from five races in 1982 to ten races in 1983, but we had overreached in Chicago. Jan Caille and his partners had tried valiantly to get the permits, but we couldn't even get a call answered, let alone a meeting to discuss proposed routes for the course. As far as the city was concerned, we were a bunch of crazy nobodies asking to shut down Chicago for a freak show.

With four weeks left, no course, and no volunteers, we decided to cancel the race. Almost immediately, we got a call from an athlete, a red-headed lawyer, who had trained during all that miserable Midwest winter to compete in the event. We explained the situation, but he wouldn't accept our excuses. "No way you're canceling that race. You wait right there, and I'll call you back." Uh-oh. Mad lawyer, paid money, trained hard. Not good.

After a short while, he called us back and gave us a number and a name. We called. It was the mayor's office. They knew who we were. We got a meeting the next day. They knew what we wanted, and they gave us everything we asked for, even though they still thought we were crazy.

In its second year, the race was the world's biggest and still is, in its eighteenth year with 5,000 athletes. There's an indescribable thrill about racing in any downtown, but especially downtown Chicago. Chicago taught us two great lessons in 1983: You ain't nobody until you're somebody; and one of the best uses for a city is as a playground.

It's a great race. Thank you, red-headed lawyer. Thank you, Jan Caille. Thank you, Chicago.

—Jim Curl

word "triathlon" thinks Ironman, and everyone who has completed a triathlon wonders if someday they might train to complete the Ironman distance. Or at least be a volunteer.

If you're interested in the history of the Ironman Hawaii, Mike Plant has the corner on the market in his classic *Iron Will: The Triathlete's Ultimate Challenge*. Read it, as they say, and weep. The book will give you everything the televised coverage doesn't. Although many of the athletes to whom he refers are now retired, the equal treatment he gives to both men and women competitors as well as the age-group athlete makes *Iron Will* stand the test of time. It's a good clue as to why everyone who has ever done an Ironman lists it as their favorite race.

Here's what the current competitors have to say about Ironman:

SALLY EDWARDS In 1980, a friend posed the following question to me: "Sally, why don't you do the Ironman?" I was 32 years old, growing an entrepreneurial business, and racing in ultramarathons of 50 to 100 miles. I didn't own a bike. I hadn't been swimming in years. It seemed too hard, too long, and would take me away from my love of running. After crunching the dimensions of the event, I passed through a convergence of thresholds—I was ready for a change. I entered. I trained with what little I knew about the event and arrived at the starting line. Here's a brief account of that experience.

After swimming 2.4 miles, I found it difficult to walk up the ramp without tottering. This was 1981, my first Ironman triathlon. Between the ramp and the finish line remained a 112-mile bicycle race and a 26.2-mile run. But I felt optimistic; I knew I would finish the race.

Of the 100-plus bicycles that had been aligned in perfect order in the swim-to-bike transition area, only a few were still standing—the bike storage area was virtually deserted. I was almost in last place. But assessing the situation and knowing that opportunities in life often disguise themselves as problems, I vowed to pass as many of my competitors as possible.

Event	Web site	Location	Hawaii slots
Ironman Florida	www.ironmanflorida.com	Panama City Beach	100
Ironman Malaysia	www.ironmanlangkawi .com.my	Langkawi Island	30
Ironman New Zealand	www.ironman.co.nz	Lake Taupo	70
Ironman South Africa	www.ironmanafrica.com	Cape Town	18
Ironman Australia	www.ironmanoz.com	Forster/Tuncurry	100
Ironman California	www.ironmancalifornia .com	Oceanside	100
Ironman Lanzarote	www.ironmanlanzarote .com	Lanzarote, Canary Islands	60
Ironman Brazil	mailto:dmadruga@ism .com.br	Florianopolis	45
Ironman Asia	www.ironmanasia.com	Jeju Island, South Korea	100
Ironman Austria	www.happynet.at /ironman	Klagenfurt	35
Ironman Japan	www.ironmanjapan.com	Goto, Nagasaki	30
Ironman USA Lake Placid	www.ironmanusa.com	Lake Placid, New York	100
Ironman Switzerland	www.ironman.ch	Zurich	80
Ironman Canada	www.ironman.ca	Penticton, BC	130
Ironman World Championship	www.ironmanlive.com	Kona, Hawaii	

By the end of the 112-mile bike race, I had moved forward a hundred places and my confidence had grown in proportion to my progress. As I started the marathon, I was the tenth-place woman, and I knew I would pass most of the runners ahead. To know, in that sense, was an act of faith. It was a feeling rather than a proven fact. I believed my positive feelings; my inner voice reinforced my optimism.

One at a time, I passed the runners ahead of me. I would imagine myself snagging a competitor and then reeling her in—catching one fish after another. There was, however, one fish I didn't catch—Linda Sweeney. Linda won first place that year. I finished second.

As I approached the finish line, the streets were crowded with jubilant spectators. Their personal passion for victory helped fuel those final steps, yet every triathlete knew that the race was a self-fulfilling prophecy. We knew before we started that we would finish—we were incurably afflicted with optimism. And we have come to realize that the finish line of any race is the start of yet another.

FRANK COKAN, M.D. (AGE GROUP 65–70) My favorite race was the Ironman Hawaii, of course. The poster says, "The Best in the World Meet Here." What is not to like? Media have blown it up a bit, so now even we're beginning to think it's some sort of miracle of human will and physical readiness.

The truth is that those who are prepared well enough and are not dying to win or dying to finish are having a very good time. What's more, the spectators are having a once-in-a-lifetime experience, which leads some into a better lifestyle.

SUE LATSHAW My favorite race is Ironman Germany. There are innumerable reasons for this vote, but the top two reasons take precedence. First, I'm "Super Sue" there! It's very inspiring to have 100,000 people make me a superhero for the day. I go really fast there in response to their urging. Secondly, Detlef Kuhnel, the race director, committed to presenting a fair and safe race for women. All the women start in the first wave, 20 minutes before the throngs of age-group men hit the water. There is little risk of a lopsided, gender-biased underwater boxing match, no good excuse for drafting on the bike, and the pro women can race head-to-head all day without losing each other in the crowds of age-group men.

DAVE MCGILLIVRAY My favorite race is the Hawaii Ironman. It was my very first triathlon, and of course the race that the sport is most associated with. The distances, the course, the elements, the history, the community support, and the organization are all reasons why it remains the most popular and prestigious triathlon in the world. Affectionately, to me, it's the Boston Marathon of the triathlon world.

When You Are Ready for More: Resources

Books

Iron Will: The Triathletes Ultimate Challenge by Mike Plant, Velo Press (1999).

Triathlon: A Personal History by Scott Tinley, Velo Press (1999).

Triathlon 2001 Directory by Katherine Williams, Katherine Williams and Sports Book Ltd. (2001).

Web Sites

Triathlonlive.com—weekly triathlon news and opinion reader

chapter 20

your triathlon community

If you come from an organized sports background, triathlon could seem fairly lonely. Triathlon is by nature a solitary sport. You swim alone, you run alone, and unless you have a tandem bicycle, you bike alone. Baseball requires you to have nine or ten players and basketball, five plus benchwarmers. In rowing, everyone pulls together at the same time, oar in the water, or the boat goes nowhere. But triathlon feels more like track and field events. Individuals either compete or make up a relay team for a particular event. If you were ever part of a team sport, triathlon can feel downright alien. In triathlon, it's everyone for him- or herself, but all of you are in it together.

There are many different ways to find help in your triathlon training. You can look for help in the sport that's your weakest, or as I prefer to say, the sport that you can improve on the most, or you can look for groups that are training for the same race you are. There are also clubs, online and live programs, camps, and coaches who can help you train for a triathlon. It all depends on what you need and, to some extent, how much you're willing to put into it in terms of time commitment, money, and soul.

Community Spirit

There's great camaraderie in the triathlon community. Triathletes support, train with, and encourage each other often. Quite possibly, this generous spirit comes from the reality that you can be the best prepared, most fit person at a race, but on the day of the race someone else might get to the finish ahead of you. Any number of factors—bike spills or flats, missed markers on the swim course, or a pulled hamstring or untied shoelace—can sideline anyone at any time. So why not grin and be cordial? It makes sense that competitors in triathlon have more of a colleague mentality than perhaps in any other sports. The triathlete community is still small enough that once you get hooked, you'll see a lot of the same people at all your local races.

Given the nature of triathlon, it's no wonder that the majority of professionals have been self-coached. They might bike, swim, or run with high-caliber athletes of single-sport fame, and that will help them in their sport-specific skills. If they need a push in one area, what better way to kick it in gear than to set up a workout with the fastest swimmers, bikers, or runners they know? The bulk of triathlon training, however, comes from the solitary run, the long bike ride, or the self-contained pool environment.

That's good news for the rest of us, because our busy lives don't adapt well to regular training time at the group workout. Kids get sick, work requires us to travel, and the weekend holds other events that take precedence over driving to the soccer field for league play. With triathlon, a long bike ride or run can be as convenient as your front driveway. There's as much time or as little time for training as you can arrange in your daily schedule. In triathlon, you have to watch out that you don't train too much, even if that sounds incredible, because the opportunities to train are everywhere, any place, and any time. And it gets into your bloodstream, because when the triathlon call of the wild sounds, it's for you.

Take, for example, the child home from school with the flu. You've missed work, but you haven't missed your chance for a track stand in front of the TV. Or put the wind trainer at the sideline of a kid's practice for their team sports. You have to travel for business? Those running shoes or goggles and a swimsuit don't take up much space in the carry-on bag. But how do you know when enough is enough or too little isn't going to get you where you want to go?

Coaching, Mentoring, and Camps

COACHING, OR HOW I STOPPED WORRYING AND LEARNED TO DO IT

There's ample opportunity for the average person to sandwich in triathlon training time. Since you've gone to a lot of trouble and effort to set aside the time, why not maximize your effort by signing up for some type of coaching? As triathlon matures, there will be more coaches certified by USA Triathlon available in your hometown. If you already live in a triathlon-oriented town, such as Seattle, San Diego, Austin, Orlando, or Chicago (the list is growing), you can get hooked into clubs that provide information on where to shop and what experts are in town. These clubs also maintain lists of triathlon resources. Coaching or joining a team or training program is a great idea for triathlon performance at any level. In making this educational investment, you protect your time spent in fitness. You can make more informed choices, work out a sensible goal for your lifestyle, and monitor your progress more closely with professional help.

There could also be local running clubs or masters swim clubs in which you can get some coaching in the different disciplines of triathlon. Groups like the Road Runners Club of America have branches all over the United States, and masters swim organizations exist in many towns and cities.

MENTORING: DOUBLE-CHECKING YOUR WORKOUTS Another option that may be less costly (but less consistent) than coaching is to find a mentor. Appropriate mentors are people who have just a tad bit more triathlon knowledge under their belt than you do. These people will have completed at least one triathlon and be interested in sharing their experience with you. Many of your triathlon plans and thoughts can be double-checked against a mentor. Mentors act as a sounding board for your concerns and build your confidence by merely talking with you. E-mail or phone calls with a mentor on a weekly or monthly basis can keep you moving toward the triathlon goal you've chosen. Unlike a coach who has the training and diagnostic tools to find and correct your training details and hopefully prescribe a solution, the mentor relationship contains a helpful quality of suggestions and a sympathetic ear.

You should be able to find a mentor through your local triathlon club, if there is one. Check your fitness club for others

The Five Basics of Triathlon Training

1. **Train to weakness.** It is easy, and tempting, to emphasize whatever it is you do best. But you will maximize your potential only if you concentrate on what you do least best. For example, Sheila Taormina entered the sport of triathlon from an elite swim background, but she spent most of her first couple of years concentrating on running and biking. The big payoff? She came in sixth at her first world championship, and sixth again at the 2000 Olympic Games.
2. **Race to strength.** This is the flip side of the coin. When the starter's gun sounds, you will perform best if you take advantage of your strengths, which means that as the primary race on your schedule approaches, your training should turn back toward your strengths.
3. **Understand the stress/rest principle of training.** Adaptation comes only if you understand and commit to both parts of the cycle. Rest without stress will not work, but neither will the reverse.
4. **Err on the side of undertraining.** Fresh and rested is a far better choice than stale or injured.
5. **Work toward being your own coach.** The best training plans depend entirely on how you react to each workout. Although an outside coach can ask how you feel, you are the one who really knows.

—Lew Kidder, founder of Triathlon Today, *which later became* Inside Triathlon, *now coaches top triathletes, including his wife, Karen McKeachie, who frequently wins the 40+ age group and was a pro for years.*

who are training for the same race or perhaps a program geared for triathlon training. You can also check online for mentors who aren't local. Many tri-focused Web sites have bulletin boards or other resources for finding people who can help you with training and questions. Check the Internet at www.mentormentee.org.

SPORTS CAMPS, OR HOW TO GET FIT ON YOUR VACATION If coaching sounds too much like a doctor's appointment and mentoring sounds too much like a good neighbor's conversation while hanging over the backyard fence, you may want to look at a sport-specific camp for your triathlon educational journey. Camps can be held over a day, a weekend, or a week. For triathlon, you'll want to look at the camp location so you can choose one that offers better opportunities for open water swimming, biking, and running than you have at your everyday disposal.

The training camp is a block of time you're setting aside for concentration on skills and workouts—why not try a fitness

Five Favorite Training Tips

1. **Change is good.** Every year add something different to your training in each of the three disciplines. I think the biggest improvements come with change as your body adapts to doing the same thing all the time.
2. **Have a friend videotape you swimming and running.** I think all of us know what a good runner and swimmer look like. Sometimes we think we are swimming like them, when we really aren't.
3. **Keep a logbook by your bed.** This way you can write in the day's training before you forget it.
4. **Have goal sets in each discipline.** Do these sets every three to four weeks so that you can see improvement.
5. **Don't just cross-train, cross-race.** It's fun to do a running race, bike race, or even an open water swim. Plus you can learn from doing a one-sport race, and you might meet new training partners.

—Barb Linquist

vacation? You'll meet others who are interested in the same things you are, learn new skills and improve your abilities, and gain some more enthusiasm for this triathlon lifestyle you're creating for yourself.

The Local Race Scene

Even if you live close to where you've always lived, you may have Planet Work blinders on when it comes to recreational activities. Many activities are still set up for the student. But there's a galaxy of opportunities waiting for you.

For now, set aside the obvious health club membership and swimming pool. With planning, you'll join these as you pursue a more active lifestyle. But where else can you get the juice on activities that will fit your time and ability?

Running Events

Running or walking a fun run 5K is one of the biggest eye-openers you'll have. Did you think that running events were only for fast runners? Nope, it's the social highlight of the week. First off, the sheer volume of events available is staggering. Road Runners Club of America estimates that there is one new marathon starting every month. Second, all sorts of people are participating. This is what you're likely to see at your first 5K: baby joggers with walkers or runners, very lean running club members, your neighbor who you never knew was a runner, people much more out of shape than you are talking about how many races they've done, high school track team members, your doctor, and lots of port-o-potties.

Look in the family features, home and community, or civic section of your newspaper to find listings of upcoming runs. Fun runs can be low-key events that stress participation, recreation, and enjoyment. Often, races are organized to benefit a charity or local organization, so not only do you get a great training day with lots of other people, but also part of your entry fee goes to benefit someone who needs it. After you do one run, you'll be on everyone's mailing list for more.

Running Shops

There are usually one or two retail stores that are very popular with runners in your area. Halt some runners as they begin their run and ask them where they buy their shoes. Go there and get race brochures and gear. Doing a 5K is great practice for the run segment of a sprint distance triathlon. You're a third of the way there!

Running Clubs

One of the most important aspects of running as a sport is the social interaction between runners. Running is fine on your own, but it's enjoyable to chat about your running goals and learn from those who are seeking to improve their performance. Some groups are primarily interested in physical fitness jogs, others in races. Group runs increase everyone's enthusiasm by creating a sense of fellowship. By running together, people can often run faster or longer than they would alone, so you might make some important breakthroughs in your training. In addition, overachievers can learn to stay within their limits and run at a reasonable pace and avoid injury. Membership fees for running clubs tend to be fairly low. If there isn't one in your area, why not start one?

Biking Events

These biking events are not the Tour de France or the time trial at your local velodrome. What you'll find is a chance to go many miles on your bike, at your pace, with organized food, water, and bathroom stops. There's even a sag wagon in most cases for some basic roadside repairs so you don't get stranded. Often, rides have a variety of routes that are 15, 30, or 50 miles long. They usually start and end at the same point. So if your training buddies can't go the distance that you can on a particular day, you can still arrange to meet them later. Many fit bikers use these organized events to push themselves on terrain they don't normally ride. Bike event organizers take special care to mark the route and to post signs warning traffic to watch for bicycles. If you're wondering how far you can go in a day, these types of bike events are low key, but they're set up for your endurance benchmarking pleasure.

Some rides travel between two cities, some ride all the way across a state or a country, some are camping oriented, and some just follow the secondary roads in your county. The rides give you an opportunity to spend a very long time with your equipment. Plus you can meet other bikers and enjoy the scenery.

Biking Shops

I've said earlier that bike shops are like auto mechanics—they're the resource for good maintenance, information, and new gear. You'll also find brochures about rides and races and maybe even repair classes so you can do the basic tune-ups yourself. Pick a bike shop that caters to or is staffed by triathletes so they'll know what you want. There are many kinds of bikers (recreational, racers, and triathletes), and not all shops can satisfy every type of customer.

Take the time to chat with your bike shop employees. There's a ton of gear produced each year, although the basic design of the bike hasn't changed in a hundred years. If you get a personal recommendation as to where you should plop down your Planet Work dough, so much the better.

Biking Clubs

They throw events, they give clinics, they stage protests on behalf of road safety for bicyclists, and they're all over the place. You can join city, state, national, international, and type of biking-specific clubs. They keep you informed on rides, routes, advocacy issues, and club events. If you're new to biking, this could be your ticket into the wide world of gear heads.

Swimming

Yes, Virginia, there are swimming events.

Not only are there masters swim teams that you can join after your days as an age-grouper (or to improve your swimming skills as an adult), but also these masters teams have swim meets. If you're so inclined, you can train for these meets and see (or return to) the world of competitive swimming from the inside.

There are also open water swim events cropping up all over the world. One of the more famous is the 65K (yes, you read that right) swim marathon in Venezuela known as Santa Fe, which takes more than 9 hours for the professionals to complete. Well, maybe you'll want to set a different goal for your first big swim event. After all, there are all kinds of events, from half-mile swims to lake swim relays.

Check at your local pool for information on these events and try asking any swimmers you meet if they can tell you about them. A half-mile open water swim doesn't need to be raced, any more than a 5K fun run does. But it could be your perfect opportunity to get in some safe open water practice without having the bike and the run immediately following to worry about.

The Web

Many fitness and recreation Web sites can search the world and find an event of any type in any city. Usually you can fill out an online entry form and pay by credit card. The event Web site might post course maps, start times, results, pictures, and phone numbers for more information. It's always fun to check out an event in an exotic location, like Maui or Disney World.

Event Web sites come and go. So rather than list a whole bunch of sites, I'll leave it up to you and your search engine. If you don't have a computer or access to the Internet, your library does. Help yourself and get the librarian to help you.

When You're Ready for More: Resources

Web Sites

Danskin Women's Triathlon: www.mentormentee.org

International Triathlon Union: www.triathlon.org

Road Runners Club of America: www.rrca.org

Slowtwitch: www.slowtwitch.com

Tri-Newbies Online: www.trinewbies.com

USA Triathlon: www.usatriathlon.org

chapter 21

WHO IS MY COMPETITION?

Now that you've read through this entire book of triathlons, I hope you know more than you did when you started. I've suggested tools and tests for basic fitness and encouraged you to get a heart rate monitor and to write a training plan. I've told you about racing, resources, and techniques. But after all that, how you view competition may keep you from enjoying all that the world of triathlon has to offer. Competition and the athletic mind-set are the last area we'll explore, because figuring out who your competition is really makes all the difference.

Find the Journey: Heading Down the Wrong Road

Beware the arrogant accounting system that measures us against the current social standards. Have you heard the sayings, "You can never be too rich or too thin," "Bigger is better," "To the victor go the spoils," "There is no second place," or even "Losing sucks"? Pithy sayings such as these echo how society defines our competitive lives. It measures us, points out our shortcomings, compares us to others, and is fundamentally a poor technique to egg us on to achieve more, build more, or buy more.

Sports talk in the media sounds a lot like those trite phrasings. Sports broadcasts are peppered with the win-lose accounts of athletic competitions. Spectators seem to love the face-off, so sportswriters and broadcasters draw out the combative aspects of any two players in a competition by talking about how many wins they had in tournament, what happened the last time they met, what injuries might figure into the match, and so on. This is a one-dimensional account of competition.

But you are a participant, a triathlete, not a spectator. When I watch sports news, I'd like to learn about the training plan of a professional sports figure contrasted with the training plan of another. I'd like to hear that one athlete ran six sets of stairs more than another one. Sadly, that's not the kind of information that can be understood or appreciated by the 90 percent of the world that doesn't view sports as more than simple competition between two players or teams.

In sports, as well as in other areas of society, we are fed information that fits the black-and-white system of win-lose. Everyone loves to think about winning. But competition can be about so much more.

The black-and-white view of competition is a difficult trap to escape. Although thinkers such as Stephen Covey are helping us to learn a new concept of team and competition, it is definitely slow going. Be careful that your internal ear isn't hearing the black-and-white summing up of your training and accomplishments.

Take a minute to write down every saying about competition that you've heard from parents, friends, or advertising. Chances are that many of the sayings are the ones with a "versus someone else" mentality, or the ones that try to put you in the conventional box, or the ones that, if you were on the downside of the quote, make you feel small or useless. Get a match and set these sayings on fire. You're now finished with arrogance, and you're ready for some reality.

Competition means doing something for yourself no matter what others might say.

Find the Joy: Unlearning What You May Have Learned

The Past

Shakespeare wrote that what is past is prologue, which means the past determines the present. Although this may be true in some instances (look at the conflicts around the world that continue to brew because of past animosities), we as individuals have many opportunities to be different in the future, despite our pasts. We do this by changing habits and making different choices so we do not relive our own past. Yet lessons learned from the past (like touching the hot stove with your finger) can serve us well.

Take stock of the lessons you think you've learned. What are the personal historical events that relate to the athlete in you? How did your fitness fit into your life at certain times? How does training bring back the past? If you were once a smoker, heavy drinker, or couch potato, does that mean you have to limit yourself to live like that today or tomorrow? The past has a powerful pull, and you'll have to choose, sometimes daily, to act as you will yourself to be, not as your past may dictate.

Competition means you can change your life, today, tomorrow, and the day after that.

Your Age Group

Another artificial standard that is sport specific is the concept of age group. When you look at race results, there's a block for either 10-year or 5-year increments. It's interesting that there's no categorization for how many kids you have, whether you're married, how many hours a week you train, how many years you've been entering races, or whether you have an elderly parent living at home or have a mortgage.

Some races are starting to have a weight categorization (self-selecting) of Athenas (women heavier than a certain weight) and Clydesdales (men heavier than a certain weight). You can choose to enter these divisions with the thought that if your body weight is sized thus and so, that puts you in a separate category to be ranked with others of that particular weight classification. This is common in sports such as wrestling, boxing, and rowing in which you find lightweight, featherweight, and heavyweight classifications.

But for the most part, you'll find the age classification to be the dominant ranking system. What this really means is that there's another artificial way to compare you with others. I've stopped counting the number of times I've been passed by older or younger folks in a race. And whenever I manage to pass someone else, you can bet that I'm way too dog tired to worry if they're in my age category or not.

"Age-grouper" is a slang term referring to people who consistently place in the top ten of their age category in an event. You may also hear about "MOPpers" and "BOPpers," which are slang for middle of the pack and back of the pack. We can use the age-group designation correctly when we're discussing how fit a person is by saying, "Do you now so and so? They're an age-grouper in triathlon in Illinois." That does suggest a certain level of racing and fitness. But for the most part, it's just another box you put yourself into. It's limited, it's arbitrary, and you won't find any lasting glory in being an age-group athlete.

A stranger can come to town, or a group of good athletes your age could sweep through that category, and what does it really mean? Show me an athlete who can remain fit and healthy for 10, 20, or 30 years with joyful racing—win, rank, or finish last. That's something to achieve.

If you measure your friendships, your wine, or your furniture in terms of age, that's perfectly normal. But if you define your athletic success as an amateur athlete in terms of age, you may find it hard to continue training when you're past your prime. Instead, focus on your own level of fitness and use a race as a measurement of your own ability. Be careful about buying into the age group or other rankings as the truest measure of your personal achievement.

Competition means finding health and accomplishment no matter what your age or size.

Fear Is the Monkey on Your Back

Many a struggle is begun before you get to a race. Some of these struggles have to do with the motivation to get out the door to train. Some are the struggles rooted in time and logistics. Many struggles are based in fear: fear of injury, failure, not finishing, being seen as comical, and all those other fill-in-the-blank fears.

There are different ways of looking at fear. It could be a feeling of disquiet or apprehension caused by the presence or imminence of danger. Feelings govern the way we act, either consciously or subconsciously, so they're not to be brushed aside. Still, another way to look at fear is the least used definition of the word, namely "extreme reverence or awe, as toward a supreme power." I like to think of the fear of a swim start as awe toward the realities of nature. That's water, and I'm a land-based mammal. Water, fire, air, and earth are the four elements of nature, so I'm going up against one of the Big Four.

But are you really in the presence of danger? Is danger present at the swim start? Sure, it is. But a healthy respect for swimming skills and swimming practice can make those dangers go away for you. If you eliminate the dangers by training properly with appropriate amounts of skills, what is left is just awesome.

Competition means transforming your fear into the fire in your belly.

Yours Truly, a Note to Me

NEGATIVE SELF-TALK "You can't do that. You're too fat. You're too short. You'll never finish. You're just showing off. Everyone will laugh at you. You run like a dork. You'll ruin your knees. It's too hard. It's too far. It's too steep. You'll come in last. You don't need this. You can do it next time."

How many times have you wanted to do something and that little voice tells you that you can't? All of us have that demon of self-doubt, the ego trying to stop us from doing new things because we might not be good at them. And that inactivity can lead to self-neglect. If you don't think you can do anything, why bother to take care of yourself at all? In fairly short order, even getting out of bed can seem like a waste of time. Your mind is a powerful weapon that you can use either to make things happen or to suck you down into a negative spiral.

Certainly no one is going to be a happy-go-lucky sort in the face of obvious disaster. But negative self-talk is not about anything really bad like death or disaster. It's just a defense mechanism you become accustomed to using so you can avoid the possibility

Five Motivational Tips That Work for Me

1. **Stop negative thinking.** For example, say, "Oh, shut up!" to yourself if the negative voice starts talking. (I use this most often to the internal voice that screams out warnings of imminent disaster.)
2. **There is power in action when faced with obstacles.** You gain a voice that says, "If you do this, you will be tougher than anyone else on the starting line and have earned the right to win."
3. **For pros, money motivates.** Before embarking on the last weeks of Ironman training, I might say to myself, "In six weeks, you may drink Hefeweissen and eat German chocolate because you will have earned plenty of deutsch marks to pay for them. If you consume those things today, however, you will be forced to retire to the life of a 40-hour-per-week drone."
4. **Joy flows from speed. Speed flows from joy.** Train and live to open the channels to joy.
5. **Expect success.** Define success by small steps that each redefines the endpoint. Failed steps define new steps to success.

–Sue Latshaw

of failure. If you always listen to the negative statements, you'll miss many wonderful opportunities. This is especially true for sports, because it's a game, it's about playing. True competition is not necessarily winning the race but rather showing up in the first place, ready to go.

You can do it. You're ready. You'll look great. You'll feel strong. You're fit. Everyone will be excited for you at the finish line. You'll have fun.

Competition means telling yourself to find the fun in training and racing.

How to Reframe and Get a Handle on Competition

Competition means doing something for you no matter what others might say.

Competition means you can change your life, today, tomorrow, and the day after that.

Competition means finding health and accomplishment no matter what your age or size.

Competition means transforming your fear into the fire in your belly.

Competition means telling yourself to find the fun in training and racing.

You are your best rival. Focus on yourself and your results, because it's all about you. Every day you have to make the choices that will lead you to a successful triathlon lifestyle. Spend some time (why not, you know you have some) considering where you're allowing your competitive juices to flow. If it's competitive energy directed at the past, your peer group, your fears, or your ego, then you're getting in your own way.

The Clock

Competition is a positive force that can be harnessed when you look at it as a test of your skill or ability. That skill comes from the daily motivation to live a balanced lifestyle, with fun-filled physical activity. The clock is your friend in the competition that life and racing bring to you. What works in the long run is to accept that your true competition is time, represented by the 24 hours in a day, or your personal best split times, or finishing times in a triathlon. You only have a certain amount of time in your life. You don't even truly know how much time you have. So use your time wisely. And as a tool to measure how competitive you are in your performance, time has no equal.

Competition in your life means setting aside slots of time for yourself and your training. The clock will allow you to be as competitive as you want to be. It's a challenge to reframe your relationship with time and how you choose to spend it—a challenge that I hope you want to meet. Competition for your time for work, family, training, sleep, and leisure is fierce. You can have many complicated negotiations in any given day to make the balance pay off for your triathlon training. We all have them.

In a race, competition is much simpler. Inner competition is less fragmented as you live in the moment of the race and are too busy going fast to worry about whether the trash got out or the dog got fed. Your competitive spirit holds you to the specific task at hand: Watch the clock and enjoy the race. You maximize every second in a race by focusing on where you are and what you're doing. It's not wrong to want to win; it's only a problem if you let that desire to win interfere with your enjoyment.

Take some of that concentration and bring it back to your lifestyle clock.

Where You Spend Your Energy and Your Thoughts

Visualize all the bad things that can happen in a race, then visualize solutions. Imagine these negative things leaving your reality, and then visualize your success. Visualize a great training ride. Visualize making a daily commitment to the triathlon lifestyle. Visualize your race from start to finish. Visualize your happiness during the race, and then visualize your success at the end. You can make it happen.

If you think you have time to train for a triathlon, then you will. If you think you have the energy to train for a triathlon, then you will. I believe you can train well, have a balanced life full of health and fitness like so many of the people I've introduced you to, and succeed.

Let the games begin.

appendix

Heart Zone Training Points Planning Table

BASE

Minutes	Zone 1 30%	Zone 2 70%	Zone 3 0%	Zone 4 0%	Zone 5 0%	HZT Points
10	3	7	0	0	0	17
15	4	11	0	0	0	26
20	6	14	0	0	0	34
25	7	18	0	0	0	43
30	9	21	0	0	0	51
35	10	25	0	0	0	60
40	12	28	0	0	0	68
45	13	32	0	0	0	77
50	15	35	0	0	0	85
55	16	39	0	0	0	94
60	18	42	0	0	0	102
65	19	46	0	0	0	111
70	21	49	0	0	0	119
75	22	53	0	0	0	128
80	24	56	0	0	0	136
85	25	60	0	0	0	145
90	27	63	0	0	0	153
95	28	67	0	0	0	162
100	30	70	0	0	0	170
105	31	74	0	0	0	179
110	33	77	0	0	0	187
115	34	81	0	0	0	196
120	36	84	0	0	0	204
125	37	88	0	0	0	213
130	39	91	0	0	0	221
135	40	95	0	0	0	230
140	42	98	0	0	0	238
145	43	102	0	0	0	247
150	45	105	0	0	0	255
155	46	109	0	0	0	264
160	48	112	0	0	0	272
165	49	116	0	0	0	281
170	51	119	0	0	0	289
175	52	123	0	0	0	298

ENDURANCE

Minutes	Zone 1	Zone 2	Zone 3	Zone 4	Zone 5	HZT Points
	10%	40%	50%	0%	0%	
10	1	4	5	0	0	24
15	1	6	8	0	0	37
20	2	8	10	0	0	48
25	2	10	13	0	0	61
30	3	12	15	0	0	72
35	3	14	18	0	0	85
40	4	16	20	0	0	96
45	4	18	23	0	0	109
50	5	20	25	0	0	120
55	5	22	28	0	0	133
60	6	24	30	0	0	144
65	6	26	33	0	0	157
70	7	28	35	0	0	168
75	7	30	38	0	0	181
80	8	32	40	0	0	192
85	8	34	43	0	0	205
90	9	36	45	0	0	216
95	9	38	48	0	0	229
100	10	40	50	0	0	240
105	10	42	53	0	0	253
110	11	44	55	0	0	264
115	11	46	58	0	0	277
120	12	48	60	0	0	288
125	12	50	63	0	0	301
130	13	52	65	0	0	312
135	13	54	68	0	0	325
140	14	56	70	0	0	336
145	14	58	73	0	0	349
150	15	60	75	0	0	360
155	15	62	78	0	0	373
160	16	64	80	0	0	384
165	16	66	83	0	0	397
170	17	68	85	0	0	408
175	17	70	88	0	0	421

STRENGTH

Minutes	Zone 1	Zone 2	Zone 3	Zone 4	Zone 5	HZT Points
	10%	10%	70%	10%	0%	
10	1	1	7	1	0	28
15	1	2	10	2	0	43
20	2	2	14	2	0	56
25	2	3	17	3	0	71
30	3	3	21	3	0	84
35	3	4	24	4	0	99
40	4	4	28	4	0	112
45	4	5	31	5	0	127
50	5	5	35	5	0	140
55	5	6	38	6	0	155
60	6	6	42	6	0	168
65	6	7	45	7	0	183
70	7	7	49	7	0	196
75	7	8	52	8	0	211
80	8	8	56	8	0	224
85	8	9	59	9	0	239
90	9	9	63	9	0	252
95	9	10	66	10	0	267
100	10	10	70	10	0	280
105	10	11	73	11	0	295
110	11	11	77	11	0	308
115	11	12	80	12	0	323
120	12	12	84	12	0	336
125	12	13	87	13	0	351
130	13	13	91	13	0	364
135	13	14	94	14	0	379
140	14	14	98	14	0	392
145	14	15	101	15	0	407
150	15	15	105	15	0	420
155	15	16	108	16	0	435
160	16	16	112	16	0	448
165	16	17	115	17	0	463
170	17	17	119	17	0	476
175	17	18	122	18	0	491

SPEED/INTERVAL

Minutes	Zone 1	Zone 2	Zone 3	Zone 4	Zone 5	HZT Points
	0%	20%	60%	10%	10%	
10	0	2	6	1	1	31
15	0	3	9	2	1	46
20	0	4	12	2	2	62
25	0	5	15	3	2	77
30	0	6	18	3	3	93
35	0	7	21	4	3	108
40	0	8	24	4	4	124
45	0	9	27	5	4	139
50	0	10	30	5	5	155
55	0	11	33	6	5	170
60	0	12	36	6	6	186
65	0	13	39	7	6	201
70	0	14	42	7	7	217
75	0	15	45	8	7	232
80	0	16	48	8	8	248
85	0	17	51	9	8	263
90	0	18	54	9	9	279
95	0	19	57	10	9	294
100	0	20	60	10	10	310
105	0	21	63	11	10	325
110	0	22	66	11	11	341
115	0	23	69	12	11	356
120	0	24	72	12	12	372
125	0	25	75	13	12	387
130	0	26	78	13	13	403
135	0	27	81	14	13	418
140	0	28	84	14	14	434
145	0	29	87	15	14	449
150	0	30	90	15	15	465
155	0	31	93	16	15	480
160	0	32	96	16	16	496
165	0	33	99	17	16	511
170	0	34	102	17	17	527
175	0	35	105	18	17	542

PEAK

Minutes	Zone 1	Zone 2	Zone 3	Zone 4	Zone 5	HZT Points
	0%	10%	60%	20%	10%	
10	0	1	6	2	1	33
15	0	2	9	3	1	48
20	0	2	12	4	2	66
25	0	3	15	5	2	81
30	0	3	18	6	3	99
35	0	4	21	7	3	114
40	0	4	24	8	4	132
45	0	5	27	9	4	147
50	0	5	30	10	5	165
55	0	6	33	11	5	180
60	0	6	36	12	6	198
65	0	7	39	13	6	213
70	0	7	42	14	7	231
75	0	8	45	15	7	246
80	0	8	48	16	8	264
85	0	9	51	17	8	279
90	0	9	54	18	9	297
95	0	10	57	19	9	312
100	0	10	60	20	10	330
105	0	11	63	21	10	345
110	0	11	66	22	11	363
115	0	12	69	23	11	378
120	0	12	72	24	12	396
125	0	13	75	25	12	411
130	0	13	78	26	13	429
135	0	14	81	27	13	444
140	0	14	84	28	14	462
145	0	15	87	29	14	477
150	0	15	90	30	15	495
155	0	16	93	31	15	510
160	0	16	96	32	16	528
165	0	17	99	33	16	543
170	0	17	102	34	17	561
175	0	18	105	35	17	576

Index

About the Authors

Sally Edwards is one of America's leading fitness authorities and triathlon experts. She is a member of the Triathlon Hall of Fame, the former Ironman Master's world record holder, and the National Spokesperson for the Danskin Women's Triathlon finishing more than 75 Danskin triathlons. As one of triathlon's pioneers, today she is the head heart of Heart Zones, an international health, fitness, and sports training company headquartered in Sacramento, California, and dedicated to helping individuals lead a lifetime of fitness.

Rebecca Brocard Yao graduated from Annie Wright (Tacoma, WA), where she received the Sportsmanship Award and was captain of the tennis team. She rowed novice crew at Georgetown University before derailing her athletic opportunities for a job on Capitol Hill. Many years, a husband, a child, and several businesses later, Rebecca rediscovered her love of sports when training for the Seattle Danskin Women's Triathlon. After that fateful day, she inaugurated the National Danskin Mentor Mentee Program (www.mentormentee.org), which links first-time women triathletes with their more experienced peers. As national coordinator, Rebecca has seen this program grow to become one of the largest peer-to-peer female athlete mentoring programs in the country.

Kaari Busick, a graduate of the Annie Wright School in Tacoma, Washington, is a technical editor and writer. She swam competitively for twelve years, including a stint at Colby College, and has competed in several triathlons and numerous road races. She practices Heart Zone Training and recommends it highly to anyone returning to fitness or looking for increased performance. For all your technical editing needs, she can be reached at ottertri@hotmail.com.

Other Triathlon Books by Sally Edwards